The CEO's Blueprint

ISBN: 1-4196-1610-2

To order additional copies, please contact us.
BookSurge, LLC
www.booksurge.com
1-866-308-6235
orders@booksurge.com

The CEO's Blueprint

10 Steps to Constructing Company Culture

David A. Monte

2006

The CEO's Blueprint

TABLE OF CONTENTS

☆☆☆

"All people dream, but not equally. Those who dream by night in the dusty recesses of their mind, wake in the morning to find that it was vanity. But the dreamers of the day are dangerous people, for they dream their dreams with open eyes, and make them come true."
T.E. Lawrence

☆☆☆

Explore, Create and Achieve

To Evelyn and Eileen

INTRODUCTION (WHY ARE WE HERE?)

Imagine if you will an organization where every employee understands the company's annual goals and long-term vision as well as their role in helping the company realize success. Then imagine a level of commitment from employees that rivals that of a small business owner's commitment to their own family business. Imagine what can be accomplished with energetic teams comprised of diverse employees who are engaged, excited, committed; and who give 120% every day….. because they want to; because they believe in their company; because they feel valued; because they understand their role; and because they believe in their leadership and themselves.

The business concepts and maxims to accomplish this are simple and well known. Almost everyone that has ever picked up a book on business has heard of them; and most who've read them also believe in them—at least intellectually. The key differentiator is that very few business leaders truly understanding their importance deeply enough to commit to them absolutely and implement a plan (a Blueprint) that allows them to turn those very simple, basic business beliefs into an organizational reality.

This is a blueprint for transforming any organization. If followed, it will improve results in every facet of your business. It will increase your profits, position your organization to implement change, and execute your strategic initiatives. It will create a superior work environment; a place where employees want to work and a place everyone wants to work.

Following the CEO's Blueprint will take a lot of work, personal energy, and unwavering commitment. Initial construction will be challenging, it will require some of the most difficult decisions you'll make in business and perhaps in life. The initial framework is critical and must be structurally sound. Once constructed, it will require on-going maintenance (the kind that can't be sub-contracted) in the form of deliberate management and leadership actions by you (the CEO) and your leadership team.

Should you and your team commit to following the CEO's Blueprint to build and maintain a positive culture as defined by its core plans, it will deliver immediate results in performance, profits, teamwork, and employee commitment. It will allow you to execute your strategy, build your brand, and define your success well into the future. So let's go!

CHAPTER I

The Two Most Important Things

Congratulations! You have arrived, landed that top spot, and climbed the last step of the ladder. You've worked hard, persevered, learned from your mistakes, and delivered results time and again. Now you get to do things your way: correct all the problems you've observed that were previously out of your influence; implement the overlooked business strategies that are sure to deliver profits; capture the untapped market opportunities; and take your company to a higher level of performance, success, and share price.

As you unpack the files, place the pictures on the desk, and admire the new view from your top floor corner office window; you know that you've just inherited a number of business issues, challenges and opportunities requiring your immediate attention. But this time it's different. You are at the top! Everything you do; how you react or don't react; the way you prioritize; the decisions you make; and where you focus key resources will reverberate throughout your organization. Every move you make is amplified like never before. A question, an idea, or request will send resources into action for hours, days, or perhaps weeks.

Each time that happens you've made an investment of time, money, and energy. You've also sent a message to employees throughout the organization. This message spreads out through formal and informal channels. It is modified, interpreted, and spun by employees in meetings, in casual conversations, and on the production floor. What was the effect? Was it positive or negative? What conclusions did employees draw about you, the company; and what they will do today and tomorrow? Whether this knowledge fills you with excitement at the thought of welding such new power, humbles you into thoughtful contemplation, or simply scares the hell out of you; you need to recognize it as a reality of your position. Everything you do or say will now build, shape, mold, destroy, shift, and/or create not only <u>your</u> reputation, but also your company's culture.

So what will come first? Developing a new strategy, addressing an operational problem, initiating new product development, updating an outdated IT system, selling off under-performing assets, dealing with a performance issue on your staff, positioning against a competitive threat, or preparing for your first board meeting? Chances are several of these issues will require your immediate attention. They simply can't wait and you'll have to work on many of them at the same time. It is easy to see how you can become 100% focused on the business issues that are immediately in front of you, but they are not the most important things for your company. The two most important things you need to focus on for your company is **leadership** and **creating your culture**.

But, do you really have time for all that "soft stuff" when you have all these business issues demanding your attention? Your answer is critical and the answer is "YES!" It is "YES" because leadership and culture will define "how" you address those key items. "How" you address them will greatly impact the solutions to those issues; how well they are accepted and implemented; and, ultimately, the quality of the results. If you do not make leadership and culture your #1 priority, you'll be an average CEO of an average performing company.

LEADERSHIP AND CULTURE ARE THE TWO MOST IMPORTANT THINGS FOR YOUR COMPANY

As you focus on all those business issues, whether they are problems, challenges or opportunities; you and your organization will develop solutions and strategies that will change work processes, tools, systems, job responsibilities, and organizational structures. A very simple and commonly used business formula that I was taught to use is A*Q= E. It was developed by General Electric in the mid-nineties as part of their Change Acceleration Process[I] when developing business solutions and strategies. Simply put, it is:

A * Q = E

A = Acceptance of the solution
Q = Quality of the solution
E = Effectiveness of the solution

Where A is the level of organizational acceptance of a technical solution; Q is the quality of the technical solution; and E is the effectiveness of the solution. The purpose of the equation is to demonstrate that you must not only have a strong, technical solution; but also a high level of organizational acceptance for the solution to be effective. A strong technical solution (a 10 on a scale of one to ten) that has low organizational acceptance (0) will not be very effective (0*10=0). A weak technical solution (0) that has high organizational acceptance (10) will likewise not be very effective (10*0=0). A solid technical solution (10) paired with a strong organizational acceptance (10) leads to high effectiveness of your solution (10*10=100!).

Real Examples

A company's supply chain department negotiates a cost-savings deal with a hotel chain that saves the company 5% annually in travel expenses; but it fails to explain to employees that the rebate is paid in a lump sum at year-end rather than at the time of the hotel stay. Cost-conscious employees continue to shop for the lower cost hotels and fail to comply with the deal because they don't accept the solution as beneficial to the company which results in limited effectiveness of the solution.

Real Examples

Accounting installs a new asset management system with improved functionality, but fails to include key partners in operations (who input data into the system) during the design. The design requires a process change in operations to input required data. The integrity of the data is compromised because it is problematic for operations to enter it correctly in the new system. Operations is not treated as an owner of the changes, and therefore is not compelled to accept them. This results in reduced effectiveness of the system.

Real Examples

Competitive pressures force leadership to close down a product line, reduce compliment, and move employees into different jobs. Leadership openly communicates and shares information on the financial pressures; offers voluntary packages and outplacement services; and works to move employees into new positions that best fit their interests and skills. While not everyone is 100% pleased, the majority of the employees accepts the decision and appreciates how the company handled the situation. This approach resulted in an effective solution for a difficult situation.

The equation A*Q=E is simple in concept, but challenging in practice. Most businesses focus only on the Q. They assume a solid technical solution will be accepted because it is logical; and/or worse yet, because "that's what management decided." The reality is that in organizations, employees as a group wield amazing power. If they don't accept something, they will greatly reduce its effectiveness and sometimes even stop it altogether. Conversely, employees can make almost any technical solution work if they are accepting and determined. That is the good news. That amazingly powerful group of employees can take even the poorest of technical solutions; and, if they accept, believe, and commit to it, make it work. Based on this, I believe the above formula is somewhat understated. The reality is—acceptance is twice as powerful as the technical solution. The level of acceptance will amplify the effectiveness of your technical solution. Therefore, the formula is better represented as:

2A * Q = E

Knowing that acceptance is twice as powerful as the technical solutions you'll develop, you'll want your organization to excel at building acceptance. There are several specific actions and methods to accomplish that in an organization; but, at this point, it is more important to know <u>who</u> builds acceptance. The answer is **your leaders**. Leaders build organizational acceptance. Not only are they the most important tool in building acceptance, they really are the <u>only</u> tool. This means you must have strong leaders; and you must support them in every way possible in building organizational acceptance of solutions, initiatives, and programs. In doing so, you'll also be supporting them in creating your culture.

LEADERSHIP BUILDS ACCEPTANCE; LEADERSHIP CREATES CULTURE

This equation is versatile in concept in that it can be applied many ways. As described, it is often applied at the project level to individual business solutions; but it can also be applied at the individual employee level to measure performance. In that form, it measures performance by multiplying "how" an employee does things by "what" that employee does.

2H * W = P

H= How something is done

W= What is done

P = Individual Performance

Once again, I reiterate that "how" things are done has more impact than "what" is done. This is a more difficult concept to buy into because whenever we look at achievements, we focus on "what" was achieved; and we remember people for the great things they did. It takes a lot of introspection to realize that "how" things are done is really what we remember and how we judge (or color) an achievement. The most obvious example is the businessperson that gets strong business results, but is deemed "cutthroat" in their approach because they leave a figurative trail of bodies in their wake.

Think about how the great achievements of sports figures, leaders, or business people are often tainted by their character and unethical or immoral activities that may or may not be related to the achievement. The opposite is true of individuals that we like and respect for the additional challenges they have overcome, their altruistic efforts or even simply how they make us feel. We tend to amplify their achievements and celebrate who they are as much as what they achieved. To illustrate, consider the following individuals:

1980 U.S. Olympic Hockey Team
Lance Armstrong
Bill Clinton
Ray Charles
Michael Jackson
Richard Nixon
Ronald Reagan
Franklin Roosevelt
Pete Rose
Martha Stewart
Mother Teresa
Oprah Winfry

What do you associate with these individuals in addition to their accomplishments or "what" they achieved? How much do the shortcomings, style, misjudgments, handicaps, and/or challenges associated with them impact your perception of their achievements? Great leaders are remembered and celebrated not only for "what" they did, but "how" they did it. As leaders build acceptance and lead your organization, "how" they do things will carry twice the impact as "what" they do.

These equations can also be applied to teams and the work products they produce. The 2A*Q=E equation can be applied to measure the effectiveness of a team's work product where the acceptance the team builds for their solution is twice as influential as the quality of their technical solution. The second equation, 2H*W=P, can be used to measure team performance where "how" the team worked together, influenced stakeholders, communicated, and built acceptance for their work product was twice as influential as "what' the team accomplished.

The highest-level application of this equation is at the organizational level. In this form, it predicts company performance by multiplying "organizational culture" by "business strategy." The same principal prevails because culture has twice the impact as "business strategy." It is the primary driver and predictor of company performance and success.

2C * S = P

C= Culture

S= Business Strategy

P = Company Performance

The beneficial connection between culture and strategy is logical and generally accepted in the business world; however, you may be challenged by the concept that culture carries twice the weight as strategy. Proven examples are harder to find because building truly strong cultures requires a rare level of commitment and focus. A good rule of thumb is that if you notice or know of another company's culture, it is a very strong culture and it significantly impacts that company's business results and performance. A few examples of notably strong cultures:

Southwest Airlines

Disney

Enron

THE CEO'S BLUEPRINT
General Electric
IBM
Microsoft

These companies are famous (and some infamous) for their business results and they are also examples of noticeable, well-defined, and effective cultures.

THE STRENGTH OF YOUR CULTURE WILL DETERMINE YOUR COMPANY'S LEVEL OF PERFORMANCE

In the book, *Good to Great,* Jim Collins' presents research undertaken to determine what makes companies dramatically outperform their competitors and identify the differences that make good companies become great companies. His team reviewed the performance of over 1400 companies to identify the ones that made the jump from average performer to superstar. They found 11 companies that generated cumulative stock returns 6.9 times the general stock market for 15 years (performance was normalized for market trends common to their industries). In examining these 11 companies, they found six common characteristics, some of which we'll discuss later. Of equal interest is what expected characteristics they did not find. They did not find "superior strategy" or "focus on what companies did" to be key differentiator.

> "Strategy per se did not separate the good-to-great companies from the comparison companies. Both sets of companies had well-defined strategies, and there is no evidence that the good-to-great companies spent more time on long-range strategic planning than the comparison companies. The good-to-great companies did not focus principally on what to do to become great; they focused equality on what not to do and what to stop doing."[2]

The quality of your business strategy, technical solutions, and what individuals do everyday is important; but it is not a distinguishing factor in determining company performance and in becoming a great company. One of the six common characteristics they identified was that great companies focus first on "who"—getting the right leaders in place and the wrong leaders out; and then later on "what"—vision, strategy, mission, and goals.

> "We expected that the good-to-great leaders would begin by setting a new vision and strategy. We found instead that they first got the right people on the bus, the wrong people off the bus, and the right people in the right seats—and then they figured out where to drive it."[3]

Leadership creates culture and culture is the distinguishing factor in determining company performance. This is why it is so important to first get the right people, the right leaders, "on the bus" and "in the right seats" (positions). It is the key differentiator between companies with equally strong strategies. To be successful, you need to have both sides of the 2C*S=P equation. Most companies only focus on the strategy (the "what") side of the equation and, as described, it has less impact than culture (the "how") by a factor of two! Great companies understand and capture the value of culture.

Leadership and culture are the two most important things for your company's success. The strength of your culture, the level of acceptance you build with employees, and how individuals get things done have twice the impact as your business strategy, the quality of your technical solutions, and what individuals do. Culture is created by leadership; and leadership builds acceptance. Leaders build acceptance by "how" they do things everyday at the individual level, which in turn creates your culture. The strength of your culture will determine your company's level of performance.

CHAPTER II

The Value of Culture (Your Foundation)

So you now know that the strength of your culture will determine your company's level of performance and that it is twice as powerful as business strategy. But what is organizational culture? Your culture is the foundation of your company. It's the base and internal structure that supports and shapes everything you do. Culture is the key to business execution and strategy execution. It defines for an organization how projects get completed; how customers are served; how and what gets communicated internally and externally; how people work together; their business ethics; and the rules and boundaries of all business interactions. In its simplest form, your culture is what it *feels* like to work for your company. Your culture can propel you forward, hold you back, or leave your spinning your wheels.

In defining all of these things, your culture also provides an identity for your company and an identity for your employees. It's the personality of your business and it's shared by each and every employee. Culture is very powerful in that it is in part how employees define who they are as people. That is why it is so hard to change, merge, or mold. Most people like, or at least are comfortable with, who they are. When you try to change their culture, you are in fact changing an important part of them.

It is also why a negative culture is so damaging. If employees feel bad about their company's culture, they also feel bad about themselves; and they'll try to change that by rebelling against the company in many ways. These ways will impact morale, productivity, and business results. That is why a common culture is so critical; why a positive culture is such a powerful business advantage; and why a negative culture is such a significant business disadvantage.

YOUR CULTURE IS THE FOUNDATION OF YOUR COMPANY. IT DEFINES WHAT YOU DO, AND HOW YOU DO IT

Your culture will determine your employees' level of excitement, commitment, and engagement. The Gallup Organization has conducted extensive research on employee engagement since 1997 and studied the responses of 3 million employees who have participated in their Q12 survey. Their Q12 survey is a 12 question assessment on employee engagement, community, life satisfaction, and the economy. The survey grouped employees into three categories: Engaged, Not-Engaged, and Actively Disengaged as defined below:

<u>The Three Types of Employees</u>

1. **Engaged** employees work with passion and feel a profound connection to their company. They drive innovation and move the organization forward.
2. **Not-engaged** employees are essentially "checked out." They're sleepwalking through their workday, putting time—but not energy or passion—into their work.
3. **Actively disengaged** employees aren't just unhappy at work; they're busy acting out their unhappiness. Every day, these workers undermine what their engaged coworkers accomplish.[1]

The results of this survey reveal that there is a connection between workplace engagement and outlook on life. It shows that people don't separate out work and home life. Level of engagement in the workplace affects their attitudes towards family and friends, expectations for personal success, quality of life, and their employer.

<u>Gallup Findings</u>[2]

- Engaged employees are 4.5 times more likely to be satisfied with where they live than disengaged employees.
- Engaged employees are more optimistic about their personal lives than actively disengaged employees

It stands to reason that if you feel good about what you do 50% of your waking hours for five out of seven days of the week, you are going to feel good about yourself, your social life, your community, and your future. Unfortunately, the converse is also true. Since your culture provides an identity for your company and an identity for your employees; if your work culture is negative, it will negatively impact how employees feel about themselves and their work life.

YOUR CULTURE IS AN IDENTITY FOR YOUR COMPANY AND YOUR EMPLOYEES

The Gallup research also confirms the intuitive link between employee engagement, worker productivity, employee retention, and business results. If you are an engaged employee, you will be a productive employee. You will value your job and support your company.

<u>Gallup Findings</u>[3]

- Engaged employees are 4.9 times as confident in their company's financial future than actively disengaged employees
- Engaged employees are 5.3 times as likely to recommend their company's products and services to family and friends than actively disengaged employees
- Engaged employees are 2.2 times as likely to think their job performance has improved in the last year than actively disengaged employees
- Engaged employees are 2.6 times as likely to plan on working for their current company one year from now than actively disengaged employees
- Engaged employees are 4.3 times as likely to plan on spending their careers with their current company than actively disengaged employees
- Engaged employees are 2.6 times as likely to plan on working for their current company one year from now than actively disengaged employees

If you are engaged, you will believe in your company and what you are doing; therefore, you will support your company in and outside of the workplace. Simply put, if you feel good about what you do everyday; you will feel good about yourself and you are going to want to keep doing it. There are very few things that impact day-to-day operational cost for businesses as much as worker productivity. Worker productivity can easily mean a 5% to 15% differential in daily operating costs. Imagine increasing your bottom line by 5% to 15% of your company's annual operating costs!

As a consumer, think about who influences the product selection and buying decisions the most in your life? Is it newspaper ads, telemarketers, and what you see on TV? Or is it the experiences and recommendations of your family and friends? Just think if your company's products were used, recommended, and positively promoted by every one of your employees? It is possibly one of the most powerful marketing tools you could have; and, if you create a culture that builds employee engagement, it is also free.

Lastly, what does employee retention do for the bottom line? When you consider the cost of hiring, relocating, training and potential rehiring (if it doesn't work out); the true cost has been estimated at double to triple the annual salary of the candidate. In his book, *Topgrading*, Bradford Smart quantifies the expense of a hiring the wrong person. He includes both the direct costs like recruiting fees, the signing bonus, the compensation for someone who does not make a contribution, and severance package along with the indirect costs such as disruption and lost time. He concludes that a mistake at the $100,000 to $250,000 salary level costs a company a total of $4.7M.[4]

To further reinforce this point, in the book, *The Human Capital Edge: 21 People Management Practices Your Company Must Implement (or Avoid) to Maintain Shareholder Value,* Bruce N. Pfau and Ira T. Kay document the results of Watson Wyatt's Human Capital Index research which showed that, all else being equal, companies having better recruiting and retention are worth 7.6% more in the market."[5]

New hires are a good thing because they bring new ideas, different perspectives, and new life into your company; but you want to hire them for the right reasons. Employees jumping ship because they dislike your culture and their work environment is not only the wrong reason to lose an employee, it is indicative of a deep-seeded problem, a problem that is very costly to your business.

Culture is created by leadership; and leadership builds acceptance. Leaders build acceptance by "how" they do things everyday at the individual level, which in turn creates your culture. The Gallup research also confirms that leaders have a tremendous influence on building employee engagement.

Gallup Findings[6]

- Employees with leaders who focus on their strengths or positive characteristics are almost 13 times more likely to be engaged.

We'll cover the topic of leadership more in depth in the next charter; but the simple fact is how employees feel about their company and their job is most strongly influenced by their immediate "boss" or the leader they work for day in and day out. Your decisions as the CEO impact your company and your culture everyday. One of the biggest decisions you will make are the leaders you choose; the kind of culture you ask them to create; and how well you support them in that endeavor.

The last Gallup findings we'll consider are the actual breakdown by percentage of engaged employees for U.S. companies.

Gallup Findings[7]

- In the United States, 17% of employees are actively disengaged, 54% are not engaged and only 29% are engaged.

These results are simultaneously energizing and depressing. They are depressing when you think about that fact that on average 81% of employees in our economy are not engaged in what they do; therefore, they do not feel good about their company, their job, and to some degree, themselves. However, it is energizing when you consider the tremendous opportunities that are out there in the business world. Opportunities to recruit, engage, and revitalize so many companies, their profits and most importantly, their employees. For a corporation of any size, it is not realistic to get 100%; but it is possible to get to 80% and potentially even 95% employee engagement. It is possible to change the way 50% or more of your employees feel about their company; and that equates to raw, untapped opportunity!

MOST COMPANIES HAVE A LOW LEVEL OF EMPLOYEE ENGAGEMENT BECAUSE MOST COMPANIES DO NOT HAVE A POSITIVE CULTURE

Gallup estimates that there are more than 22 million employees in the United States that are "actively disengaged," costing business between 250 and 300 billion annually in lost productivity. This estimate is conservative and increases when you consider the added effects of workplace injury, illness, turnover, absences, and fraud. Not to mention that this estimate only covers employees who are "actively disengaged." If you were to also add in the cost impact of employees who are "not engaged," the estimate becomes staggering, and could surpass $1 trillion per year (~10% of the U.S. Gross Domestic Product).[8]

Think about this opportunity in terms of increased productivity, the kind of advertising money can't buy, low turnover, and a place where employees want to work because they feel good about their company and themselves. **Imagine if even half the corporations in the U.S. focused on building and creating a positive culture. Imagine what they would accomplish if 80% of their employees were engaged. What would that mean for their profits, for the stock market, and the U.S. economy? Creating a positive culture is the single most unrealized opportunity to improve the bottom line in the business world today. The opportunity and potential consequences of capitalizing on it is staggering.**

As the CEO, you will begin to change your organization's culture the first day on the job; either through action, inaction, or accidental action. In ideal situations, the aware leader will begin to take deliberate actions to positively change culture when opportunities arise through thoughtful, well-planned, and even orchestrated events. Conversely, the poor or unaware leader will not take any deliberate action; and most likely through accidental actions, start to form what is a negative culture. Lastly, the unaware but strong leader will begin to change a culture for the better through positive, but accidental, action. While this is good and will most likely lead to a beneficial culture, it is sub-optimal; because through awareness and deliberate action, that strong leader could build a strong and very positive culture. Culture is a key business advantage, you need it to be as strong as possible and have it ready for use as quickly as you can.

As with most things in a company, the CEO has control. Culture is no exception. You may want to believe that because culture is shared by every employee and is difficult to change because employees strongly identify with it; that ultimately they have more control and influence then the CEO given their proportionally greater numbers; but they do not. This is true because building a positive culture that is shared by the majority of employees is very difficult, whereas having a fractured or negative culture is very easy. Like so many things in life, it is easy to do something wrong; but it is much more challenging to do something right.

The CEO controls communications, resources, budgets, personnel (hiring and firing), and those key decisions that send cultural messages to all employees. Control of these things combined with decisions that are made regarding these areas, send messages about values. What do your decisions say you value or don't value? Do they build upon the belief that your company respects and values employees? Do they recognize and reward behaviors that are reinforcing the type of culture you are trying to create? If the CEO makes decisions or does not take appropriate actions, it will send the wrong messages and negatively impact morale, teamwork, and employee engagement. The CEO will single-handedly start to create a negative culture.

Next we need to discuss the three main types of cultures: positive, negative, and split (a mix of both) cultures. Of course there are many different flavors of both positive and negative company cultures that emphasize different business attributes and traits. I like to use the term "flavor;" because while the differences are noticeable, they don't change the fact that the culture is either positive or negative. These different flavors can also appear as sub-cultures within one company. Often these will be cultural differences and nuances that are noticeable across different functions, departments, geographies or subsidiaries. It's easy to see how business functions or companies that focus on customer service, product production, or commodity trading will have a different look, feel, and culture because they are valuing different skills, have different areas of focus, and methods of getting things accomplished.

While cultural flavors vary dramatically, for the purposes of our focus on building and creating a powerful business advantage; we really only need to understand the three main types of cultures: positive, negative and split. The flavor of your culture can be added in later and will typically evolve quite naturally.

Positive Cultures

Positive cultures are cultures where the majority of employees are engaged, committed, supportive, and excited about the company as well as their profession. Even though positive cultures come in many flavors, there are core attributes that are shared by every positive culture. Positive cultures have strong leaders that communicate and build trust. They focus on their employees, leverage their talents, and succeed through teamwork. I've seen companies communicate their vision and annual goals at the beginning of the year; and then proceed to make decisions and send messages that demonstrate support for, and reinforce progress towards, realizing their vision and goals. These actions create a positive culture. They demonstrate that you really believe in your vision. It reinforces what employees must focus on; what they will be rewarded for; and what they must believe is good for them and their company. It builds trust; it builds respect; and it creates focus. To be fair, it is not always this simple. There will be many business situations that require decisions that will seem to be (and may in fact be) in conflict with the vision or goals you have established for the company. That makes the decision and how it is communicated extremely critical. It's where the "how" comes in. Successfully figuring out "how" to communicate and explain that type of decision indicates that you are actively working to manage, build, and create your positive culture.

Negative Cultures

Negative cultures are cultures where the majority of employees are not engaged or are actively disengaged from the company and their job. Negative cultures do not focus on leadership or their employees because they do not understand their value. They "tell" instead of communicate. They create distrust through their actions as well as show a preference for commanding and controlling rather than collaboration and teamwork. I've seen companies communicate their vision and annual goals at the beginning of the year, and then proceed to make decisions and send messages that both ignore and conflict with their vision and goals. These actions create a negative culture. It means that you really don't believe what you said in the first place and it erodes employees' trust. Employees will question your sincerity in what you value and what you said you wanted the company to value. It does nothing to get employees engaged and supportive of what you asked them to do; and they will feel "cheated" if they had bought in and were actively working on the goals you laid out for the company within the cultural environment you said you wanted to create.

Split Cultures

Split cultures occur when a positive and negative culture exist in about equal strength in the same company. This situation is common after a merger. Split cultures must not be confused with the different cultural flavors of sub-cultures. Sub-cultures can exist as organizational or functional nuances within the same overarching culture. Having sub-cultures can be absolutely fine, if they are connected at the top by one cultural vision that is positive. Having split cultures is very destructive. If you have a split culture at every interface, the positive and negative compete against each other. As they do, every business decision will be influenced; not by what is best for the company, but rather its implications for the opposing culture. There will constantly be winners and losers, fractured teamwork, and low employee engagement.

***

The good news is—regardless of what you are starting with, cultures can be changed and new ones created. A positive culture can be constructed around core attributes and then further developed over time. As you create your culture, you are working towards the point where you reach a "critical mass" of employee engagement and acceptance. Critical mass occurs when a significant majority of your employees are engaged, excited, and committed to the company and their profession.

As discussed, split cultures will naturally lead to competition between the different cultures. Whereas in most things competition is good; it's not when it comes to culture. In the case of cultural competition, competition is counterproductive and destructive. The last thing you want is your employees putting energy into winning a cultural battle. You must aggressively act to prevent cultural competition. If your multiple cultures are positive, you need to bring them together at every opportunity where they share cultural commonalities. You must work hard to emphasize that they share the important core attributes of a positive culture while you acknowledge that it is acceptable to have different positive sub-cultures (flavors).

If one or more of your cultures are negative, destroy it as fast as you can and replace it by building a positive culture. A negative culture is a cancer in your organization. You should fear it. If not addressed, it will grow, spread, and eat away at everything that is positive until your company is consumed. You might not go bankrupt; but you will be ineffective and a below average performer. You'll have 29% or less of your employees engaged and working to make the company a success. As the negativity remains, your number of engaged employees will dwindle down further and further until only you and a few of the highly compensated of your employees are left engaged in what they do because of the personal wealth they have at stake. That is the worst reason possible to be an "engaged" employee. I'd even argue that these types of employees are really just fooling themselves. Money can't buy happiness; it can't buy (true) love; and it can't buy truly engaged employees.

You not only have to address a negative culture, you must remove it.

Containment is not an option. Allowing it to exist is a compromise that will undermine all your other efforts. The engaged employees will notice; wonder why you allow it; and begin to question your commitment, integrity and beliefs. Being an engaged employee feels better for employees, but it also requires employees to work harder and give more of themselves. If they question your commitment, they'll question what they are putting their energy into and then you'll start to lose them. Lose them in terms of losing their acceptance, buy-in, support, and level of engagement. You must recognize and reward your engaged employees as well as punish and remove a negative culture.

One key point to highlight as you begin to create your positive culture is that you must understand your starting point (positive, negative or split). Although it won't change the mechanics of what you do to construct your positive culture, it will define the amount of effort and focus you need to put into different areas. For example, destroying a negative culture will require you to eliminate the things (the culture killing actions, situations, and attitudes) that are causing the problems as you begin to put into place the key actions to build a positive culture. Starting with a positive culture will mean you will put more energy into reinforcing and adjusting the positive actions and much less energy into eliminating the problems. In addition to knowing where you'll have to focus, understanding your starting point is important; because it will allow you and your leadership team to set appropriate expectations regarding the effort, energy, and resistance associated with your pending cultural change.

CEOs, don't wait to create your positive culture. It should and will be "flavored" somewhat by you and your style. It can come before everything else, even your vision, mission, strategy, brand, or annual goals. It <u>must</u> come before all things on the priority list. If not, you are not putting enough focus on it.

One of the most advantageous things about creating your culture is that unlike so many other business initiatives, the timing is not dependant on other things. You can begin before, after, or at the same time as you create your vision, mission, strategy, or goals. If you already have these other things in place, you can focus in on your culture; build your leadership team; and then reaffirm and adjust them as needed to increase and build leadership buy-in. If you are starting from scratch (or need to), you then have a great opportunity to build and create your culture as you create your vision, mission, strategy, and goals. In doing so, you will build a tremendous amount of acceptance and buy-in. You will have a company full of "owners" who chose to buy-in because they helped create what they bought into.

So your immediate focus is to begin building a positive culture where the significant majority of employees are engaged, commitment, supportive, and excited about the company and their profession. To truly have a positive culture you must have better than 51% employee engagement. You must have a significant majority, and you must reach the point of critical mass. Critical mass is the point at which the positive culture you have created overwhelms all the other cultural forces in your company. They still may be out there, but they are fragmented and so comparatively small that they are barely noticeable. If I were to put a number on significant majority, I'd say it is between 65% and 95%. Once you've created your culture and reached critical mass, you should be able to maintain 65% to 95% of your employees engaged; accepting of your culture; and in agreement that you and your leadership team are doing the right things in the right ways.

During times of great change such as major reorganization, merger, or significant change in strategic direction; it is ok to be on the low end of the employee engagement scale (65%) working back towards the high end. However, in the absence of any significant change, if you start dropping down towards 65% you've got a problem; and you'll need to figure it out fast. Over time you'll want to, and be able to, maintain your organization in the 85% to 95% range. This is the desired end-state that will deliver a significant competitive advantage. It is optimal in terms of energy, engagement, productivity, and profits.

YOUR CULTURE WILL DETERMINE YOUR EMPLOYEES' LEVEL OF EXCITEMENT, COMMITMENT, AND ENGAGEMENT

Defining your culture for a large organization may seem daunting and overly complex, but it is not. It is not complex because you get to start by defining it with the five broad core attributes of any positive culture. Over time, defining the subtleties or flavor of your culture will be a conscious effort; and you will get there quite easily with the support of your staff of superb leaders. Later, I will discuss how to measure, define, and communicate your culture; but for now let's define culture at a very high level.

Every positive business culture will have the following core attributes. A positive culture is:

FORGED BY LEADERSHIP
SUSTAINED BY TRUST
DRIVEN BY TEAMWORK
FUELED BY DIVERSITY
FOCUSED ON EMPLOYEES

Forged by Leadership

Your culture will be forged by your leadership. We've discussed the fact that you, the CEO, are in control of your culture. You have the greatest amount of influence and you are in control because you control the key resource for building and maintaining a positive culture. That key resource is leadership. You can't create a positive culture without it. It is simply too much work and requires too much input, feedback and communication for one person. But, believe it or not, you (the CEO) can single-handedly create a negative culture by what you do and/or don't do. Unfortunately it is just that easy and all too common.

How employees feel about their company and their job is most strongly influenced by their immediate "boss," the leader they work for every day. That person is the primary resource for communication as well as building acceptance and gaining employees' commitment to the organization's mission, vision, strategy, and goals. It is important to realize that who that leader is and the skills they possess, has been directly influenced by their leader and their leader's leader, and so on until it gets to you, the CEO. In this way, the CEO controls the key resource—leadership, for building and maintaining a positive culture. One of the biggest decisions you will make as CEO are the leaders you choose; what kind of culture you ask them to create; and how well you support them in that endeavor. A positive culture is forged by leadership.

Sustained by Trust

Like all other relationships, work relationships are built on trust. The minute you start to lose the trust of your employees, you'll begin to lose your positive culture. Then the level of employee engagement will drop along with commitment and energy. If you can't be trusted and you don't follow through on your commitments, you'll lose employees faster than if you fire them. At a company with a positive culture, employees don't want to lose their job because they are a part of something that is important to them. They believe in what they are doing. It is a part of their identity and losing that is more significant than losing a paycheck. When your actions or the actions of the company tell employees they cannot trust you or the company, they start to lose all those things. Ultimately, not being able to trust in your company or its leadership feels worse than being fired.

Trust between you, your leaders, and all employees will maintain and sustain your culture. It will allow you to work together in an open, honest environment where everyone feels safe and respected. A high level of trust also means that employees will have a clear understanding of their role in the company and what is expected of them. Trust promotes two-way communication. It demonstrates respect and keeps people from wasting precious energy on hidden agendas and meaningless, unproductive, turf battles. A positive culture is maintained by trust.

Driven by Teamwork

We have all seen what tremendous teamwork can achieve, in our sports, in the business world, and in our personal lives. Few things can be as exciting, energizing, and fulfilling as being a part of a great team. Conversely, we have also seen "teams" fall apart and crumble from within. We have seen top performers and superstars fall short of goals and expectations because they couldn't be a part of a team.

Teams are an absolute necessity in today's business world. They far outpace the smartest CEOs in terms of diversity, ideas, and results. Teamwork creates energy and builds respect among team members. It sparks creativity as well as provides balance for business solutions and initiatives. Being a part of a great team where team members share a common vision and work towards a common goal can be an incredibly fulfilling experience for employees. Teams in the form of your leaderships' direct staff, cross-functional teams, or special project teams will make your decisions, collaborate, communicate, and solve your businesses problems. If you don't have time for teamwork, you don't have time for a positive culture. A positive culture is driven by teamwork.

Fueled by Diversity

The business world and the problems, challenges, and opportunities it creates for your company are complex and diverse. No single person is smart enough or experienced enough to deal appropriately with all the problems; develop the optimal strategies for opportunities; and plan for all the challenges the average business will face. Diversity of thought, diversity of experience, and diversity of perception are the fuel that fires your company's problem solving and creative furnaces.

Singularity of thought will never produce the best outcome. A team of people who all think the same will never produce the best outcome. How could they? If you only populate a team full of people that think the same, have the same work experience, and share the same perceptions about business, life and community; that team will leave the majority of questions unasked, the majority of solutions unevaluated, and the majority of perceptions unconsidered.

At every opportunity fill your company full of smart people that think differently, have lived differently, come from different backgrounds, and have experienced different things. In a team environment, they will design better products; develop better plans; respond better to crisis; and create better solutions. Woodrow Wilson, the 28th President of the U.S., once said, *"I not only use all the brains that I have, but all that I can borrow."* Use all the brains you have in your company and make every effort to make sure those brains come from multiple backgrounds, experiences, and ways of thinking. A positive culture is fueled by diversity.

Focused on Employees

Your culture is the foundation of your company, the key to long-term success, and one of the most unrealized competitive advantages in the business world today. Your culture provides an identity for your company as well as your employees. Your entire focus on building a positive culture is in fact a focus on employees. Creating for them a business environment where they can optimize their success and in turn optimize your company's success.

Employees are an organization's most valuable assets. Machines, equipment, tools, products, and market share will change, wear out, become obsolete, and deteriorate over time. None of those assets help you adapt, grow, or adjust your business to keep up with the changing world. Nothing is more flexible, adaptable, creative, or capable than the human mind. No other assets can assure continued growth. A focus on employees is a focus on growth and on your company's future. This is underscored by the widely known, yet under practiced, management truism called Packard's law. Developed by the cofounder of the Hewlett-Packard Company, David Packard, Packard's law states:

> "No company can grow revenues consistently faster than its ability to get enough of the right people to implement that growth and still become a great company. If your growth rate in revenues consistently outpaces your growth rate in people, you simply will not—indeed cannot—build a great company."

Creating a positive culture means creating a high level of employee engagement. Creating a positive culture is managing, focusing, coaching, developing, and rewarding your employees, your "human" assets. Focusing on employees is not difficult. While you can never please everyone all the time, you can seek feedback, listen to concerns, acknowledge what you hear, and always make an effort to communicate. If you do these things well, you'll go a long way towards creating an environment that employees will respect and can thrive in personally and professionally. How well you focus on employees, their concerns and perceptions, their work environment, and their ideas will determine the strength of your culture, the strength of your company and your future share value. A positive culture is focused on employees.

***

Forged by leadership, sustained by trust, driven by teamwork, fueled by diversity, and focused on employees are the core attributes of a positive culture. By understanding and using these core attributes, you can build a positive culture that delivers superior results. These core attributes are not specific enough to define your culture in detail. For that you'll want to create your own culture survey. As an example, the Gallup Q12, the 12 key employee focused questions that were used to conduct their survey, contains many of the specific components that help define a positive culture[9]. They provide a great starting point for developing your own culture survey for your company.

> **"Engagement in the Workplace: 12 Measures that Matter**
> To indentify the elements of worker engagements, Gallup conducted hundreds of focus groups and many thousands of worker interviews in all kinds of organizations, at all levels, in most in-

dustries, and in many countries. Researchers then pinpointed 12 key employee expectations that form the foundations of strong feelings of engagements—the Gallup Q12.

The Gallup Q12 Items

1. I know what is expected of me at work.
2. I have the materials and equipment I need to do my work right.
3. At work, I have the opportunity to do what I do best every day.
4. In the last seven days, I have received recognition or praise for doing good work.
5. My supervisor, or someone at work, seems to care about me as a person.
6. There is someone at work who encourages my development.
7. At work, my opinions seem to count.
8. The mission or purpose of my company makes me feel my job is important.
9. My associates or fellow employees are committed to doing quality work.
10. I have a best friend at work.
11. In the last six months, someone at work has talked to me about my progress.
12. This last year, I have had opportunities at work to learn and grow.

Copyright © 1992-1999 The Gallup Organization, Princeton, NJR[10]

We've discussed the fact that culture is more important than business strategy. We've talked about the fact that culture must be your first priority, focused on before your vision, mission, strategy, and goals. So with all this focus on culture you may be wondering, "What about profits, what about stock price?" "If I put so much emphasis and focus on culture, how can I then turn around and tell employees that financial performance is critical without them feeling that the bottom line is all I care about?" The answer is **it's not only ok to tell them, it's important to tell them.**

The more honest you are about what you want to achieve with your positive culture, the more employees will respect you for that honesty and the more engaged employees will try to help you get it done. Remember, your culture isn't about the goals you have or the work you do everyday, it is about "how" your employees achieve them and "how" they get the work done everyday. It is the positive and optimal means to the desired end state.

The strength of your culture will determine your company's level of performance and it is twice as powerful as business strategy. Your culture is the foundation of your company; it defines what you do and how you do it. It is also the identity for your company and your employees. Your culture will determine your employees' level of excitement, commitment, and engagement. A positive culture is a significant business advantage and the key to business and strategy execution. Most companies have a low level of employee engagement because most companies do not have a positive culture. The core attributes of a positive culture are: forged by leadership, sustained by trust, driven by teamwork, fueled by diversity, and focused on employees. Creating a positive culture is the single most untapped bottom line opportunity in the business world today.

CHAPTER III

Leadership is Everything (Build and Maintain)

Leadership is everything because leadership builds and maintains positive culture; and, in turn, determines your company's performance. Leaders build acceptance for solutions, ideas, and changes (2A*Q=E). In building that acceptance, they amplify the effectiveness of everything they do. The level of acceptance is twice as powerful as the quality of the solution itself in determining the overall effectiveness.

You also know that "how" leaders do things is twice as powerful as "what" they do everyday in terms of results and individual performance (2H*W=P). As leaders build acceptance; as they emphasize the "how" they do things; they build and maintain a positive culture. A positive culture is the key to company performance because it's the key to executing your strategy. A positive culture is twice as powerful as strategy when it comes to impacting company performance (2C*S=P).

Leadership is everything when it comes to building a positive culture. When you consider the activities leaders actually perform and how often they do those things, their awesome potential for impact becomes clear. Almost all leader activities are opportunities to affect culture; and as a result, leaders are the ones that have <u>almost all the opportunity</u> to mold your culture. They have opportunity to make an impact (positive or negative) based on "how" they do those things. How they manage, how they communicate, how they develop and lead their teams, define an organization in terms of a positive workplace and a positive culture; and they take their lead and direction from you (the CEO).

LEADERS BUILD ACCEPTANCE BY "HOW" THEY LEAD; AND, IN TURN, BUILD AND MAINTAIN YOUR CULTURE

Consider for a moment all the activities leaders perform. They are the ones that execute the tactical day-to-day operation of your business. Leaders are on the ground solving problems, working with employees, as well as managing performance and production. They interface with customers and resolve the daily challenges that often go unnoticed. Leaders coach, develop, and improve employee performance every day. They communicate every significant and insignificant piece of information and policy change to employees in addition to providing feedback on morale, reactions and perceptions. They control your resources (employees, materials, equipment), your budgets, and the quality of your product or service. In doing all these things, leaders are the ones that execute your strategy; build your brand; improve the bottom line; and drive you closer to realizing your mission, vision, strategies and goals.

As they do their job every day, each communication, each decision, each customer or employee discussion, phone call or email is an opportunity to lead, an opportunity to build and maintain a positive culture. To demonstrate the impact of leadership, take an average workweek of one of your leaders on the front line and have them collect the following data:

- Number of emails they sent and number of employees that received them
- Number of meetings they held or attended and the number of employees attending (include one on one meetings)
- Number of phone calls or teleconferences they participated in and the number of employees attending
- Number of decisions they made or participated in that impacted employees in some way

As an organizational leader, I once collected this data personally to discuss and demonstrate the point for my staff and other leaders. This is what I found.

- 106 emails sent to 152 employees
- 24 phones calls or conversations involving 30 employees
- 6 meetings involving 24 employees
- 10 employee based decisions involving 15 employees

When you extrapolate the weekly totals into a full year's timeframe by multiplying the numbers by 48 work weeks (excludes vacations and holidays), you start to build an understanding and appreciation for the potential leadership impact that each individual leader commands.

- 46 weekly opportunities to impact culture through 221 employee interactions
- 7008 annual opportunities to impact culture through 10,608 employee interactions

One leader on the front line has over 7000 opportunities each year to positively impact your culture and over 10,000 employee interactions (some being repeat interactions with the same employees) in which to influence employees. That is over 7000 opportunities to demonstrate leadership, to communicate, to build trust, to build acceptance, to gain commitment, to engage employees, to demonstrate respect and to build and maintain your positive culture.

Now remember, this is the potential impact of just <u>one</u> leader. So how many leadership positions do you have in your company? Let's assume there are 200. So in this example, your leadership will have 1,400,000 opportunities in a year's time to build and maintain your culture. That is about 5,700 leadership opportunities per day on average. Strong leaders recognize and optimize these bountiful opportunities and consistently use them to build your culture and leverage them to make your organization a place where people want to work. Imagine if every day, all your leaders are doing and saying the right things in the right way to create a positive culture in your company. It wouldn't take long for the organization to get the message, to start to feel the difference, and to believe. Everyday, 1000's of times a day, "how" leaders do things impacts your culture.

This of course was not an in-depth study involving leaders at all levels from multiple industries and different size companies, so my example numbers could be off in the case of your company. Perhaps for your company, the number of opportunities is half as much.... or twice as much. Regardless, if you give this exercise a try, you'll discover that the number of opportunities and employee interactions add up to be a big number; but the most important thing to remember is that no matter what the numbers are for your company, your leaders have 100% of them. Your leadership, defined as anyone who has another employee working for them or holds a leadership title from the CEO to the front line leaders, not only have a tremendous number of opportunities to impact your culture, they have <u>**ALL**</u> the opportunities to impact your culture.

LEADERS HAVE TREMENDOUS OPPORTUNITY EACH AND EVERY DAY TO MAKE YOUR COMPANY A PLACE WHERE PEOPLE WANT TO WORK, A PLACE WHERE EVERYONE WANTS TO WORK

The sheer volume of daily and annual leadership opportunities are rarely considered and for the most part overlooked. Your role as CEO is to not only to raise awareness of these numerous opportunities, but to also create expectations for your leadership to take advantage of them. Imagine if you asked each leader during their annual performance review to describe how they used their 5000+ employee interactions/leadership opportunities to build trust, build employee engagement, gain commitment, and reinforce the vision and your strategy? This action alone would dramatically change how your leadership viewed and conducted employee interactions. This is why leadership is everything and leveraging this knowledge with a plan to build a positive culture is a major business advantage. It will make you and your company unique, exceptional and much farther ahead of your culturally challenged competitors.

***

So we understand that leaders are important. We understand all the things they do and that "how" they do those things will build and maintain culture. But what is leadership really? How do you define it? What kind of leaders do you need for your company and how do you find them?

You can read thousands of books on the subject that will cover different leadership styles and philosophies, review case studies linking leadership to performance/results, and examine the achievements and styles of great leaders past and present. When we consider leadership examples throughout history we look to the epic battles, the historic struggles for freedom or equality, the visionary giants of industry, the nations and empires that have risen and fell, and world changing historic moments like the moon landings, splitting the atom, or the fall of communism. We often define these events by the leaders involved in these great achievements or monumental failures. Throughout history, leadership is defined by the builders of nations; the people who persevered to overcome oppression and persecution; and the intellectual and creative leaders who have changed our world with their ideas and values. Yet the traits of these successful leaders vary so greatly, it almost seems that any type of personality or style can work to deliver great leadership.

One of the best articles on the subject of effective leaders' styles comes from a Harvard Business review titled, "Leadership that Gets Results." The article is based on research performed by the Hay/McBer consulting firm in which they analyzed a database of 20,000 executives to identify and categorize six distinct leadership styles. They then verified the effectiveness of these styles in a variety of business situations. Their conclusion was that leaders have six distinct leadership styles (Coercive, Authoritative, Affiliative, Democratic, Pacesetting, and Coaching), all of which are effective during different business situations and environments.

> "Coercive leaders demand immediate compliance. Authoritative leaders mobilize people toward a vision. Affiliative leaders create emotional bonds and harmony. Democratic leaders build consensus through participation. Pacesetting leaders expect excellence and self-direction. And coaching leaders develop people for the future. The styles, taken individually, appear to have a direct and unique impact on the working atmosphere of a company, division or team, and in turn on its financial performance. And perhaps the most important, the research indicates that leaders with the best results do not rely on only one leadership style; they use most of them in a given week—seamlessly and in different measure—depending on the business situation. Imagine the styles, then, as the array of clubs in a golf pro's bag. Over the course of a game, the pro picks and chooses clubs based on the demands of the shot. Sometimes he has to ponder his selection, but usually it is automatic. The pro senses the challenge ahead, swiftly pulls out the right tool, and elegantly puts it to work. That is how high-impact leaders operate, too."[1]

The best leaders understand and are able to adjust and select the best style given the business situation. You want to have leaders with different styles (or different clubs in their golf bag) and the ability to use various styles when the circumstances dictate. However, in addition to the ability to effectively use multiple styles, strong leaders must possess the same core skills or competencies.

For the purposes of leadership and building and maintaining a positive culture, you do not have to assess and identify styles. You need to identify and assess leadership competencies. Simply defined, leadership competencies are varied descriptions of skills and/or activities that can be assessed in terms of a leader's ability to perform them. When you consider everything you want and need your leaders to do and do well, it may seem like a long list for even one leadership position; however, you must keep in mind that you are not trying to define *everything* a leader does in terms of competencies, you are just trying to define the leadership actions that will be most relied upon for a given position in a given industry.

Customizing your leadership competencies for your different leadership levels (team leader, team manager, VP), functions (operations, finance, sales, etc.) and your business type (manufacturing, service, consulting, etc.) will require careful thought and consideration. You will identify between eight to fourteen competencies to define any given leadership role, and six of them will be the same for every leadership position in your company. These are the six core leadership competencies leaders must have to build and maintain a positive culture. They are the six core competencies that every leader in your organization must not only possess, but be able to execute daily at a proficient or strength level of competency.

Later, I will discuss the customizing of your leadership roles with an extensive list of competencies; but for now, we need to define and discuss the importance of the six core competencies for leadership. Every positive business culture must have leaders that are proficient or excel at the following six core leadership competencies:

COMMUNICATION
BUILDING TRUST
GAINING COMMITMENT
BUILDING A SUCCESSFUL TEAM
LEVERAGING DIVERSITY
DEVELOPING EMPLOYEES

Communication

As a leadership competency, communication is defined as the ability to clearly convey information and ideas through a variety of media to individuals or groups in a manner that engages the audience and helps them understand and retain the message. Strong communicators organize their communications by clarifying purpose and importance, and by strongly emphasizing key points in a logical sequential format. They develop and format messages to their audience based on their background, experience, and sensitivities to communicate and ensure understanding. They seek input during communication, check understanding, listen to audience feedback, and adjust accordingly to optimize the message and information. Strong communicators identify communication needs and opportunities as well as create routine communications such as staff meetings or update calls as appropriate.

Effective communication is truly the lifeblood of a positive culture. An organization and its culture will thrive, be sustained, and nourished by effective communication; or it will be weakened, reduced, and limited by a lack of it. Effective communication enables employees to understand mission, vision, goals, and strategies. It allows employee and teams to share ideas, identify problems, overcome challenges, and develop solutions more quickly and effectively. It enables leaders to tap into and understand key employee perceptions and concerns so they can address them. It also allows leaders to mine the employee base for creative ideas and opportunities, as well as to optimize innovation and improvement efforts at all levels. Effective communication by your leadership is a critical component of building and maintaining a positive culture.

Conversely, ineffective communication, in the form of poor communication or lack of communication, is a culture killer. Wherever you find a negative or struggling culture, you will also find ineffective communication. Poor communication by leaders not only impairs the information and the understanding or context in which you would like it to be received; but it also sends a message, a negative communication of its own. The negative message is that the information being communicated isn't really important because leadership didn't make the effort to effectively communicate it. Making an effort to communicate and doing it poorly is worse than not communicating at all because it also sends a message to employees that their time isn't valuable and what you made a point to tell them really isn't important to you (the leadership) or the organization.

Real Examples

A company conference call is scheduled with all company leaders to launch a new leadership development program. The call is planned to begin with senior executives sharing the basics of the program, emphasizing its importance to company goals, and encouraging leader participation. The senior executives did not coordinate with each other and some of them arrived late to the meeting, delaying the start time by 15 minutes. By the time they began, the audience is no longer engaged; the messages are not well delivered or coordinated; and their desired emphasis on the importance of and enthusiasm for the program is not well conveyed or believed. Their actions communicated that their time (the executives' time) was more important than every other leaders' time that were participating on the call. It communicated that the leadership development program was not important enough for them to be on time or prepared for the meeting. They negatively impacted employees' perceptions on the importance of the program through poor communication.

Whenever there is a lack of information, employees will attempt to read between the lines and fill in the gaps. What they fill in can be complete speculation or directionally correct; but regardless, it will generally be perceived in a much more negative light. General speaking, your employees will always think the worse when something obvious is left unanswered. The resulting concern and churn can impact productivity. It can lead to employee relations and morale problems that will lead to increased costs to correct and address.

Real Examples

A company issues a mandate for the organization to reduce expenses by restricting all travel, meetings, and non-mandated spending in the fourth quarter. They establish lower budget targets for each department, but do not provide leaders with an explanation that can be shared with the organization. Employees are willing to help, but they are also concerned with the action. They begin asking questions concerning annual performance numbers, financial stability, and potential job reductions. In this situation, the lack of information creates negative employee concerns leading to reduced productivity and morale. In addition,

> the company also loses the opportunity to take full advantage of employee saving ideas and efforts. Had they effectively communicated, explained the need for the reduction, and made an effort to recruit employees' assistance; they would have achieved additional savings and avoided the productivity and morale impacts.

Communication is how information is delivered to employees and information is power. If you have information and when you have it determines your status and importance. If you find out someone else has information and you don't, you may feel left out and disrespected. It is a leader's job to assure that their employees get information in a reasonable amount of time to avoid these perceptions. When information is poorly communicated or not communicated at all, it undermines respect, trust, and how individual employee's feel about the value they bring to the company.

An organization must be full of leaders who are strong proactive communicators, know how to deliver messages, and work as a team to create and deliver them. This ability allows them to achieve a higher level of trust, respect, and employee engagement. In business there are many different issues and decisions that will occur each day that impact people, employees, or customers in many different ways. Employee groups can, and will, react very differently to the same information. What may seem positive to one group may seem very negative to another. This alone requires that your leaders be astute in their communication abilities and approach; because regardless of how employees feel about an issue, if it is well communicated, they will still feel respected and they will accept it. They may not like it or welcome it with open arms; but they will understand, accept it, perhaps support it, or more importantly not appose it.

One theory that I also subscribe heavily to is this: "50% of all resistance to an idea by individuals is a result of them not being asked their opinion or reaction to it." Consider that when selling your idea, half the resistance you will encounter can be eliminated if you simply ask people what they think about it ahead of time. When people are surprised and don't have all the facts, they get concerned and defensive about issues they otherwise would not have any significant concern about. Simply communicating proactively can save your company significant amounts of energy, resources, and cost.

Regardless of the news, if it's good or bad, direction changing or mundane, each and every communication is an opportunity to build and maintain positive company culture. Every time your leaders effectively communicate they build respect, they build trust and they emphasize the value of informed and engaged employees. Communication is a leadership competency every one of your leaders must possess and perform well.

Building Trust

As a leadership competency, building trust is defined as the ability to interact with others in a way that gives them confidence in one's intentions and those of the organization. Leaders who build trust demonstrate their honesty and integrity by consistently keeping their commitments; treating people with dignity, respect, and fairness; and standing up for others regardless of resistance or adversity. They disclose their thoughts, feelings, and ideas so their position is known while remaining open to, encouraging the sharing of, and listening objectively to, the ideas of others even when they conflict with their own. They make themselves available to listen. They follow up with related outcomes and information to ensure individuals know they were heard; and they positively reinforce open communication of concerns, new ideas, and diverse thinking.

A positive culture is sustained by trust. Trust is a core attribute of a positive culture and building trust is a core competency each of your leaders must possess and perform well. Trust between you, your leaders, and all employees will maintain and sustain your culture. It will allow you to work together in an open, honest environment where everyone feels safe. A high level of trust will also mean that employees will have a clear understanding of their role and what is expected of them. Trust promotes two-way communication; it demonstrates respect; and keeps people from wasting precious energy on hidden agendas and meaningless, unproductive, turf battles. Trust also allows you to effectively manage and lead through difficult business issues. Your leaderships' ability to build trust is a critical component of building and maintaining a positive culture.

Like all other relationships, work relationships are built on trust. In creating a high level of organizational trust, you are establishing a necessary platform for productive working relationships and a productive working environment. Inherently, most employees want to believe in and trust their leaders and their coworkers. They want to be able to share their thoughts and ideas in an open environment with freedom from hidden agendas or motives. This type of environment allows you to leverage the diverse ideas and creativity of your workforce. While this might seem naive on the surface because individual motives and company politics are a reality, an environment that is built on and sustained by trust is attainable through deliberate actions and focus. It is attainable because it does not eliminate the reality of motive or politics, rather it constructively encourages them by making it acceptable to have positions and motives when they are disclosed, shared and discussed openly. It is leveraging the trust you've built into your working environment.

One of the most significant advantages to building trust is simply not having distrust. Distrust, simple put, is a culture killer. It is staggering to consider the level of distrust inherent in the working relationships throughout the business world. Distrust limits communication, creativity, innovation and opportunity to improve your business. It negatively impacts your ability to leverage the diversity of your workforce, to gain acceptance of new ideas and initiatives, and to build your level of employee engagement. Distrust places a stranglehold on all these things by adding costly overhead to each and every employee interaction. In building trust, your leaders are avoiding the debilitating effects of organizational distrust.

Real Examples

A company is engaged in a legal dispute with a union in one of their subsidiaries over the payment of their annual bonus that is based on achieving earning targets. The union's contract language is upheld in court; the company in loses the legal dispute; and is forced to pay the disputed bonus amount to employees (with interest). The outcome of this situation taints all employee perceptions (union, non-union and salaried employees) of the company's wiliness to pay annual bonuses and honor their established incentive plan. This situation alone not only creates distrust of the company's intentions related to the incentive plan, it calls into question motive, fairness, and integrity on every issue. There are, of course, two sides to every story; but in this situation, the company did not do the right things in terms of interpreting the contract language, building and communicating understanding around the issue, and acting in a way that builds trust.

Trust is about consistent, predictable, dependable behavior and attitudes by leaders over time. In reality, there is no difference between a lack of trust or distrust. You might have situations where you do not yet have enough trust and are working to build it; but for the most part it is all or nothing, either you have trust or you have distrust. The tricky thing is trust can turn on a dime; and if your don't have enough of it built up, one wrong decision or one significantly large, poorly managed issue can compromise you and put you not only in a situation where you need to build trust, but you also have to overcome distrust. It's much easier to build a relationship than to repair one. It takes time (months and months) to build trust through deliberate, repeated, and consistent actions; but only one decision or action to create distrust and nullify previous gains. Your starting point has then been compromised and it will take even longer to overcome the distrust that was created and return to your previous level. The minute you start to lose the trust of your employees, you'll begin to lose your positive culture; and then the level of employee engagement will drop along with their commitment and energy.

An interesting concept that also applies to building trust is that of social capital amongst employees in an organization. In Harvard Business Review, Laurence Prusak's article, *How to invest in Social Capital,* presents the concept of social capital as analogous to each working relationship having its own bank account. As you work with an individual or employee group, you are either adding funds to that account or drawing funds from it. Every time you have a positive outcome or interaction, you have added funds to the account. Over time the account builds and you can more easily tap into it and leverage what you have saved. Two people who have never worked together will begin with a balance of zero. Two people who have had difficultly working together might be starting with a negative balance.

> "Every manager knows that business runs better when people within the organization know and trust one another—deals move faster and more smoothly, teams are more productive, people learn more quickly and perform with more creativity. Strong relationships, most managers will agree, are the grease of an organization.... Scholars have given a name—social capital—to

> the relationships that make organizations work effectively. The term nicely captures the notion that investments in these relationships return real gains that show up on the bottom line."[2]

The article goes on to discuss that social capital is under assault by increased volatility (change, mergers, restructuring) and virtuality (remote leadership, virtual workforces, outsourcing, etc). These business trends serve to break down social capital, further reinforcing the need to have leaders that are capable of building trust. The building of organizational trust is the building of social capital, with the understanding that it takes significant effort to save or build up your account; yet it is very easy to drain the account down to almost nothing with one mistake.

Every time your leaders effectively build trust, they are sustaining and maintaining your positive culture by defining the necessary platform for productive working relationships while minimizing the debilitating effects of distrust. The ability to build trust is a leadership competency every one of your leaders must possess and perform well.

Gaining Commitment

As a leadership competency, gaining commitment is defined as the ability to use appropriate interpersonal styles and techniques to gain acceptance of ideas or plans and modifying one's own behavior to accommodate tasks, situations, and individuals involved. Leaders who effectively gain commitment are able to describe goals, possibilities, expectations, and future opportunities in a way that provides a high level of clarity while generating interest and excitement. They are able to leverage their interpersonal skills and relationships and utilize others' ideas and input to make people feel valued, appreciated and included. They are able to facilitate genuine acceptance and work to help people understand and adapt to changes and new ideas by using various influences, strategies, and approaches.

Gaining commitment is all about the power of people, the power of employees. It is about understanding just how powerful individual commitment and acceptance can be when trying to make a new idea, process, or organization work. It is also about how lack of commitment can be so ineffective, draining, and resistive. Gaining commitment is the essence of the "A" in the formula **2A * Q = E**. Where "A" is the level of organizational acceptance of a technical solution, "Q" is the quality of the technical solution, and "E" is the effectiveness of the solution. Leaders who are able to gain the commitment of employees as individuals and groups are leveraging that very important part of the equation, acceptance. The ability of your leadership to gain employee commitment is a critical component of building and maintaining a positive culture. Most businesses focus only on solutions—what is to be done (the Q) because they assume a solid technical solution will be accepted because it is logical and because they, the executives, decided upon it. They overlook the power of employee commitment; the reality that if employees do not accept a new idea or process change they will greatly reduce its effectiveness and sometime even stop it altogether. They leave untapped the power of employees to make almost any technical solution work when they are committed and determined. In the book, *The Human Capital Edge: 21 People Management Practices Your Company Must Implement (or Avoid) to Maintain Shareholder Value,* Bruce N. Pfau and Ira T. Kay document the results of Watson Wyatt's WorkUSA® 2000 study to quantify the shareholder value of employee commitment.

> "The numbers in Watson Wyatt's WorkUSA® 2000 survey of 7500 workers show that companies whose employees are highly committed to their employers deliver dramatically higher returns to shareholders. Firms with a high employee commitment index rated 36 percentage points higher total return to shareholders than those with a lower employee commitment. Firms with a high employee commitment index actually outperformed the S&P 500 by 24 percentage points."[3]

It is amazing how little effort is put into gaining commitment and building employees' level of acceptance by the typical organization. So often, organizations simply tell employees what to do; what has been decided; or what will be done to them. They mandate, edict, and command their way through the business day because they are the boss. They have the title and the ability to hire, fire, and roadblock careers. This truly is the lowest level of passion or engagement that can be obtained from employees. This approach means that employees will do only what they were told. It means they will have no personal stake in the success or failure of your idea. Their only concern is completing the commanded task as required. It also means if they don't like, accept, or understand the importance of what they have been asked to do; they will gladly let it fail even if they could have put forth the extra effort to make it work. There are also several ways to convince oneself that you do not need to gain commitment on a particular issue. "I don't have time to convince everyone of everything," is one of them. "Everyone knows their role and what they are supposed to do; they need to go do it," is another. There are times to command and to act fast—in emergencies, in times of great financial duress where time is short, when immediate action is needed for safety, customer service, financial viability, compliance to regulations, or when you are positive you already have a high level of commitment.

Other than emergency situations, commanding people what to do is the ultimate in ego, laziness, and ignorance. Whenever something new is introduced that employees have any type of personal stake in, they will resent the fact that it was mandated or that they were simply commanded so their level of commitment will be low or nonexistent. Failure of your leadership to build and gain commitment on key issues at critical times is a culture killer.

Gaining commitment is not about getting 100% acceptance on everything 100% of the time. Rather, it is about ensuring as much commitment and acceptance from your employees as possible in everything they do for your company. It is about knowing where to focus energy and where to gain commitment. A leader seldom needs to gain commitment for a basic job task that is routinely performed; but whenever there is a change, a new policy, process or idea, the need to put time and energy into gaining commitment must be carefully considered.

Dwight D. Eisenhower was quoted as saying, *"Leadership is the art of getting someone else to do something you want done because he wants to do it."* This quote captures the essence of a leader's ability to gain commitment, champion change, and lead. It points out that leadership is not an exact science or method. It is in fact, an art. It communicates that action must be taken by the leader to make others not only follow, but believe and want to follow because they are committed. Leaders gain commitment; leaders build acceptance. Gaining commitment is a leadership competency every one of your leaders must possess and perform well.

Building a Successful Team

As a leadership competency, building a successful team is defined as the ability to use appropriate methods and a flexible interpersonal style to help build a cohesive team and facilitate the completion of team goals.

Leaders who successfully build teams develop clear direction for the team in terms of purpose and importance as well as specific and measurable team goals and objectives. They create appropriate structures by establishing team member roles and responsibilities, and defining formal steering, review and support functions. They are able to facilitate goal accomplishment; involve team members in discussion, decisions and actions; share information that is important to the team; leverage the team members' diversity; and model commitment for the team itself.

A positive culture is driven by teamwork. Each and every day teams in every form across an organization are driving results. Too often we only focus on teams that come together for a specific purpose, project, or initiative. These types of teams are extremely important for both the business issues they address and for the high organizational visibility they have. The success of these types of teams and the business results they achieve can be a tremendous advertisement for teamwork and your culture. But as important as these teams are, the day-to-day teams and teamwork are even more important.

The employees that report directly to each leader in your organization are a team. Across the organization the individual employees from different areas that come together to deal with a specific process, problem, or function represent teams. These types of teams are much more numerous; therefore, their issues and work are much more frequent. They are in operation every single day running your business. How they function and how well they execute as a team will drive the pace of your organization and your results. Having each and every employee understand positive team dynamics, practice good teaming skills, and participate as a team member on a positive team is vital. Employees can only get to that point if leadership values teams and teamwork, and has the skills to build them. Your leaderships' ability to build successful teams is a critical component of creating and maintaining a positive culture.

When you don't have teamwork, you don't have participation; you don't have acceptance; and you don't have diversity of ideas, solutions, or outcomes. Organizations can survive with little or no teamwork, but they will be highly ineffective compared to what they could be because they are missing the opportunity to have engaged and energized teams of employees driving the organization.

> Real Examples
>
> A front line worker on the production floor is given the plans to manufacture a new part for a component of an automobile body. In reviewing the design, the employee realizes the dimension of the component will not allow it to function properly once installed. The employee's job function gives them this unique perspective and exposure to recognize this situation even before the part is manufactured and tested. The employee says nothing and just builds the part because that is their job. The result is time, material, and energy is needlessly wasted.

I guarantee this happens with alarming frequency across all industries because of lack of teamwork and a lack of a positive culture. In this example it is easy to say there are many reasons for this problem. The least likely of them is that the employee is a bad employee and didn't do their job. Very, very few people go to work each day and don't want to do the right thing. It is more likely that this result is due to poor leadership and a negative culture in the form of poor communication, lack of trust, low employee involvement, and of course, teamwork. Lack of teamwork embodies all these ills. This employee was not part of the team; not invited, nor encouraged, to be part of a team; not part of the initial design team; not part of the stakeholder team; not encouraged to communicate ideas and concerns; not trusting that the feedback would be received positively; and not valued or respected as an individual.

Of course, not everyone can be involved in everything 100% of the time; but everyone can be a part of a team in what they do every day. Leaders must make all employees feel they are a part of a team. They must assure strong team dynamics and assure participation. They must build successful teams in every form: project teams, direct staff teams and cross-functional teams.

Few things can be as exciting, energizing, and fulfilling as being a part of a great team—a winning team. Of course, there are also times when teams lose or fall short of their goals. Sometimes teams make mistakes and could have performed better; other times they are simply outplayed or overcome by the circumstances. Strong teams take their licks and bounce back. However, weak teams or teams in name only fall apart, erode from within and become even more dysfunctional. Being a part of a losing team because it is dysfunctional is a huge morale killer. In a dysfunctional team, the team members feel bad about the team and themselves. Employees know when they are not working together and they recognize when a team is dysfunctional. Lack of teamwork and/or dysfunctional teams are culture killers. Each and every leader must have the skills and ability to assure they have a solid team in place.

Teams are an absolute necessity in business. They will always outpace individual efforts in terms of diversity, ideas, and results. Teamwork creates energy; it builds respect among team members; it sparks creativity; and provides balance for business solutions. Being a part of a great team where team members share a common vision and work towards a common goal can be an incredibly fulfilling experience for employees. It is every leader's responsibility to make each employee feel part of a team and to make that team successful. The ability to build a successful team is a leadership competency every one of your leaders must possess and perform well.

Leveraging Diversity

As a leadership competency, leveraging diversity is defined as the ability to recruit, develop, and retain a diverse high quality workforce; and to lead and manage an inclusive workplace environment that maximizes the talents of each person to achieve sound business results. Leaders who are able to effectively leverage workforce diversity respect, understand, value, and seek out individual differences and ideas to achieve the mission and vision of the organization. They recognize diversity in employees as an organizational asset that creates competitive advantage and set standards of behavior for treating all employees with respect and dignity. Leaders hold themselves and others accountable for increasing diversity by recruiting and developing individuals from varied backgrounds, experiences, cultures, and functional areas.

A positive culture is fueled by diversity. It is fueled by creativity, innovation, new ideas, and approaches. It is fueled by looking at opportunities and problems from as many different perspectives as possible. This is important not only to exhaust all the possible ways of accomplishing a goal, but to also structure and position your solution for a variety of issues and outcomes. The business world is very diverse. Today's companies operate in a connected, full-time access, on-demand, completely wired global economy that is, as a result, a sea of diversity and complexity. No one person regardless of their experiences has enough diversity of thought to deal appropriately with all the problems, develop the optimal strategies for all opportunities, and plan for all contingencies. Your leaderships' ability to leverage the diversity of your workforce is a critical component of creating and maintaining a positive culture.

Singularity of thought in a person, in a team, or in a company will never produce the best outcomes. Leaders who know how to leverage diversity understand that a team full of people that think the same, have the same work experiences, and share the same perceptions about business, life and community will not consider all the potential outcomes from all the possible perspectives. The majority of business challenges that companies face today reflect a diverse business environment. In today's world no company can afford to leave the majority of questions unasked, the majority of solutions unevaluated, and the majority of perceptions unconsidered.

Leaving the benefits of diversity untapped and unrealized is a culture killer. It is a culture killer not for the loss of the things left undone or sub-optimized (which are performance killers), but for what it communicates to employees when you disregard the benefits of diversity. If you ignore diversity, employees will see it; they will feel it; and they will lose respect for you and the company as a result. Ignoring diversity sends a powerful negative message that not every employee is valued. It is a message you cannot afford to send and you must never send.

Your leaders need to know how to leverage diversity and at the same time select people with the same core leadership skills and competencies. Your leaders need to respect and take advantage of diversity of thought and ideas while at the same time build commitment and acceptance of a common vision, strategy and goals. Your leaders need to know how to encourage and respect diversity while aggressively managing and removing employees who don't get results by doing things in the right ways that support your positive culture. As you can see, this requires skill, judgment, and a crystal clear understanding of the difference between diversity of thought and lack of acceptance, commitment, and sharing cultural values. It is one of the most challenging components and reoccurring questions you will have as your build and maintain your positive culture.

Make sure your leadership understands and has the skills to leverage diversity. If you do, they will fill your company full of leaders that think differently, have lived differently, come from different backgrounds, and have experienced different things. The result will be teams that design better products, develop better plans, respond better to crisis, and create better solutions together. Diversity of thought, diversity of experience, and diversity of perception are the fuel that fires your company's problem solving and creative furnaces. The ability of your leaders to leverage diversity is a leadership competency every one of your leaders must possess and perform well.

Developing Employees

As a leadership competency, developing employees is defined as the ability to plan and support the development of individuals' skills and abilities so that they can fulfill current or future job roles and responsibilities more effectively. Leaders who develop employees, co-develop development plans with their employees and have awareness and understanding of each employee's career goals. They provide employees with challenging and stretching tasks and assignments and frequently meet with them to discuss progress and development.

Development isn't a special effort to address a problem or need. It is a continual process of growth and improvement. It is also happening to everyone all the time. As employees, all of us are always learning, changing, and adapting in some way. The business world is not stagnant; nor are the challenges or situations that employees face every day. The situations employees face each day are ever changing; and everyone is to some extent changing or developing to address them. Even people who are staunchly resistant to all change do in fact change or develop over time in some way, shape, or form. The question is, is it conscious, well focused and optimized? Everyone has new challenges in their job; but are they actively working to develop themselves to address them and are they being activity supported their leadership? Your leaderships' ability to develop employees is a critical component of building and maintaining a positive culture.

Developing employees isn't about being a tremendous coach or teacher; it is about leadership involvement with employees' work lives. It is about taking the time; taking an interest; and focusing in on key development challenges and opportunities as they arise. Coaches and teachers are typically expected to know the answers. The nice thing about developing employees is that the leader doesn't have to have all the answers. Leaders can develop employees by setting up a process that allows people to become more self-aware; builds on their strengths; compensates for their shortcomings; sets clear goals; and confronts development realities (both needs and opportunities).

In setting up that process, they only need to be willing to commit the time to help their employees find the answers and utilize all the available resources to do so. Resources for development include other leaders, human resource professionals, and business/organizational development books, ideas, and methodologies. Probably the most common resource that will be used is the employee-leader conversation. A conversation that is in the form of an active two-way discussion about what to do in a given situation, how to tackle that difficult relationship, or what approach to try to get different results. Leaders who are good at developing employees will find that their teams are much more productive; their inter-departmental relationships smoother and stronger; and their "difficult personnel issues" much less time consuming.

A positive culture is focused on its employees in many ways: performance, communications, trust, recognition, training, and development. One of the strongest and most impactful ways to focus on employees is individual by individual, developing them to be better at what they do everyday. Development is about developing something new or improving upon an existing skill that is valuable to you in your current work. It's very personal and one of the most individual employee-focused activities your leadership can perform.

Employees are an organization's most valuable assets. Ignoring your human assets and failing to invest time and energy into further developing them is a culture killer. It is a culture killer because it communicates to employees that you do not value them. Machines, equipment, tools, products, and market share all change, wear out, become obsolete, and deteriorate over time. None of those assets will help you adapt, grow, or adjust your business to keep up with the changing world. Nothing is more flexible, adaptable, creative, or capable than the human mind. Development is not about believing your employees are not good enough; it's about believing and knowing they can be even better. Developing employees will create strong working relationships between leaders and employees. The effort itself communicates value, appreciation, and confidence in each other. A leadership quote by John Maxwell describes this concept well, *"It is wonderful when the people believe in their leader; it's more wonderful when the leader believes in the people."* If your leadership believes in employees and makes a committed effort to continually develop them, employees will also believe in their leader, their company, and you. The ability to develop employees is a leadership competency every one of your leaders must possess and perform well.

***

If you have leaders that can do these six things (communicate, build trust, gain commitment, build successful teams, leverage diversity and develop employees) and do them well, you'll have won 90% of the battle for a positive culture and optimal company performance. You will also need technical aptitude and knowledge and additional competencies based on position, level, function, and your type of business; but these six core leadership competencies will make or break a leader every time which means it will make or break your culture every time. High performance companies are built on, and sustained by, the quality of their leadership. I've had the benefit of working for and with exceptional leaders, but never truly understood the full impact of strong leadership until I experienced truly poor leadership. Companies with poor or absentee leadership (using the term leadership meaning in title only, not practice) will be condemned to mediocrity in the short term and failure in the long term.

The fiercest business competition in the future will not be for size, scope, position, or market share; it will be for the best human assets, the best employees, and the best leaders. Leaders possessing these six core leadership competencies, the high performance leaders that can build a positive culture. As CEO, it is a competition you must win not only once, but continuously. You'll have to identify, evaluate, and hire the best; and then keep them. The good news is—the better you are at competing for and getting them, the better your culture will be and the more employees will want to stay and work for your company.

COMPETE FOR THE BEST CULTURE; COMPETE FOR THE BEST EMPLOYEES; AND COMPETE FOR THE BEST LEADERS

Leaders build acceptance by how they lead, and in turn build and maintain your culture. Leaders have tremendous opportunity each and

every day to make your company a place where people want to work, a place where everyone wants to work. ALL of your leadership must possess the ability to communicate, build trust, gain commitment, build a successful team, leverage the diversity of employees, and develop their employees. Leadership will create and maintain your positive culture; this is why leadership is everything.

CHAPTER IV

Use Teams (Diversity is Strength)

A positive culture is driven by teamwork. Positive culture and leadership are the two most important things for the success of your company. Your culture is your foundation and leadership is everything, but you cannot fully achieve a positive culture without effective teams and teamwork.

As you select, develop, and build your leadership; as you create and foster a positive culture; you must use teams effectively and those individual teams must function effectively. In so many ways teamwork will positively impact your culture and help define what it *feels* like to work in your company. Where you find effective teamwork, you will also find respect, enthusiasm, collaboration, communication, openness, trust, creativity, energy, and engaged employees. Where you find teamwork, you will almost always find a positive culture or the beginnings of a positive culture. Command and control organizations do not understand teamwork; because they do not have balanced participation, open sharing of ideas, nor diversity of thought. Teams allow you to leverage your workforce diversity, and your diversity is your strength; strength in the form of better business solutions, ideas, and approaches. A positive culture is driven by teamwork. Leaders create and lead teams, and teamwork breeds excitement, employee engagement and ultimately, success.

In terms of leveraging diversity, the value of teams is simple. Teams allow you to openly consider and debate a variety of solutions, ideas and approaches to any type of business problem, need, or opportunity. This is why teams will always outperform individuals. Even a great idea from one person can be made even better with additional input from others with different perspectives.

Singularity of thought will never produce the best outcomes; just as a team of people who all think the same will never produce the best outcome. Teams full of people that think the same, have the same work experiences, and share the same perceptions about business, life, and community will come to agreement quickly. They will have very little conflict and "they" will all be satisfied with the outcome. This approach is the easy way out; but, as a result, the team solution will be sub-optimal. It is sub-optimal because this type of team leaves the majority of questions unasked, the majority of solutions unevaluated, and the majority of perceptions unconsidered. Teams must come to consensus, AFTER they have positive conflict, debate, and compromise. After they have considered multiple options and variations to arrive at the best, most balanced, answer.

If you fill your company full of smart people that think differently, have lived differently, come from different backgrounds, and have experienced different things; you will have a diverse organization. If you build teams that reflect your diverse organization, you'll leverage the strength of that diversity.

TEAMS ALLOW YOU TO LEVERAGE YOUR WORKFORCE DIVERSITY, AND DIVERSITY IS STRENGTH

A positive culture is driven by teamwork because teamwork creates the best business solutions and results. It also creates positive culture because it creates respect, enthusiasm, collaboration, communication, openness, trust, creativity, energy, and engaged employees. All of these things are found in the core attributes of a positive culture. Where these attributes exist, you will find a company where employees want to work; where they are committed and engaged. Teamwork will be known as "how" your company does things; "how" employees work together to solve problems, make improvements, develop new ideas, and accomplish goals (2H * W = P). Team solutions and work products will be more effective because of the acceptance level the team builds for their diverse, balanced, and high quality technical solutions (2A * Q = E).

Being a part of a great team where team members share a common vision and work towards a common goal can be an incredibly fulfilling experience for employees. You and your leadership must promote teamwork, commit to educating the organization on how to be team leaders; participate as team members; and utilize teams to generate results that positively influence your culture.

USE TEAMS TO BOTH GENERATE RESULTS AND POSITIVELY INFLUENCE YOUR CULTURE

To have an organization with effective teams and teamwork, you must understand the core attributes of teamwork and your leaderships' role in building and maintaining teams. The core attributes of teamwork are:

EFFECTIVE TEAM LEADERSHIP
CLEAR UNDERSTANDING OF ROLES AND EXPECTATIONS
SHARED VISION AND GOALS
TEAM MEMBER DIVERSITY
REWARD AND RECOGNITION OF RESULTS

Effective Team Leadership

A team cannot achieve success, realize its goals, or have positive team dynamics without effective team leadership. Each of your leaders must be assessed and reviewed for the core leadership competency of building a successful team. Every leader in your organization must have the ability to be a team leader because every leader will lead their own team of direct reports each and every day. They must also be an effective team member for the team they lead, for their leader's (their boss's) team, and for any other special project or ongoing cross-functional teams.

An effective team leader must be a sound facilitator with the ability to use appropriate methods and a flexible inter-personal style to build a cohesive team and shepherd them to the completion of team goals. Effective team leaders must establish a clear direction for the team in terms of purpose, importance, priorities and measurable team goals and objectives. They must create the appropriate structures in terms of defining team member roles and responsibilities as well as establishing formal steering, review, and support meetings and functions. As they facilitate towards accomplishment of team goals, they must skillfully involve all team members in discussions, decisions and actions; share information that is important to the team; leverage the team's diversity; and model commitment for the team itself. They must participate and guide; provide appropriate direction; and make decisions when needed without dominating or limiting discussion. They need to assess team member buy-in and acceptance in addition to acknowledging points and opinions; yet know when to invest time and when to move past non-productive areas. Effective team leadership requires focus and practice, the development and refinement of many skills, and an understanding that at times it is more of an art than a science. To have an effective team, you must have effective team leadership.

Clear Understanding of Roles and Expectations

Every team and team member must have a clear understanding of individual and team roles and expectations. When you have team members trying to fill the same role, you will have confusion, frustration, and possibly unproductive competition. This situation also breeds lack of trust because individual motives and intentions will be questioned. It brings into question accountability for results. That is why it is important to clearly define team members' roles on the team and what is expected of them. Team members' expected contribution and their area of expertise must be identified for both the individual and for the rest of the team. This does not mean however that the rest of the team cannot be involved, provide feedback or assistance into another team member's role. The clarity of role is not meant to exclude others nor censure or restrict input or participation. Rather it is meant to promote efficient teamwork and team dynamics as well as to establish appropriate accountabilities.

In defining each team member's role, you will also define the expectations associated with that role. Establishing expectations establishes team member accountably and responsibility for tasks, deliverables, and results. Clarity of individual team member roles and expectations will translate into clarity of roles and expectations for the team itself. Establishing clear roles and expectations is a building block for both accountability and trust. To have an effective team, the team and each team member must have a clear understanding of roles and expectations.

Shared Vision and Goals

A team is not a team without a shared vision and goals. At the start of any team, each individual will have their own thoughts, ideas, and desired outcomes for their team and themselves. This is normal as different things motivate different individuals; so as a result, they have individual based perceptions, goals and aspirations. This will be especially true when a team reflects the diversity of your organization. Each team member envisions the best outcomes they can imagine that align with their goals and aspirations. This diversity of thought is valuable; therefore, it should be captured and acknowledged. It is possible that many of the team members' goals and their unique vision will align with the team vision and goals. It is also likely that not everyone's goals and vision will fit perfectly with what the team needs to accomplish.

Some team members will be very focused and possibility too narrow in their desired scope, while others will want an all encompassing scope that will be unachievable. The goals you set for any team, the timeline for achieving them, and the end resulting vision must be balanced. It must be both ambitious and yet bounded by reality.

It is very important to spend time up front establishing the shared team vision and goals, and to quickly build the acceptance and buy-in of those goals. The key word is "shared." Team members must share the vision. They must share in the goals. They all must understand what the vision is and what the goals are, in order to commit to achieving them. Team members that do not share the vision and the goals will not be committed and therefore will not be part of the team. The other team members will notice and problems will result. These employees will be amongst the "not-engaged" or "actively disengaged" group of employees. At some point in time, if they can't be recruited and if they don't share the vision, they will be detrimental to your team and must be removed. An effective team will have well defined goals and a clear vision that is shared by each team member.

Team Member Diversity

Team member diversity is vital to optimizing team results. Diversity of experience, background, perception, and thought will optimize and amplify team performance. As you build a team initially or over time, you must have a keen awareness of diversity and your ability to leverage its benefits. This can be challenging because it is natural to seek someone who "fits in" with the team. In fact, we've already discussed that team members need to "fit-in" when it comes to sharing vision and goals. At the same time, team members need to think differently to challenge each other with different ideas, thoughts, and perspectives.

Select team members deliberately. Look for opportunities to include different backgrounds, experiences, cultures, races, sexes, and personality types on your team; but also look past the typical "surface features" of diversity. While it is valuable to look diverse from a culture and employee base perspective, it is more important to be diverse. Do not be afraid to take chances and step outside the norm. Everyone is influenced to some degree by stereotypes so it is important to remember that most often strength is found where stereotypes predict weakness. Always make an effort to look beyond the norm and the stereotype to find the strength and the opportunity. Regardless of what team members look like or how they may be typically labeled, an effective team will be comprised of team members who are diverse in experience, background, and way of thinking.

Diversity enables and creates opportunity for positive conflict. Positive conflict is disagreement and debate for the right reasons. It is an open, respectful, and energetic dialog/discussion of different and often opposing ideas. When it comes to effective teamwork, harmony is bad. The worst thing a team can do is to value and seek out harmony over positive conflict. Create teams that reflect true diversity, leverage strength of that diversity, and optimize your results.

Reward and Recognition of Results

Effective teams reward and recognize results—results in terms of progress, small victories, major successes, and completion of final goals. Rewarding and recognizing gives feedback to the team and to the team members. It is positive reinforcement for the team and at times individual team members as they work toward their vision and reach milestones. It allows the team leader to keep the team focused on the right things and when necessary, adjust focus or behavior. Teams must be focused on and pay attention to, results. One way to help achieve that focus is through reward and recognition of results.

Effective reward and recognition for teams builds your culture by reinforcing teams and teamwork. Every time the organization recognizes team accomplishments, it builds increased understanding of the value of, and expectation for, teamwork.

It is an opportunity to emphasize the "how" part of a team; to underscore the value of acceptance; and the value of culture. Teamwork itself is "how" the organization accomplishes its goals, focusing it further on the positive efforts of "how" a team builds consensus, leverages diversity, communicates to stakeholders; and in the process, increases the effectiveness of its technical solutions (remember 2A * Q = E and 2H * W = P).

Timeliness is a key component of recognition and rewards. Recognition and rewards need not always be monetary to have significant motivational impact for employees and teams, but they must be timely. The optimal incentive practice is to reward the extra effort and extraordinary performance that adds value to the company immediately to reinforce and promote continued positive behaviors. While that is not usually practical, efforts to recognize and reward must happen quickly to optimize effectiveness and be fair and reasonable in terms of consistent company practice.

Ideally, each leader will have budgeted reasonable resources for recognition and rewards, and be encouraged to use those resources appropriately and effectively.

Effective reward and recognition of results provides critical feedback and positive reinforcement for teams, individual team members, and the organization as a whole.

EFFECTIVE TEAMS HAVE TRUST, ACCOUNTABILITY, POSITIVE CONFLICT, COMMITMENT AND A FOCUS ON RESULTS

Dysfunctional teams lack trust; avoid both conflict and accountability; and are not truly committed to a shared vision and goals. Dysfunctional teams do not produce good results in terms of outcomes, solutions products, and positive cultural influences and benefits. In his book, *The Five Dysfunctions of a Team,* Patrick Lencioni, author and management consultant, presents a solid model for teamwork in the form of a leadership fable in which a new leader works to correct the dysfunction in her new team. In the process, he defines a strong model for successful teamwork. Lencioni's five dysfunctions are described below:

> "The first is an **absence of trust** among team members. Essentially, this stems from their unwillingness to be vulnerable within the group. Team members who are not genuinely open with one another about their mistakes and weaknesses make it impossible to build a foundation of trust. This failure to build trust is damaging because it sets the tone for the second dysfunction: **fear of conflict**. Teams that lack trust are incapable of engaging in unfiltered and passionate debate of ideas. Instead, they resort to veiled discussions and guarded comments. A lack of healthy conflict is a problem because it ensures the third dysfunction of a team; **lack of commitment**. Without having aired their opinions in the course of passionate and open debate, team members rarely, if ever, buy in and commit to decisions, through they may feign agreement during meetings. Because of this lack of real commitment and buy-in, team members develop an **avoidance of accountability**, the fourth dysfunction. Without committing to a clear plan of action, even the most focused and driven people often hesitate to call their peers on actions and behaviors that

seem counterproductive to the good of the team. Failure to hold one another accountable creates an environment where the fifth dysfunction can thrive. **Inattention to results** occurs when team members put their individual needs (such as ego, career development, or recognition) or even the need of their divisions above the collective goals of the team. Another way to understand this model is to take the opposite approach—a positive one—and imagine how members of truly cohesive teams behave:

- They trust one another.
- They engage in unfiltered conflict around ideas.
- They commit to decisions and plans of action
- They hold one another accountable for delivering against those plans
- They focus on the achievement of collective results."[I]

The core attributes of teamwork in the CEO's Blueprint are designed to create teaming environments that allow leaders to avoid dysfunctional team pitfalls while they build and maintain a positive culture. Effective team leadership and a diverse team membership must build trust while allowing for positive team conflict around ideas and solutions. Establishing clear roles and expectations along with a shared vision and goals, builds commitment to decisions and direction that establish appropriate team accountabilities. Lastly, effective reward and recognition of results assure team focus on achievement of results and success building actions.

Now that we understand the core attributes of teamwork, the value of using teams, and the opportunity teams provide to leverage diversity and dramatically influence your culture, we need to consider where teams will exist in your organization. Where are they? What kind of team are they? What form do they take? How many active teams will you have at any one time? If you value teamwork, teams are everywhere at every level of the organization. You just need to define and recognize them. They come in many different forms ranging from the informal to the highly visible special project teams. At any one time, you will have more active teams than you have leaders. All these statements are true if you make teamwork part of your culture and if your positive culture is driven by teamwork.

In business, teams exist everywhere. In a positive culture they are much more prolific than we typically realize or notice. Recognizing that teams and teamwork must exist everywhere and at all times seems simple in concept, until you look at how few companies really understand and promote effective teamwork. You must deliberately define and recognize teams and teamwork in all its forms across the spectrum of your company. To do this, we'll consider teams in three main categories: leadership's direct staff, cross-functional teams, and special project teams. Teams in these three forms will exist in significant numbers in your company all the time, if you have a positive culture. And, these teams will drive results each and every day reinforcing your positive culture in the process.

The most prolific form of team in your organization will be your leadership's direct staff. The direct reports of every leader in your organization are a team. This means that at any given time every leader belongs to two active teams. The first being their team of direct reports of which they are the team leader, and the second being their leader's (their boss's) team of which they are a team member. This is why building a successful team is one of the six core leadership competencies. Every leader must know how to be both an effective team leader and productive team member. In your organization, every employee is a team member and every leader is a team member and team leader, including you, the CEO.

Across the organization the individual employees that come together to deal with a specific, process, problem, or function represent teams. These teams can be best described as cross-functional teams. Think of these teams as a typical dotted-line team; they always exist due to necessity, but are often not formally recognized. These types of teams are much more numerous and the issues they work on are much more frequent. They are in operation every single day running your business, yet they are the least recognized of teams. They are underutilized in business because they are below the surface and not enough focus is placed on these types of teams; yet it is very important that you define these teams and set expectations for them like all others. They are dealing with the most challenging issues faced by your company each and every day; issues that cut across the organization and require the focus of multiple leaders and functions to address. These leaders and functions will most often have conflicting areas of focus so setting expectations for teamwork for these teams is critical because the results need balance and focus beyond any individual leader or function.

Lastly, the most commonly utilized, recognized, and visible type of team is the special project team. Too often, we only focus on these teams because they are formed to address a specific need, project, or initiative. These types of teams are extremely important for both the business issues they address and for the high organizational visibility they have. The success of these types of teams and the business results they achieve can be a tremendous advertisement for teamwork and your culture.

As important as these teams are, the day-to-day teams are even more important. Often there is a lot of focus on project teams and team initiatives, but the key is to ingrain teamwork and team philosophy into your culture, into your direct staff, and into your cross-functional teams. How the day-to-day teams function and how well they execute will drive the pace of your organization and your results. Having each and every employee understand positive team dynamics, practice good teaming skills, and be a part of a successful team, is vital. Employees can only reach that point if leadership values teams and teamwork and has the skills to build them. To have a positive culture that is driven by teams, you have to recognize all your teams, create awareness for all employees that they are team members, and set expectations that they work and act as a team. A critical communication for your organization is that every employee is a team member and every leader is a team leader. This is a message you and your leaders must deliver each and every day. Your leaderships' ability to build successful teams is a critical component of building and maintaining a positive culture.

EVERY EMPLOYEE IS A TEAM MEMBER, EVERY LEADER IS A TEAM LEADER

As you select, develop, and build your leadership; as you create and foster a positive culture; you must use teams. Few things can be as exciting, energizing, and fulfilling as being a part of a great team. Teamwork creates energy; it builds respect among team members; it sparks creativity; and it provides balance for business solutions and initiatives. Teams allow you to leverage your workforce diversity, and diversity is strength. Use teams to both generate results and positively influence your culture.

The core attributes of teamwork are effective team leadership; having a clear understanding of team roles and expectations; sharing vision and goals; team member diversity; and rewarding and recognizing team achievements. Every employee is a team member; every leader is a team

leader. Effective teams have trust, accountability, positive conflict, commitment, and a focus on results.

In a positive culture, teams exist in significant numbers all across the organization at all times. You must define and recognize teams and teamwork in all its forms to positively influence your culture, employee perceptions, morale, and work environment. Teamwork is how strong organizations execute and deliver better products, services, and ideas. A positive culture is driven by teamwork.

CHAPTER V

The CEO's Blueprint

Thus far we've discussed company culture, leadership, and teamwork. We will not delve much further in to the theory of these areas because this is not a book about these very important business topics. This is a book about <u>using and understanding the value</u> of culture, leadership, and teamwork to <u>build and maintain a positive company culture</u>. If you want to learn more about these topics or need to be further convinced of their value and importance, there is a vast array of great business books and resources available (see Appendix D for Suggested Reading and Reference Materials). If you believe in concept what we've discussed thus far and/or you have experienced and understand the value of culture, leadership and teamwork, then you are ready to move forward and commit yourself to creating a new company culture and a new organization.

As you have already seen, the core attributes of a positive culture, the six core leadership competencies, and the core attributes of teamwork have common themes. They are interconnected and dependent on each other for success. You and your leaders' understanding of how they fit together and the ability to select, develop, and implement these competencies and attributes throughout your organization will determine your success in this cultural transformation. The diagram below visually depicts how it all fits together. It is your new cultural organizational model and leadership philosophy combined. When someone asks to see your company organizational chart, show them this....

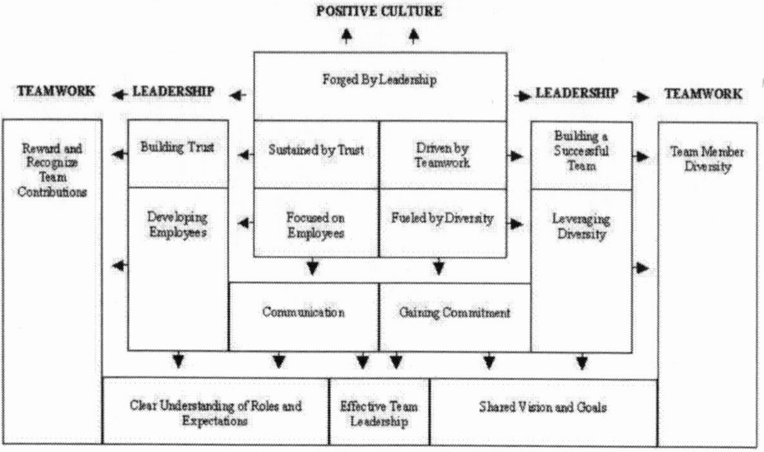

This is your **cultural organizational model and leadership philosophy.** More than any other document, this will best explain your new company once your have implemented the CEO's Blueprint. It is more valuable than a traditional organizational chart because it doesn't focus on your current structure or who reports to whom. It explains clearly and concisely "how" your company works and "how" you get things done. It is independent of the "what" in your current goals, business plans, and strategies. It represents your culture and your leadership values. It is your, your employees', and your company's business identity. Combined with your mission and vision, it communicates where your company will go and how it will get there.

***

Now let's get started. The following ten steps are a Blueprint for transforming your organization. If you follow these steps, you will improve your company and your business results. You will create a positive culture and a terrific work environment—a place where employees want to work and a place <u>everyone</u> wants to work. Your employees will be engaged, commitment, and excited about what they are doing. They will understand the company's annual goals, long-term vision, and their role in achieving those goals. They will utilize diverse teams and teamwork daily to develop new ideas, solve problems, and execute your business plans and strategy. Your employees will believe in their company, feel valued and respected, understand their role, and believe in their leadership, themselves, and in you (their CEO).

The CEO's Blueprint—10 Steps to Constructing Company Culture

1. Commit at the Very Top
2. Define your Leadership Needs in Terms of Competencies
3. Define a Selection Processes
4. Reselect and Realign Leadership (Make No Excuses, Make No Exceptions!)
5. Build Staff and Cross Functional Teams
6. Communicate, Communicate, Communicate (Your Mission, Vision, Strategy, and Goals)
7. Develop Teamwork and Team Building
8. Create Development Plans for Leadership
9. Reassess Leadership for Results, Vision, and Acceptance (Make Changes!)
10. Establish Annual Processes to Solidify and Develop a Positive Culture
    a. Review Mission and Vision, Share Strategy and Goals
    b. Develop Team Operating Plans and Initiatives
    c. Develop Individual Performance Expectations
    d. Communicate Company Performance Review
    e. Conduct Individual Performance Reviews
    f. Reward and Recognize Teams and Employees
    g. Conduct Annual Culture Survey
    h. Develop Individual Leadership Development Plans
    i. Develop Culture Action Plans
    j. Provide Training and Education on Teamwork and Leadership
    k. Conduct Leadership Reassessment and Adjustments

Following the CEO's Blueprint will take a lot of work, personal energy, and an unwavering commitment. Steps 1 through 5 involve the initial construction; Steps 6 through 10 define the on-going maintenance and development. I wish I could tell you that these are 10 *easy* steps; and once they are completed you'll be done with the hard stuff. But the fact is these steps are not easy and you'll never be done with the hard stuff. Once you achieved a positive culture, you will have succeeded in developing a tremendous business asset and competitive advantage; but you'll have to continue working hard to maintain and further develop that culture. There is also nothing easy about the steps themselves. Each one will take your and your leaders' time, energy, and attention. Additionally, you and your leaders will have to develop some new skills and improve upon others to implement them successfully.

The ten steps in the CEO's Blueprint combine an understanding of culture, leadership, and teamwork together to create a positive culture. As you implement them, you will define how you, your leaders, your teams, and your employees will do business each and every day. When you follow the CEO's Blueprint, you will be one of the few visionary leaders in the business world today. You'll have a true understanding of the value of a positive culture, leadership and teamwork and a deep commitment to transforming that understanding into an organizational reality.

STEP I—COMMIT AT THE VERY TOP

Step I: Develop your understanding of the decisions you'll have to make and the leadership actions you will take; and then make a commitment to build, maintain, and develop a positive culture. Make your commitment a very visible top priority by communicating it and modeling it for your organization.

Commitment. For so many of our endeavors in life, it takes commitment. Think of the things you've achieved in your life. Obtaining that degree, learning to play a musical instrument, keeping in touch with that best friend, running a marathon, commitment to marriage, family.... It all takes a commitment of self..... time, energy, practice, hard work, willingness to self-sacrifice, and prioritization of certain things ahead of others.

How many times have you heard, been asked or asked the questions: "What is your level of commitment on this?" "How committed are you to making this happen?" "Is he/she really committed to making this thing work?" In the business world commitment and priorities are clearly important. We are constantly assessing and reassigning where to focus our energy, time, and resources. In doing so, we are strongly influenced by the actions of leaders and our CEO. This is why commitment at the very top is critically important. It communicates priorities. It defines where resources, time, and energy should be focused. It communicates when we can make trade-offs and where not to compromise.

Following the CEO's Blueprint is no exception; it requires commitment. In fact, it requires a level of commitment above all other business priorities. It requires this level of commitment because you are creating a company culture, the foundation of your organization, its personality, and the identity you and your employees will share. You will ask everyone in the organization to not only support but to believe; and to put their time, energy, and passion into its creation. You will discover that your leadership and employees are willing to do this; but you can never afford to have them question your level of commitment. What you'll be asking them to do is difficult because it requires sacrifice and hard work. They must believe strongly that you support and care deeply about what they are doing everyday. Your commitment must be unwavering, unquestioned, and relentless.

Of course, this does not mean that you must implement every last detail of the CEO's Blueprint exactly as recommended. In fact, you'll see there are many details that you and your leaders must develop and define along the way. It means that you'll have to first understand the big issues that will require commitment and resolve, the issues that cannot be compromised. You'll have to understand what messages key decisions will send and know when those decisions will undermine or draw into question your commitment. You need to know that whenever you make a decision that appears to be in conflict with your culture, compromises your core beliefs or processes, or appears to put you or your leadership team "above" the rules, employees will notice. They will notice and they will want to know why you allowed it so they will begin to question your commitment, integrity, and beliefs. Remember, you are asking them to work very hard for you. You've communicated your highest level of priority and commitment; and you asked them to share in it.

If employees question your commitment, they'll question what they are putting their energy into and then you'll start to lose them. You may not lose them in terms of employment; but you'll lose them in terms of true support and commitment. Like every other corporate initiative or program, this organizational undertaking will require the participation of hundreds or perhaps thousands of employees. If you want them to differentiate this initiative from all the past ones that have come and gone, you must demonstrate a level of commitment that they have never seen before. To accomplish this, you need to clearly understand what you are committing to do.

So, what are you committing to? You are committing to making tough decisions about people by putting the right people in leadership and moving the wrong people out of leadership. You are committing to a new leadership and management philosophy that will guide your actions every day. You are committing to new tools, techniques, and methods and to instituting standard processes and programs that will build and maintain your positive culture. You are committing to openness and to continual review of not only "what" you do, but also "how" you do things before you do them. You must be willing to open yourself and your decisions to constructive challenge, review, and influence. You are making a 100% commitment to these things, knowing full well that the majority of the issues and challenges you will face will not be "black and white," but various shades of "gray."

Committing to putting the right people in leadership may sound like an easy commitment to make, but it is far from it. Your leadership selection process will uncover many things, and you'll end up having to make some tough decisions to remove or demote some very experienced people. Some of the people you remove from leadership will be long-term managers and content experts—people with significant experience. You will also have to take risks on new people—unproven leaders. It will require you to be committed to the process, committed to your core leadership competencies, and committed to your selection process. CEOs often appears ruthless and heartless because they will downsize, outsource, early retire, and fire anyone to increase profits. The reality is they are often ruthless in the wrong places...they need to be ruthless about leadership selection. They need to be ruthless about sharing vision, developing culture, and creating high performance teams. You, the CEO, must be ruthless about putting the right people in leadership.

However, being ruthless about putting the right people in leadership does not mean you or your culture will be perceived as ruthless. Another finding of Jim Collins in his research of good-to-great companies is that they all have cultures that are rigorous in their people decisions.

> "The good-to-great companies probably sound like tough places to work—and they are. If you don't have what it takes, you probably won't last long. But they are not ruthless cultures, they are rigorous cultures. And the distinction is crucial. To be ruthless means hacking and cutting, especially in difficult times, or wantonly firing people without any thoughtful consideration. To be rigorous, not ruthless, means that the best people need not worry about their positions and can concentrate fully on their work. To be rigorous in people decisions means first becoming rigorous about top management people decisions. To let people languish in uncertainty for months or years, stealing precious time in their lives that they could use to move onto something else, when in the end they aren't going to make it anyway—that would be ruthless. To deal with it right up front and let people get on with their lives—that is rigorous."[1]

COMMIT AT THE VERY TOP TO MAKE THE RIGHT DECISIONS ABOUT PEOPLE AND LEADERSHIP

Committing to a new leadership and management philosophy that will guide your actions means committing to modeling new actions for the organization on a daily basis. You are committing to new tools, techniques, and methods and to instituting standard processes and programs that will build and maintain your positive culture. It means you have to model for the organization how you want them to lead and the tools and techniques you want them to use as they do it. It is showing them by personal example how you want them to build your culture.

CEO's and executives get used to having special privileges. They often believe their time is more critical than everyone else's and that the typical rules don't apply to them because they have big jobs and because they run the company. If this applies to you even a little, you have to make a commitment to change your mindset. If you want an organization with strong leadership and a positive culture, you and your team have to be strong leaders and exhibit strong leadership. If you expect leaders to be strong communicators, you and your staff must be models of strong, proactive communication. If you expect superior teamwork, you must show your organization that you and your direct reports are a great team. You must use the same selection processes, the same programs and employee policies, and you and your staff must have an annual personal development plan like the rest of leadership. You must participate in culture surveys and share your individual performance goals. You cannot send a message that the people at the top of the organization do not need to do these things while the rest of the organization does and still expect to get the level of acceptance that you need. In the book, *The Human Capital Edge: 21 People Management Practices Your Company Must Implement (or Avoid) to Maintain Shareholder Value,* Bruce N. Pfau and Ira T. Kay emphasis this point as part of their overall findings.

> "One of the surest ways to torpedo faith in senior leadership is clear evidence that management does not practice what it preaches. In contrast, companies that get high marks for leadership make it a habit to develop and showcase ways in which the company stands behind everything it says......There are plenty of companies out there with inspiring mission statements posted

on the wall. Most of the time, those statements do more harm than good. When they're not backed up by obvious, definitive action by a committed leadership, those posters inspire ridicule rather then commitment."[2]

You and your team must be in practice and belief what you want the rest of the organization to be in terms of culture, teamwork, and leadership. This is a lot of work. It takes commitment not only to do the work, but also to make that work a priority over other demands on your time. If you and your team put the important things that build and maintain a positive culture first, so will the rest of the organization.

COMMIT TO A NEW LEADERSHIP AND MANAGEMENT PHILOSOPHY, TO NEW TOOLS, AND TO NEW TECHNIQUES AND METHODS

Lastly, you are making a commitment to openness and to continual review of not only "what" <u>you</u> do, but also "how" <u>you</u> do it. Both before and after you act, you must open yourself and your decisions to constructive challenge, review, and influence. This is the only way you will get enough variety of perspective to not only make the right things happen for your company, but also make them happen in a way that builds and does not retard your positive culture. Various employee groups often perceive broad organizational decisions and issues that appear straightforward very differently. What one group of employees could perceive as a positive impact, another group of employees could perceive as a negative impact. The classic example of this is overtime. Some employees want and depend on the additional income they get from overtime. Other employees do not want any overtime because they value their non-work time more than the extra income. These types of issues require you to carefully consider how they will be implemented and how they will be communicated. To be successful at this, you have to open yourself up to a lot of questions and challenges from your employees.

CEO's and their staff don't like to be questioned. They don't like to be humbled and they don't like what they perceive as a challenge to their authority. You need to get past this! If you are able to, you will get better results, better decisions, and better communications. You'll demonstrate that you are willing to listen, to learn, and to admit when you could have been better. This will not undermine your authority; rather, it will add to it. Regardless of position or title, nothing builds quiet contempt more quickly than someone who never admits they are wrong. Nothing builds visible respect more quickly than openness, honesty, and admitting a mistake while correcting it. Let your leaders and your employees make you better at what you do.

COMMIT TO OPENING YOURSELF AND YOUR DECISIONS TO CONSTRUCTIVE CHALLENGE, REVIEW, AND INFLUENCE

The difficult part is that despite all of this effort to describe the level of commitment you need to have, you really won't know what it means until you do it and live it. When you are challenged; when you are faced with a "gray" issue that needs to be addressed and you are concerned about the organizational and cultural impact—that is when your commitment will be tested the most. It will be ongoing and it will be hard work. If you feel tested; if you live it everyday; you'll also know you are doing it right.

Another finding of Jim Collin's team in their effort to define what makes companies go from good to great was the type of leader at the top, the CEO. They found leaders of good-to-great companies could be described as "Level 5 Leaders," as defined below.

> "The term Level 5 refers to the highest level in a hierarchy of executive capabilities that we identified in our research.. ... Level 5 executive builds enduring greatness through a paradoxical blend of personal humility and professional will. Level 5 leadership is not just about humility and modesty. It is equally about ferocious resolve, an almost stoic determination to do whatever needs to be done to make the company great.. ... Level 5 leaders channel their ego needs away from themselves and into the larger goal of building a great company. Its not that Level 5 leaders have no ego or self-interest. Indeed, they are incredibly ambitious—but their ambition is first and foremost for the institution, not themselves."[3]

To do this right; to execute the CEO's Blueprint; to build and then maintain a positive culture; this is the type of leader you, the CEO, must be—relentless in your commitment, exhibiting great resolve with balance and humility, always putting the organizational needs ahead of any self-interest.

Here is a quick checklist of questions for you and your leadership teams that will help you ensure that you are maintaining a high level of organizational and cultural awareness, actively communicating, and demonstrating your commitment.

Tactical Commitment Questionnaire

- What have I learned this week about our recent successes, failures, concerns or perceptions?
- What decisions have I made, or will I have to make, that will communicate my commitment to developing our positive culture?
- What are we doing this week as a leadership team to reinforce, develop and build our positive culture and level employee engagement?
- What sensitive issues or decisions do I have to address and communicate strategically to the organization?
- What opportunity do I have this week to reinforce positive leadership and employee behaviors through reward and recognition?
- What communication opportunities do I have to share to reinforce my vision, strategy and goals?

Review these questions during your weekly staff meetings to assess your and your team's level of tactical commitment. The questions will serve to both measure your level of cultural awareness and communication and to prompt appropriate culture forming actions from you and your team.

YOUR COMMITMENT MUST BE UNWAVERING, UNQUESTIONED AND RELENTLESS.... YOUR FIRST ORGANIZATIONAL PRIORITY MUST BE A POSITIVE CULTURE

Step I is to commit at the very top. The very top is you. Your commitment means your direct staff and all of your leadership will commit and must commit. If they don't, it means you've either placed some of the wrong people in leadership and you need to make changes, or you have failed to demonstrate your own highest level of commitment to creating a positive culture. Commit at the very top to make the right decisions

about people and leadership. Commit to opening yourself and your decisions to constructive challenge, review, and influence. Remember that nothing builds quiet contempt more quickly than someone who never admits they are wrong; and nothing builds visible respect more quickly than openness, honesty, admitting a mistake, and correcting it. Commit to a new leadership and management philosophy, to new tools, to new techniques and new methods. Commit to these things and take the first step!

STEP 2—DEFINE LEADERSHIP NEEDS IN TERMS OF COMPETENCIES

Step 2: Define your leadership needs in terms of leadership competencies. Begin with the six core leadership competencies for building a positive culture and customize by level, function, and your business with an additional four to eight competencies.

Now that you have taken the first step and made the "commitment at the top," you are ready to move onto Step 2, Define Leadership Needs in Terms of Competencies. Before you are ready to hire and populate your organization with leaders that build and maintain your positive culture, you need to further define your leadership needs in terms of leadership competencies. Competencies are best described as varied descriptions of skills and/or activities that can be assessed in terms of a leader's ability to perform them at an insufficient, proficient, or strength level. You now understand the six core leadership competencies every leader must possess so you next need to consider what additional competencies you need your leaders to possess to define a complete leadership competency model for your organization.

In defining your leadership needs in terms of competencies, your challenge is to not over-think the details. You do not need to hire a consultant to construct an elaborate leadership competency model for you. Nor do you need to have finished developing your mission, vision, strategy, or goals. Lastly, do not get slowed down in restructuring positions, titles, roles, and responsibilities. You know your company. You know your industry. Therefore you will intuitively know what key leadership competencies, skills, and abilities are important for success.

The six core leadership competencies have already been defined for you. You and a diverse team of your employees will have enough experience and understanding of your company and its leadership needs to complete a leadership competency model for the levels, functions, and for your type of business. A first draft for all leadership positions should take at most a few days. After which the majority of your time will be spent sharing, discussing, generating interest among employees, and building understanding of the model and why it is important.

Do not wait until you have defined your mission, vision, strategy, or goals to begin defining your leadership needs. Your leaders will get you where you want to go regardless of the destination if you select leaders that have the six core leadership competencies. In fact, you should not customize your leadership around mission, vision, and strategy because those things can and will change over time. You must select leadership that can execute any strategy, drive towards any mission, and realize any vision that you create for them.

Do not let reorganization or restructuring efforts delay efforts to define your leadership needs. Delaying the creation of your leadership competency model because you plan to change the number, scope, or alignment of leadership positions in your organization is a mistake. Your leadership needs are not dependent on your structure. Any organizational structure will work well if you have the right leadership in place. Having the right leadership means you have leaders that can do the most difficult things (building trust, gaining commitment, developing employees leveraging diversity, building teams, and communicating). They have the skills and ability to lead through any challenge organizational structure can create.

Regardless of organizational structure, all organizations benefit from strong leadership; however some organizational structures are more dependent on strong leadership to optimize results. A matrix or team-based organizational structure that distributes responsibility, empowers employees, and creates the need for collaboration requires strong and talented leaders to optimize results. A command and control structure where a few people have all the control and no one steps on their turf requires the least amount of leadership skill, but the capabilities of this structure are limited. Command and control structures limit the exchange of ideas and are severely lacking in diversity of thought. They are typically only as good as the few individuals who are in command because their ideas are the only ones that are considered.

You are building an elite collection of leaders who will have the skills to make any type of organization structure succeed because they will be equipped to lead through and manage the nuances and challenges that any organizational design can create. In fact, given the type of leadership you are going to populate your organization with, you want to design a challenging structure to optimize results and performance.

If you need to restructure, do it in layers and get past it as quickly as you can by restructuring as you reselect your leadership layer by layer.

The two efforts can run in parallel. If you are restructuring as you reselect leadership, build the best team you can and design it for positive tension and a balance of the power in your team.

Your direct reports must be the best possible team you can create. You must have the strongest leaders, a good mix of diversity, and people who can model the leadership competencies you've identified. All of your team's actions will be amplified and replicated throughout the company. You and your direct reports will be the most visible team in the organization and are therefore the model for teamwork for your organization. Generally speaking, I don't think it is a good practice to create jobs for individuals with one exception, an exceptional leader. If you identify an exceptional leader or leaders, find a way to get them on your team. Your team of leaders that report directly to you must be united in their efforts and they must be the best at creating a positive culture.

Design your organization to have positive tension. Positive tension exists when leaders have interlocking, though at times opposing, areas of focus. This is where they have situations where they must work together to solve problems and get things done where they need to be involved in each other's business. Positive tension will exist when you create situations that require your leaders to look beyond the focus of their function or their departmental goals to realize the best solutions and outcomes for the company. This is how solutions and decisions become balanced and optimized in a positive culture.

The other organizational design component you should consider is that of common titling for leadership positions. I am a proponent of the commonly used business title standards such as Vice President, Director, or Manager with one exception, the title of "supervisor." A supervisor by definition is a person that has direction or oversight over the performance of others. While that definition is applicable to your leaders on the front line as a definition, it is too narrow because it fails to communicate the true nature of that role in a positive culture. Use the title "team leader" for all your front line leaders or any leadership positions that lead employees who are not in leadership positions. The team leader title communicates your expectation for teamwork across the organization each and every day as it sends the message that leaders must lead.

Lastly, you, the CEO, need to balance out the power in the organization among your direct reports. You can do this in part by how you align responsibilities and resources; but the reality is that not every position can have the same number of employees and equal size budgets. You need to guard against giving some of your staff significantly more power than others. You do not want a team of "haves" and "have nots," insiders and outsiders. The inequality or perceived inequality among team members will be counterproductive to the trust, respect, and teamwork that you want to create and maintain with your team. You'll have to be attentive to these issues and make a conscious effort to balance power across your team members with your involvement, support, and focus.

CREATE A CUSTOMIZED LEADERSHIP COMPETENCY MODEL FOR YOUR COMPANY DELIBERATELY AND EXPEDIENTLY; AVOID THE POTENTIAL DELAYS AND DISTRACTIONS

The material, formats, and examples in this section are designed to facilitate you through a thoughtful, straightforward, and expedient process to create your leadership competency model. To define your leadership needs and create your leadership competency model, you'll want to begin with your general thoughts and ideas on the specific skills and actions your leaders must perform at the various leadership levels in your company. This task is made easier for you as the majority of this effort has already been completed with the identification of the six core leadership competencies. The six core leadership competencies will be included in the definition for every single leadership position in your company, including yours.

Your challenge is to consider an expanded list of additional competencies to further customize and define the various leadership positions across your company. The following table provides a comprehensive list of **leadership competencies.** While many of these may seem self-explanatory by name, you'll want to reference the definitions in Appendix B as you work through this section to better understand the leadership skills and expectations associated with each competency. As you review, you'll see that the competencies are defined broadly. Some are similar but have slightly different focus; and many are linked, interrelated, and/or supportive of each other.

Communication and Acceptance	**Teamwork and Development**	**Managing and Executing**	**Relationships**	**Personal Traits and Abilities**
Communication Oral Communication Written Communication Informing Listening *Gaining Commitment* *Building Trust* **Strategy Focused** Vision Building Strategic Thinking External Awareness Strategic Agility Entrepreneurship	Manage Diversity *Leveraging Diversity* Interpersonal Skills Employee Relations *Developing Employees* Personal Development Continual Learning Coaching Sizing Up People Self Awareness Personal Disclosure *Building a Successful Team* Motivating Others Rewarding and Recognizing	Aligning Performance for Success Managing and Measuring Work Accountability Drive For Results Planning and Organizing Delegating Responsibility Decision Making Problem Solving Analysis Initiating Action Setting Priorities Time Management Process Management Innovation Management Conflict Management Facilitating Change Managerial Courage	Political Savvy Interpersonal Savvy Working Collaboratively Building Strategic Working Relationships Organizational Agility Dealing with Ambiguity Dealing with Paradox Influencing & Negotiating Partnering **Customer Focused** Building Customer Loyalty Customer Service Service Motivation	Perseverance Resilience Standing Alone Flexibility Composure Humor Creativity and Innovation Perspective Patience Judgment Work-Life Balance Integrity & Honesty Compassion Approachability

This is not an extensive list of all possible leadership competencies. As you and your Human Resources team review other resources (See Appendix D, Suggested Reading and Reference Materials), you will find that this list captures the majority of the most commonly utilized competencies with minor modifications in description or definition. Ultimately you may decide to add additional competencies that are not on this list or revise some of the definitions; but, overall this list is broad enough to allow you to define your company's leadership needs and design a leadership competency model for your organization.

LEVERAGE THE SIX CORE LEADERSHIP COMPETENCIES AND CUSTOMIZE YOUR LEADERSHIP COMPETENCY MODEL FOR YOUR BUSINESS

Customizing your leadership competencies for your different leadership levels (team leader, team manager, team director, vice president, etc.), functions (operations, finance, sales, etc.), and your business type (manufacturing, service, consulting, etc.) will entail some careful thought and consideration. You will have eight to fourteen competencies for a given leadership position, six of them being the core leadership competencies shown below.

Core Leadership Competencies

Communication
Gaining Commitment
Building Trust
Building a Successful Team
Leveraging Diversity
Developing Employees

For the remaining competencies you'll be identifying two to eight more competencies based on level, function, and your business. In identifying your additional leadership competencies, you'll want to consider one to three competencies for both level and function in addition to as many as two competencies that are unique to your business. For any given leadership position in your company, the simple formula for defining the leadership needs of that position is:

Leadership Position =

Core Competencies (6) +
Level Based Competencies (1-3) +
Function Based Competencies (1-3) +
Business Based Competencies (0-2)

Your various leadership levels and functions may differ enough in scope, responsibility, and perspective that it will be necessary to define specific competencies to differentiate your leadership needs for those positions.

Defining a business-based competency is optional. You'll want to consider the use of a competency to define how the core focus of your business or industry is of value to your leadership competency model.

To identify your level based competencies, review the list of competencies and select the ones that you feel are critical to the success of each of your leadership levels from team leader to CEO. This will be challenging because you expect a lot from each level and you'll be tempted to include about 20 different competencies for each. Force yourself to prioritize and get the list down to 10 or less competencies for each level on your first review. As you do so, keep in mind that this exercise is not intended to define every skill a leader at a certain level will need. It is about defining what they need more of and what they need to comparatively do better than leaders at other levels. As you review, keep in mind your first level team leaders will have a more day-to-day tactical and execution focus compared to the more strategic focus of your last level consisting of you and your executive staff. As you move through the leadership levels, it is acceptable to overlap as you move from mostly tactical and execution focused competencies to more strategically focused competencies at the CEO level. After your first pass, you should have developed a list similar to this...

	Team Leader	**Team Manager**	**Team Director**	**Vice President**	**CEO**
Level Based Competencies	Informing Listening Personal Development **Coaching** **Motivating Others** **Managing and Measuring Work** Accountability Drive For Results Problem Solving Service Motivation	Employee Relations Motivating Others Aligning Performance for Success Managing and Measuring Work **Drive For Results** **Decision Making** Initiating Action Setting Priorities **Facilitating Change** Working Collaboratively	**Aligning Performance for Success** Accountability Drive For Results Planning and Organizing Delegating Responsibility Decision Making Interpersonal Savvy **Working Collaboratively** Building Strategic Working Relationships **Strategic Thinking**	Self Awareness Rewarding and Recognizing **Accountability** Delegating Responsibility Conflict Management Political Savvy **Organizational Agility** Vision Building Strategic Agility **Judgment**	Listening **Vision Building** **Strategic Thinking** **Manage Diversity** **Sizing Up People** **Self Awareness** **Conflict Management** Perspective Integrity & Honesty Approachability

Now force yourself to carefully consider and choose from one to three competencies for each level. For the CEO level you can chose from two to six because the CEO won't have a single function associated with their position (example choices shown in bold). Once you make your choices, you will have your first draft of your level based competencies.

To define your function based competencies, start by creating a list of the functional areas in your organization. Then review the full list of competencies and make notes on the ones that will be most critical to the success of each function. Again, it is acceptable to overlap between functions and choose some of the same competencies identified under your level based competencies. Remember this is not about defining every skill that is important for each function; rather it is about defining in terms of skills the comparatively stronger leadership focus for a specific function. For example, for your Operations you may determine a need to focus strongly on

"Process Management" whereas your Sales may require a strong focus on "Interpersonal Skills" and "Building Customer Loyalty". After your first pass, you'll have developed a list similar to this...

	Operations	Human Resources	Finance & Accounting	Legal	R&D	External Affairs	Communications	Sales and Marketing
Function Based Competencies	Manage Diversity **Managing and Measuring Work** Accountability **Planning and Organizing** Problem Solving Initiating Action Time Management **Process Management** Working Collaboratively Service Motivation	Listening Interpersonal Skills **Employee Relations** **Coaching** Sizing Up People Conflict Management Integrity & Honesty Compassion Approachability **Interpersonal Savvy**	**Accountability** Process Management Working Collaboratively **Planning and Organizing** Integrity & Honesty Managerial Courage **Analysis**	**Accountability** Working Collaboratively Standing Alone Flexibility **Judgment** Composure Dealing with Paradox **Integrity & Honesty** Managerial Courage	**Continual Learning** **Innovation Management** Analysis **Problem Solving** Perseverance Resilience Creativity and Innovation Partnering	**External Awareness** Interpersonal Skills **Political Savvy** Working Collaboratively Analysis Interpersonal Savvy Building Strategic Working Relationships **Organizational Agility** Dealing with Ambiguity Partnering	Oral Communication Written Communication External Awareness **Working Collaboratively** Building Customer Loyalty **Informing** **Listening** Rewarding and Recognizing Interpersonal Savvy Interpersonal Skills	Entrepreneurship Working Collaboratively Influencing & Negotiating **Building Customer Loyalty** Creativity and Innovation Humor **Drive for Results** **Interpersonal Skills** Approachability Customer Service

Once again, choose from one to three leadership competencies for each function (example choices shown in bold). Once you have selected them, you've completed your first draft of your function-based competencies.

The last component to consider is if you need to select business based competencies that you believe are a vital focus for all your leadership. Similar to the six core leadership competencies, these competencies would be included in your model for all leadership positions. The key question to consider is, "Will your company, type of business, or mission statement focus benefit from having one specific competency that is critical for every leader in your organization to possess?" For example, if your customers are dependent on you helping them manage business ethics issues and deploy sound judgment in difficult situations (perhaps your business is a law firm, financial advisors, or environmental consultants), you may want to consider "Honesty," "Integrity," or "Judgment" as a core business competency for every leader. These traits are obviously always important for leaders to possess; but in this example they are core and so very important to business reputation and brand that they need to be a constant and visible focus of every leader. If you are in the healthcare industry, "Compassion" is a likely core business competency every leader should possess. If your business is known for creating new products and solutions such as an advertising agency, software developer, or manufacturer you may choose "Creativity" and "Innovation" as core business competencies.

Once you've selected one or two business based competencies or determined you do not need them, you now have your first draft of a **leadership competency model** that defines the leadership needs of your organization.

Core Leadership Competencies	*Communication* *Gaining Commitment* *Building Trust* *Building a Successful Team* *Leveraging Diversity* *Developing Employees*

	Team Leader	**Team Manager**	**Team Director**	**Vice President**	**CEO**
Level Based Competencies	Coaching Motivating Others Managing and Measuring Work	Drive For Results Decision Making Facilitating Change	Aligning Performance for Success Working Collaboratively Strategic Thinking	Accountability Organizational Agility Judgment	Vision Building Strategic Thinking Manage Diversity Sizing Up People Self Awareness Conflict Management

	Operations	**Human Resources**	**Finance & Accounting**	**Legal**	**R&D**	**External Affairs**	**Communications**	**Sales and Marketing**
Function Based Competencies	Managing and Measuring Work Planning and Organizing Process Management	Employee Relations Coaching Interpersonal Savvy	Accountability Planning and Organizing Analysis	Accountability Integrity & Honesty	Continual Learning Innovation Management Problem Solving	External Awareness Political Savvy Organizational Agility	Working Collaboratively Informing Listening	Building Customer Loyalty Drive for Results Interpersonal Skills

Core Business Competencies (Optional)	Creativity and Innovation

With this model you can now define the leadership selection criteria for the **leadership positions** in your company.

Leadership Position = Six Core Competencies (6) + Level Based Competencies (1-3) + Function Based Competencies (1-3) + Business Based Competencies (0-2)

Leadership Position	Core Leadership Competencies	Level Based Competencies	Function Based Competencies	Business Based Competencies
Team Leader, Operations	Communication Gaining Commitment Building Trust Building a Successful Team Leveraging Diversity Developing Employees	Coaching Motivating Others Managing and Measuring Work	Planning and Organizing Process Management	Creativity and Innovation
Team Manager, Finance	Communication Gaining Commitment Building Trust Building a Successful Team Leveraging Diversity Developing Employees	Drive For Results Decision Making Facilitating Change	Accountability Planning and Organizing Analysis	Creativity and Innovation
Team Director, R&D	Communication Gaining Commitment Building Trust Building a Successful Team Leveraging Diversity Developing Employees	Aligning Performance for Success Working Collaboratively Strategic Thinking	Continual Learning Innovation Management Problem Solving	Creativity and Innovation
Vice President, Sale & Marketing	Communication Gaining Commitment Building Trust Building a Successful Team Leveraging Diversity Developing Employees	Accountability Organizational Agility Judgment	Building Customer Loyalty Drive for Results Interpersonal Skills	Creativity and Innovation

YOUR LEADERSHIP COMPETENCY MODEL WILL DEFINE YOUR LEADERSHIP NEEDS AND DETERMINE THE SELECTION AND ALIGNMENT OF LEADERS ACROSS YOUR COMPANY

When your first draft is completed, you'll want to gather input and reactions; discuss and adjust; and then finalize and communicate the model to your organization. Assemble a small change team to review, consider, and react to your proposed model. Populate your team with employees from different levels and functions to assure balanced feedback and an informed perspective on your proposed model. Meet with your change team and ask for input and suggestions. Be flexible on the design, but establish upfront that the six core competencies are non-negotiable and required for every leadership position in the company. Also, hold firm on 14 as a maximum number of competencies to define any given position. Use the team to provide you with additional insight from their diverse perspective, work to facilitate them to acceptance of a final model within a few days, and develop a communication plan for sharing the model with the organization. Move quickly in developing a communication plan and communicating your model because the more organizational awareness you can generate the better.

USE YOUR NEW LEADERSHIP COMPETENCY MODEL AS A COMMUNICATION TOOL TO EDUCATE EMPLOYEES ON YOUR EXPECTATIONS AND GOALS FOR LEADERSHIP AND CULTURE

Communication of your company's leadership model is a great first opportunity to demonstrate your commitment and prepare the organization for your leadership selection process. Additionally, each and every leadership competency in your model communicates to every employee what you value in terms of leadership and company culture. In the book, *The Human Capital Edge: 21 People Management Practices Your Company Must Implement (or Avoid) to Maintain Shareholder Value,* Bruce N. Pfau and Ira T. Kay discuss the value of defining your organization's positions in terms of competencies.

> "Identifying and communicating competencies helps to define and communicate an organization's strategy. It helps employees to understand the strategy and achieve its goals. The many roles that competencies can play in an organization include:
>
> - Articulating what the organization values
> - Proving a common language for employees and managers to describe value creation
> - Linking pay, promotions, and growth directly to what the organization values
> - Guiding employees and managers regarding what is expected and how value is defined even in times of dramatic change and restructuring."[4]

Over time your leadership competency model will become much more than a tool for your selection process. It will become part of your leadership language.

Create a customized leadership competency model for your company deliberately and expediently; avoid potential delays and distrac-

tions. Leverage the six core leadership competencies and customize your leadership competency model for your business with additional leadership competencies. Your leadership competency model will define your leadership needs and determine the selection and alignment of leaders across your company. Use your new leadership competency model as a communication tool to educate employees on the expectations and goals for leadership and culture.

STEP 3—DEFINE A SELECTION PROCESSES

Step 3: Define your selection process in terms of standards, steps, and timing. Develop and incorporate processes to assess the six core leadership competencies, your level and function based customized leadership competencies, personality preferences, job fit, experience, and performance.

Now that you have defined your leadership in terms of competencies and created your company leadership competency model, you are ready to define and plan your selection process. Leadership is everything when it comes to creating a positive culture. Finding the "right" leadership, leadership that is skilled in the six core leadership competencies, is critical to creating a positive culture.

To find the right leaders, you have to be able to assess them with a high degree of confidence in a relatively short period of time with limited information and exposure. To accomplish this, you need to gather more data than you ever have before in your selection processes. This is necessary to determine to the highest degree possible the leadership skill level of your potential leaders. It will not be perfect for no selection process is, but it will maximize your percentage of leaders who have the right skills and abilities.

Even though the primary focus of this step is the selection of leaders, it is important to note that the selection process you establish will be used for all jobs and leadership positions. When used for leadership selection, the amount and type of information you gather will be different; but the methods, formats, and timelines for gathering information and completing the process will be the same. The process must be effectively communicated and well understood by employees. It is the doorway to advancement and career development for all your employees. A key component to building trust and gaining commitment is a standardized, predicable, and fair process of selection. Employees must understand your selection process and have confidence in it, and be assured that you and the organization will abide by it.

One very significant culture building action you must take as CEO is to follow this process for <u>your</u> direct reports to select <u>your</u> team. If you do not, you will have already headed down the path of putting the wrong people in the wrong positions for the wrong reasons. You will have sent your first message that you don't really believe in the core attributes of a positive culture and that "leadership is everything" because you've put yourself and your team outside of the process and above the rules. Don't be a typical CEO, be an exceptional CEO. Design a solid selection process and follow it for selecting your team and all your leadership.

The leaders you need to create a positive culture are out there, and they are willing to lead; you just need to have the courage to find them and to let them

In defining your selection process, it is important to first understand what the process must achieve for you and your leaders. Your selection process must be designed to:

- Collect key information about the candidates using methods that increase the accuracy of the information and the overall assessment
- Provide flexibility to the hiring manager while guaranteeing that standards and requirements are met including leadership proficiency in the six core leadership competencies
- Promote and demonstrate fairness, consistency, and respect
- Be efficient for the organization and timely for everyone involved
- Allow you to select the right employees for leadership and put them in the right position

If your selection process meets the criteria defined above, it will enable you to effectively staff your organization with the right leaders, fill all your positions, and reinforce your positive culture in the process. A predictable, robust, and consistent selection process is a key building block process for your organizational culture.

The "key information" to be collected by your selection process is as follows:

- Proficiency in the six core leadership competencies
- Proficiency in the function, level and business based leadership competencies

- Professional experience, performance and education
- Personal preferences and job fit information

First and foremost, you must collect assessment information on the six core leadership competencies. This information is critical as it will be used exclusively to determine which candidates "make the cut" for leadership positions. You will establish a minimum score in your assessment process based on the six core leadership competencies and those that fall below it will not be considered for leadership positions. Only those that score above that threshold will be considered for leadership.

You will also collect assessment information for the level, function, and business based competencies in your leadership model. This information will assist in determining leadership alignment (level and function) along with the information collected on experience, performance, job fit, and preferences. Experience and performance information will also be used to determine if a candidate meets the minimum required skills and experience to be considered for a position.

In determining the methods for collecting this data, it is important to realize that the core of a successful selection process is what information you gather and how you gather it. You need to invest time and resources to gather the right data upfront to find out as much as possible about potential candidates. To collect this data, you will utilize several different methods to collect the same information in different ways. This redundant approach allows you to build a higher degree of accuracy in your overall assessment results. The standard methods I recommended are as follows:

- **Panel Role Play**—Two assessors collaboratively assess a candidate during a role play exercises with a third role playing assessor where the candidate is asked to react to, and lead through, a situation with an employee, peer, or boss to demonstrate their leadership abilities.
- **Panel Behavioral Interview**—Two to three interviewers collaboratively assess a candidate by conducting a behavior-based interview where the candidate is asked to answer questions by giving actual examples that demonstrate proficiency.
- **Written Application**—Written submission from the candidate in response to a set of specific skill based questions that focus on leadership, competencies, experience, and performance.

- **Standard Resume**—Standard resume chronicling work history, professional experience, education, and references.
- **Preference Assessment Tool**—Assessment tool that identifies a candidate's preferences in terms of thinking, communication, work tasks, and approaches. There are no right or wrong answers, nor are these tools customized for any particular job or field of study; rather they are helpful in determining job fit, diversity of thought process, and at times, candidate self-awareness. (See Appendix D, Suggested Reading and Reference Material for common preference assessment tools.)
- **Hiring Manager Interview**—One-on-one interview between the last one or two strongest candidates to exchange information, answer and/or confirm any remaining questions, and contribute to overall job fit assessment.

This will appear to be a tremendous amount of information requiring both effort and resources; but if designed and executed properly, it will be a fair, reasonable, and even enjoyable process for most candidates. Granted it may be intimidating or overwhelming to some, but that response in itself provides insight into the candidate's preferences and abilities. It also demonstrates how seriously you and the organization take this process. It shows that you are making a significant effort to truly understand the strengths and qualifications of the candidates and are determined to assure a good job fit. It also demonstrates that you understand the value to your company of finding the right leaders and placing them in the right roles.

You will want to include each of the above methods in your selection process. Each provides information in a different form, delivered to you by the candidate in different ways. Utilized together these methods allow you to collect a variety of information for different areas in your assessment (leadership abilities, experience, job fit) as well as redundant information to validate critical areas (leadership abilities and performance).

The six core leadership competencies are examples of where you will assess the same skill using multiple methods. When assessing a candidate's skill, a written response describing a situation in which they for example, effectively "gained commitment" is good information and provides a reasonable degree of certainty that the skill is present. Verbalizing that same situation in an interview provides a higher degree of certainty that the skill is present. Demonstrating the skill live in a role-play situation provides the best possible information and the highest degree of certainty.

Panel Role Play

Role-playing a situation is a great assessment tool because it is very real. Candidates must respond to an actual situation with a real person and show you what they have or do not have in terms of skills in real time. You'll utilize two assessors to watch the role play and document the candidate's performance while a third assessor acts as either the employee, peer, or occasionally the boss. As the candidate interacts with the role player to address and respond to a real life business situation, they will demonstrate their communication style and interpersonal skills as well as their leadership competencies. It will happen fast so it is critical to have two assessors to document the interaction and capture both the positives and the negatives that are discovered and observed.

You will utilize role-playing to directly assess proficiency in leadership competencies as well as oral communication ability and interpersonal skills. Gather information on the core leadership competencies that are best assessed using this method such as gaining commitment, building trust, and communication. While it is not impossible to role-play competencies like team building, leveraging diversity, and employee development, the first three of the six core competencies are better suited for this method. You may also include a leadership competency from your leadership competency model; keeping in mind that it isn't practical to role-play every competency, and different methods may better suited for a particular competency.

Panel Behavioral Interview

A behavioral based panel interview is another great interactive assessment tool. Using two to three interviewers to collaboratively assess a candidate's answers to questions that require actual examples of situations allows you to assess almost any competency as you gain insight into work experience and performance. Use this method to assess your six core leadership competencies and the level, function, and business based competencies you identified for a given leadership position using your leadership competency model. In doing so, you'll also utilize this method to overlap and verify the competencies you assessed using the role-play assessment method. You need not include a specific question on communication skills because the interview itself provides an opportunity to assess proficiency in oral communication ability and interpersonal skills.

Written Application

For each position, develop a specific set of skill-based questions designed to provide information on leadership competencies, work experience, and performance. Like the behavioral interview format, you will provide instructions to the candidate to respond by giving actual examples that demonstrate proficiency. A common approach is to ask the candidate to provide answers in a generic outline that first defines the situation or work task, the action they took, and the results they achieved. This method is valuable as it allows a candidate to provide a level of detail and thought regarding their achievements that typically cannot be provided in a live interview situation. In many ways it is an extended, more detailed, and more focused version of a resume. Use this method to overlap and verify the some of the competencies you assessed using the role-play and interview assessment methods. Additionally, this method along with the candidate's resume allows you to assess written communication skills.

Standard Resume

As a common standard, all candidates should submit a resume chronicling their work history, professional experience, education, and references. In addition to the background information on each candidate, a resume allows you to assess their written communication skills, look for job fit indicators, determine experience, review education requirements, and develop a sense for the candidate's overall professionalism. It also provides the hiring manager with background for more in-depth questions and clarification should the candidate advance to a hiring manager interview.

Preference Assessment Tool

Preference assessment tools help candidates self identify their preferences in terms of thinking, communication, work tasks, and approaches. In these "tests" there are no right or wrong answers, nor are they customized for any particular job or field of study; rather, they are focused on determining job fit, diversity of thought, and at times, candidate's self awareness. These tests are also helpful beyond the selection process in developing an understanding of team diversity and interactions. Understanding individual employees' preferences for thinking, working, and decision-making can often improve team member interactions. Use of these tools often come later in the process and may be limited to the top two or three candidates under consideration.

Hiring Manager Interview

The hiring manager interview is typically a one-on-one interview between the last few candidates or at times the single top candidate to exchange information, answer remaining questions, and confirm overall job fit. This interview provides an opportunity for the hiring manager and prospective employee to ask each other questions about expectations and particulars of the position. It may be the first opportunity for the two individuals to directly interact and clarify questions or concerns related to the assessment process. The hiring manager will also use the interview as an opportunity to fill in any remaining informational "blanks" or seek additional information based on questions raised during the overall assessment process.

***

The following template provides a **sample selection assessment plan** for a team leader in operations. It includes the six core leadership competencies as well as the functional, level, and business based competencies from the leadership competency model. The template defines from which part of the process certain information will be obtained and assessed using the various assessment methods.

Selection Information	Use/Purpose	Area of Assessment	Role Play	Panel Interview	Written Application	Resume	Preference Assessment Test/Tool	Hiring Manager Interview
Six Core Leadership Competencies	Meets the Minimum Skill Level for Leadership	Communication	*	*	*	*		
		Building Trust	*	*	*			
		Gaining Commitment	*	*	*			
		Building a Successful Team		*	*			
		Leveraging Diversity		*	*			
		Developing Employees		*	*			
Experience & Performance	Meets the skills level for experience and performance Organizational Alignment	Experience			*			*
		Performance		*	*			
		Education				*		
		References				*		*
Level, Function and Business Based Leadership Competencies	Organizational Alignment	Coaching	*	*				
		Motivating Others		*				
		Managing and Measuring Work		*	*			
		Planning and Organizing		*	*			
		Process Management		*	*			
		Creativity & Innovation		*	*		*	*
Job Fit	Organizational Alignment					*	*	*

This template helps to illustrate the selection process information needs and goals; and the methods you plan to utilize to obtain assessment information for any given leadership position. This part of your selection process is clearly work intensive in both upfront planning and execution, but the type and quality of information you collect directly correlates to the quality of your assessment and the future success of the leaders you choose. This is the place to invest your organization's time and energy. It will pay dividends and minimize the personnel mistakes that will eventually cost you time, performance, results, and money.

A WELL EXECUTED, INFORMATION INTENSE SELECTION PROCESS DEMONSTRATES THAT YOU UNDERSTAND THE VALUE TO YOUR COMPANY OF FINDING THE RIGHT LEADERS AND PLACING THEM IN THE RIGHT ROLES

Defining a selection process that provides flexibility to the hiring manager while guaranteeing that standards and requirements are met is a challenge. Hiring managers never want to be told who to hire for a job. They know they are responsible for goals and performance so they usually have strong opinions on who are the best people to help them get there. Many will prefer to choose who they know and/or rely on their own individual assessment and judgment of candidates. If left to their own judgment, they will make mistakes and put the wrong leaders in place.

To neutralize this, you must utilize a team-based hiring approach consisting of the hiring manager, Human Resources, and internal peer resources to balance out your selection decisions and drive to the best results. This may seem on the surface to be a minor point, but it is actually a very critical component of your positive culture. Your organization uses and depends on teamwork not only for day-to-day execution and special projects, but also for executing your very important process of selection. In the book, *The Human Capital Edge: 21 People Management Practices Your Company Must Implement (or Avoid) to Maintain Shareholder Value,* Bruce N. Pfau and Ira T. Kay documented this key point.

> "Particularly in organizations that emphasize the team concept—whether officially moving to "self directed" teams or not—it is critical to use a team approach to hiring. If a new team member is thrust upon an existing group, it clearly communicates that management's commitment to the team concept is shallow. If the employees are to work as a team, they should choose their members as a team."[5]

Hiring managers must be convinced of the value of the process and the value of the information it provides. They need to collaboratively work to discuss the best candidates with the other assessors and Human Resources partners involved in the process. Their Human Resources partners and the other assessors need to hold firm on making sure the best candidates rise to the top and that candidates who do not make the cut for leadership are eliminated from the process. The key to achieving this is making your Human Resources professionals a partner in the process and giving them an equal voice. They should not be given the power to choose the candidate, but they should be able to remove candidates that fall short of the requirements and influence areas of diversity and job fit. This is a critical design component of your selection process.

Your selection process must promote and demonstrate fairness, consistency, and respect. Employees have a vested interest in their company's selection process, because it is a doorway to advancement and career development. They may not always agree with the results, but they need to have a clear understanding of how the process works as well as the timeline and the expectations of them as they move through the process. They have to have confidence that you and your leaders are committed to following the process. The best way to build that confidence and demonstrate fairness is to utilize the process without exception. In doing this, you are taking advantage of a very simple and direct opportunity to build trust and gain commitment through your consistent, predicable, and fair process of selection.

Your selection process must be respectful to candidates by providing them information and feedback at the appropriate times throughout the processes. For example, you never want a candidate to hear the results of the process from another source before they hear back from the hiring manager. The process itself must be an efficient and respectful of the use of candidates' time. It should not "string candidates along" if they do not have a realistic chance of being the successful candidate. The candidate may not like hearing that they are not qualified or ready for the position, but it is best to tell them this when it becomes apparent rather than at the very end of the process. It is also important to realize that candidates will be asked to do a lot in a very short period of time regardless of the outcome their participation and interest. Their effort must be acknowledged with thanks.

One of the biggest design challenges is to make a process that is information intensive and requires a lot of personal interaction efficient for the organization and timely for those involved. The time required to complete the hiring process is always a challenge. It is critically important to get the right leaders in the right place; however, the realities of business today are that companies cannot afford to take months to find the right leaders. Things move too fast and the demands are too great. The more quickly you are able to fill key positions with the right people, the sooner your important business needs can be addressed. As a starting point, define a process that allows you to have a job accepted by the successful candidate within 17 days of posting the position. Based on your preferences and needs, you may wish to shorten or lengthen this timeline.

This may appear to be a very aggressive timeline, but it can be made to work well once the organization thoroughly understands the process.

Prior to reselecting your leadership you will formally communicate your new selection process to the organization and provide the opportunity for employees to ask questions on process specifics. Build as much understanding of the process and the associated expectations of the candidates as possible before beginning to use your selection process. The following outlines a high level timeline and key actions required for a 17-day selection process.

<u>**Selection Process Timeline (17 days)**</u>

Days 1-7: Post the complete job description and written application questions. Provide information about competencies, expectations, experience and response requirements (include the hiring process timeline and interview time blocks).

Day 7: Accept and process application materials

Days 3-8: Assess and rate resumes and written applications. Determine interview list (three to five candidates) and schedule interviews.

Days 9-13: Conduct behavioral interviews and role playing sessions.

Days 12-14: Determine final candidates list (one to two) and schedule hiring manager interviews and job fit tests.

Day 15: Complete hiring manager interviews(s), assess final results and make offer to successful candidate.

Day 17: Fill position, communicate to all candidates and formally announce new assignment to the organization.

Your process will begin with posting the complete position description, the written application questions, and detailed information about the competencies, expectations, and experience requirements. You will also include the deadline for receiving application materials and the overall hiring process timeline including interview time blocks to allow candidates to plan to make themselves available for interviews.

Require that application materials be received seven days from the posting date. This provides candidates a full week and a weekend to work on materials and consider their candidacy. You can begin assessing the materials as soon as they are received, grading and ranking them as they are submitted up to day eight. On day eight you will assess the rest of the applicant's materials and arrive at your interview list of candidates. You'll want to force yourself to work the list down to five candidates or less. If you are realistic about qualifications, experiences, and written assessment results this will not be difficult. The efficiency and expediency of your process is dependent on interviewing only the candidates that realistically have a strong chance of being successful.

Once you complete your interview list and schedule interviews, you are ready to complete your behavioral interviews and role-playing sessions during days nine through thirteen of your process. This is where you can provide limited flexibility to candidates by scheduling their time within these six days. In doing so you will still front-load the days as much as possible and attempt to get all the interviews and role plays scheduled in the first three days (days nine through eleven), leaving the next three for reviewing results and hiring manager interviews.

On days twelve through fourteen, you'll review the results of your interviews, role-plays, written applications, and resumes and then determine final candidate(s). Depending on need, you'll schedule and complete your hiring manager interview(s), complete your final assessment, and make your offer on day fifteen. At this time, administer any job fit assessment tests you plan to use. At most, these tools will take 30 to 40 minutes to administer so they can be quickly assessed and reviewed the same day by the hiring manager.

The hiring manager interview is an excellent opportunity to fill in any "blanks" and reaffirm what has been learned about individual candidates. Typically it will not change your initial ranking or outcome, but in some situations it will influence selection and prove vital to making the right choice. In either situation it is a valuable step because it gets the successful candidate face to face with the hiring manager for some one-on-one discussion. It is an opportunity to start off what will be an important and hopefully very successful, working relationship.

Once the hiring manager interview is complete you will be able to finalize your selection; perform all the necessary due diligence that precedes hiring (references, drug tests, background checks, etc.); and finalize the details of the offer (salary, relocation, starting date, etc.). Now you can contact the successful candidate to make the offer. You will have communicated upfront to the candidate that if offered the position, their answer is required within one to two days. If your offer is accepted you can then communicate to the remaining unsuccessful candidates with an offer to provide them with feedback and thank them for their participation. You will then formally fill and communicate the new assignment to the organization on day seventeen.

Clearly this process as described requires upfront coordination and careful resource planning. This is an area where you must either have a well-staffed and flexible Human Resources organization or utilize external resources for material preparation, interviewing, and role-playing. It is recommended that you utilize an external Human Resources consultant as a resource provider to execute this process. You will benefit from their ability to provide expertise on assessment of competency in addition to the development and execution of both the role-playing and interview formats. As your organization gains experience and expertise utilizing the process, you could need less external resource depending on the size of your Human Resources staff. This is an area where you could utilize an external consultant to assist you, particularly during Step 4, Reselect and Realign Leadership, when you will be executing your process for a large number of leadership positions.

For your non-leadership positions, the selection process will be the same, only the type of competencies and skills will be customized for the position you are filling. Depending on the position, role-playing will be optional though it may still be desirable for certain positions such as sales or external affairs. If you can effectively execute leadership selection in 17 days, you will definitely be able to fill non-leadership positions in 17 days or less as they will require less information. The ability to fill key positions or any position in 17 days or less is most definitely a competitive advantage for your company. Instituting this process and making it part of your culture will be difficult because you could meet with resistance even if you are the CEO and you will have to dedicate time and resources to do it right.

Using these steps, methods, and suggested timing as guidelines you must develop and define your selection process. After this, you can begin communicating it to the organization and building employees' understanding of the process components and timing. Your selection process is critical to finding the right employees for leadership; putting them in the right positions; and finding the right employees for all positions. The ability to execute an effective and timely selection process will greatly benefit your company and your culture.

Leadership is everything when it comes to creating a positive culture. Finding the leaders who are skilled in the six core competencies is critical to your organization's future. Your leaders are out there and are willing to lead. You just need to have the courage to find them and to let them. Design a collaborative selection process that collects accurate information about candidates; provides flexibility; assures standard requirements are met; and is fair, consistent, respectful, efficient, and timely. A well executed, information intense selection process demonstrates that you understand the value to your company of finding the right leaders and placing them in the right roles.

STEP 4—RESELECT AND REALIGN LEADERSHIP (MAKE NO EXCUSES, MAKE NO EXCEPTIONS!)

Step 4: Reselect and realign all your leadership positions in the organization from the top down. Utilize your selection processes to identify the leaders that make the cut for proficiency in the six core leadership competencies. Then utilize the position and company customized competencies, personal preferences, job fit, experience, and performance to align those leaders into positions across the company. Do not make excuses or exceptions for previous leaders who do not make the cut in the six core competencies. Regardless of their other qualifications, move them out of leadership and/or out of the organization.

Now that you have designed your selection process and communicated it to the organization, you are ready to reselect and realign your leadership from the top down. This step is one of the most critical and the most difficult because it requires you and the leaders you hire to take some risks and make some very difficult decisions.

The difficult decisions will be making sure every leader in your organization "makes the cut" for leadership by removing or demoting the former leaders who do not. If your organization has historically hired and promoted leaders based on what they know and the results they achieved without consideration of "how" they get those results, you will find yourself making a lot of these difficult personnel moves.

Remember, how employees feel about their company and their job is most strongly influenced by their immediate "boss," the leader they work for day in and day out. Your decisions as the CEO impact the organization and the culture every day. One of the biggest decisions you will make are the leaders you choose and what kind of culture you ask them to create.

The risks you and your leaders will be taking involve the selection of strong leaders and only strong leaders, the leaders who "make the cut" and possess the skills associated with the six core leadership competencies. This involves a leap of faith for some regarding your selection process; but even more importantly, your leadership philosophy. There will be plenty who disagree with the approach; who do not believe in the value of culture, leadership, and teamwork as you are defining it. This is all the more reason to not make excuses or exceptions for previous leaders who do not make the cut in the six core competencies. Regardless of their other qualifications, move them out of leadership and/or out of the organization.

AS CEO, THE BIGGEST DECISIONS YOU WILL MAKE ARE THE LEADERS YOU CHOOSE AND WHAT KIND OF CULTURE YOU ASK THEM TO CREATE

Everyone has seen the impact and cost of a bad hiring decision, assignment, or promotion. These will happen as no process is perfect, but your selection process is your advantage in minimizing bad hires and the associated cost. It is your best chance to make as many good upfront decisions as possible, using a consistent model and approach for your organization. If you waver in this, you will compromise your process from the start and negate your advantage. Your company will not crumble and whither away, but you will incur greater cost than you need to in the form of bad hires. It will also require more effort to correct these mistakes and you will fail to realize the cultural results you desire.

YOUR SELECTION PROCESS PROVIDES YOU THE ADVANTAGE OF SELECTING THE RIGHT LEADERS THE FIRST TIME AND MINIMIZING COSTLY PERSONNEL MISTAKES

Your goal in this part of the process is to find leadership ability; then position and align it for success. To find your leadership, you'll utilize your selection process and its evaluation of candidate's skill level in the six core competencies. One of the six key findings of Jim Collin's research team's review of good-to-great companies was finding the right leaders and putting them in the right positions.

> "When we began the research, we expected to find that the first step in taking a company from good to great would be to set a new direction, a new vision and strategy for the company, and then to get people committed and aligned behind that new direction. We found something quite the opposite. The executives who ignited the transformation from good to great did not first figure out where to drive the bus and then get people to take it there. No, they first got the right people on the bus (and the wrong people off the bus) and then figured out where to drive it. If we get the right people on the bus, the right people in the right seats, and the wrong people off the bus, then we'll figure

> out how to take it someplace great.....The good-to-great leadership understood three simple truths. First, if you begin with "who", rather than "what", you can more easily adapt to a changing world. If people join the bus primarily because of where it is going, what happens if you get ten miles down the road and you need to change direction? You've got a problem. But if people are on the bus because of who else is on the bus, then its much easier to change direction...Second, if you have the right people on the bus, the problem of how to motivate and manage people largely goes away. The right people don't need to be tightly managed or fired up; they will be self-motivated by the inner drive to produce the best results and to be a part of creating something great. Third, if you have the wrong people, it doesn't matter whether you discover the right direction, you still won't have a great company. Great vision without great people is irrelevant."[6]

Great companies focus first and foremost on finding the right leaders. As you do this, it is important to remember that leadership cannot be created in people. Like every gift or talent, you need to have the both the raw ability and the will to use it. There must be some innate ability, some raw material—the "right stuff" if you will, to be a leader. To be a professional athlete you must have the raw material, strength, size, speed, skill, and the desire to use it. You will of course be coached. You will learn and expand your talents further; but if you don't have the superior physical attributes for that sport, you'll simple never be able to be a professional. The same holds true for many professions. Whether you are an artist, a musician, or a nuclear physicist you must have the raw material and the desire to use it to be successful. Leadership is no different. Not everyone can be a leader so do not try to create leadership if the raw material is not there. You won't be successful. Your selection process assessments will show you who has the raw material, the right stuff, to be a leader.

LEADERSHIP CAN'T BE CREATED, YOU HAVE TO FIND IT, SELECT IT, POSITION IT, AND COACH IT FOR SUCCESS

In Step 3 we discussed designing your selection process, but we did not discuss evaluation rating methodology. To illustrate the critical process of determining what candidates make the cut for leadership, we need to define a rating methodology for use when assessing leadership competencies. In doing so, the goal is to bring clarity and simplicity to an information intensive process; therefore I recommend the following levels to rate candidate's skill.

Level 4 (highest)—Candidate demonstrates very strong evidence of the skill and associated results. This is clearly an area of high proficiency and a comparative strength for the candidate. In a leadership role the candidate is expected to be a visible and easily identified model for top performance in this area.

Level 3—Candidate demonstrates strong evidence of the skill and associated results. This is an area in which the candidate is clearly and completely proficient. In a leadership role the candidate is expected to perform this skill solidly and with relative ease.

Level 2—Candidate demonstrates partial or some evidence of the skill and associated results. This is an area in which the candidate has demonstrated some aptitude and skill, but not enough to indicate proficiency and therefore will most likely be challenged by some situations associated with this skill. In a leadership role the candidate is expected to need support, coaching, and further development in this area to be successful.

Level 1—Candidate demonstrates none or an insignificant amount evidence of the skill and associated results. This is an area in which the candidate has not provided information that demonstrated aptitude or has provided information to confirm the absence of the skill. In a leadership role the candidate is expected to be severely lacking in this area, most likely beyond the ability to support or even coach to success.

Level 0—Candidate demonstrates definitive evidence that the skill and associated results are absent. This is an area in which the candidate has provided information that demonstrates the lack of a skill or the "opposite" actions associated with the skill (for example, actions that create distrust rather than build trust). In a leadership role the candidate is expected to be severely lacking in this area; may actually create the opposite of the desired results; and is far beyond the ability to support or coach to success.

These ratings are intended to be distinct for a process that entails a significant amount of observation, judgment, and consensus. Requiring the assessors to utilize these rankings will, in the long run, simplify and provide clarity to the selection process. These ratings should be used for both the leadership competencies assessments as well as the experience and performance assessments.

When applying these ratings, each assessor will individually rate a candidate at a 0-4 level for any particular assessment methods (role play, panel interview, written application, etc.). After the assessment is completed, each assessor will discuss their individual ratings and then come to consensus on a single 0-4 rating. Once the overall assessment is completed, the assessors can integrate all the information in a similar manner driving to a 0-4 level consensus for each competency, experience, and performance requirement. The ratings for the individual competencies can then be averaged together to determine an overall core leadership competencies rating. The following is an example of **rating outcomes for the six core leadership competencies.**

Selection Information	Area of Assessment	Role Play Rating	Panel Interview Rating	Written Application Rating	Overall Rating
Six Core Leadership Competencies	Communication	4	3	4	**4**
	Building Trust	3	3	4	**3**
	Gaining Commitment	-	2	3	**2**
	Building a Successful Team	-	3	2	**3**
	Leveraging Diversity	-	3	3	**3**
	Developing Employees	-	2	2	**2**
Overall Core Leadership Competencies Rating					**2.83**

Utilize a similar process and complete a results table for the remaining level, function, and business based leadership competencies from your leadership competency model and for your **experience and performance requirements.**

Selection Information	Area of Assessment	Role Play Rating	Panel Interview Rating	Written Application Rating	Overall Rating
Level, Function and Business Based Leadership Competencies	Coaching	3	3	-	3
	Motivating Others	-	4	-	4
	Managing and Measuring Work	2	3	2	2
	Planning and Organizing	-	3	2	2
	Process Management	-	3	3	3
	Creativity & Innovation	-	4	3	3
Remaining Leadership Competencies Rating *					2.83

* Job/Position dependent based on your leadership competency model

Selection Information	Area of Assessment	Panel Interview Rating	Written Application Rating	Resume Rating	Overall Rating
Experience & Performance	Experience (2)	-	3	-	**3**
	Performance (2)	3	4	-	**4**
	Education	-	-	3	**3**
	References	-	-	3	**3**
Overall Experience and Performance Rating (1)					**3.25**

(1) Job/Position dependent based on your leadership competency model
(2) These items may be split into more specific descriptions of required experience and performance based on the position being filled.

For selecting your leadership and determining who makes the cut, you'll utilize the overall rating for the six core leadership competencies in addition to the experience and performance rating. While the level, function, and business based leadership competencies and job fit information are valuable for alignment and final selection, they will not be used to "make the leadership cut." To make the cut, leaders must reach a certain level of performance rating for both the six core leadership competencies and the experience and performance assessments. To illustrate how to evaluate these two areas together, we will utilize a two by two **leadership selection matrix** (see below). The vertical axis shows the rating for the six core leadership competencies and the horizontal axis shows the rating for experience and performance. This matrix allows you to plot a candidate's performance, apply common standards to your selection, and categorize assessment results into seven distinct outcomes (discussed below).

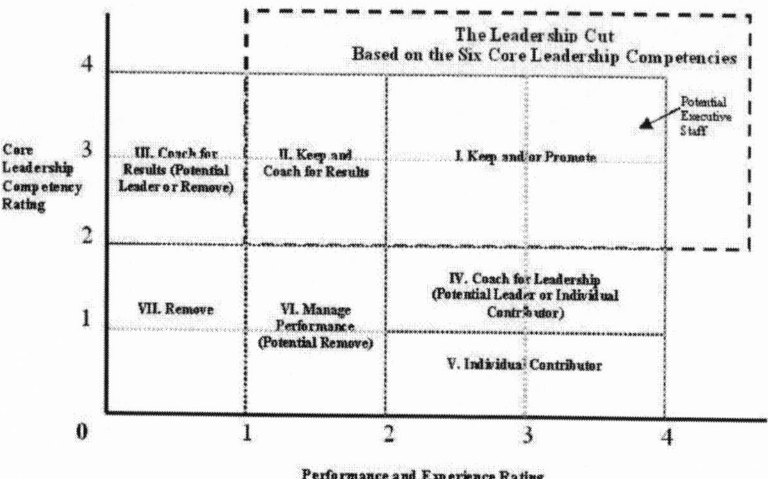

I. Keep and/or Promote

Candidates that rate 2 or above in leadership and 2 or above in experience and performance are your top leaders. They have the leadership skills you require and the experience and performance to match. You need to keep them and/or promote them in leadership. Your team, your executive staff, will come from this level of candidates as will most of your leadership. All of these candidates "made the leadership cut" in terms of the six core leadership competencies. They also have a valued track record of performance and the experience.

If a candidate scores in this range, wants to be a leader, and can commit to sharing the cultural values, you must find a leadership position for them somewhere in your organization. They are simply too valuable not to utilize in leadership. These leaders are the best because they have made the leadership cut. Ultimately, you want all of your leaders in this category.

II. Keep and Coach for Results

Candidates that rate 2 or above in leadership and between a 1 and a 2 in experience and performance also make the leadership cut. These candidates are strong leaders and are too valuable not to consider for a leadership role even through they currently do not meet the experience and performance levels you desire. Keep them in leadership and/or place them in a position where they can build experience as you coach them to deliver results.

These candidates, regardless of whether they are selected for leadership at this time, must be coached for results. They must be nurtured and given the opportunity to gain more experience and achieve the performance results you need. It is also possible they were not in the right role and can perform better if aligned to a position that better suits their present skills and abilities. These candidates have made the leadership cut and can be considered for leadership; but like all leaders if they ultimately do not perform; if they do not meet both sides of the equation 2H * W = P and achieve success both by "how" they do things and "what" they do; they will need to be removed from leadership.

It is important to note that these leaders should be placed in leadership where needed <u>even if they do lack experience</u>. It is better to have a strong leader who is technically inexperienced than a technical expert who is not a strong leader. It is rare to find an organization of any size where there is a lack of organizational knowledge. With support, strong leaders will tap into internal knowledge resources and quickly learn to compensate in areas where they lack experience.

<u>III. Coach for Results</u>

Candidates that rate 2 or above in leadership and 1 or less in experience and performance do not make the leadership cut and therefore will not be considered for a leadership position. Their experience and/or performance level is simply too low to be considered for leadership; and depending on their current role, may be potentially too low to even keep in your organization. If they are currently a leader and their performance level is clearly below expectations, they must be removed from leadership. Employees can easily identify under-performers; and leaders who are under-performers are extremely visible within the organization. To leave them in place would undermine your process and the culture you are trying to build. These candidates are fairly rare unless they are new to the working world; because it's not often that you will find someone skilled in leadership who simply cannot perform in term of results.

If a candidate is not currently a leader in your organization, it is possible that they could be developed into a solid leader. While these candidates are not ready for leadership, they must be coached and monitored to see if they can become strong leaders. If they are coached and given the opportunity to gain more experience, they may achieve the performance results you need. If they are successful, you've realized another high performance leader. If they are not successful, you must place them in a less challenging role where they can succeed or remove them from the organization.

IV. Coach for Leadership

Candidates that rate between a 1 and a 2 in leadership and above a 2 in experience and performance have not made the cut for leadership, but clearly are of value to your organization in terms of experience and performance. If they have an interest in leadership and have some ability in the six core competencies although not yet enough, it is worth working to coach them to determine if they can improve upon their leadership skills. If they can improve and a future job fit opportunity presents itself, you've found another solid internal leader. If not, you still have a solid, experienced, and strongly performing individual contributor and team member.

V. Individual Contributor

Candidates that rate a 1 or below in leadership and above a 2 in experience and performance have not made the cut for leadership. Even though they clearly are of value to your organization in terms of experience and performance, they do not have enough of the raw leadership talent to invest time coaching them for leadership. They are a solid, experienced, and strongly performing individual contributor and team member and should be valued as such.

VI. Manage Performance

Candidates that rate between a 1 and a 2 in leadership and between a 1 and 2 in experience and performance have not made the cut for leadership and are not making the cut for experience and performance. While they may have some capability in both areas, clearly their performance must be managed and improved. This may be a "coaching to improve" situation or it may require managing performance up to an acceptable level. If their performance doesn't improve to an acceptable level, you must place them in a less challenging role where they can succeed or remove them from the organization.

VII. Remove

Candidates that rate below a 1 in leadership as well as in experience and performance have not made the cut for leadership nor for experience and performance. These employees must be removed from your organization. In fact, they should be removed quickly, particularly fast if they were a leader. If you have any of these types of leaders, they are extremely visible in the organization because they are deficient in every area. They are the managers that everyone scratches their head over and wonders, "How did they get that job?" and "Why are we keeping them?" It would be great if your company has effectively managed leadership and performance such that all these situations have already been addressed; but more likely, you will have some of these leaders at every level in your organization even at the top. Remove them and the quicker, the better. Employees will take notice and respect the change.

***

The leadership selection matrix represents a critical point in this process of implementing the Blueprint's 10 Steps because it is your best chance to make the right leadership choices upfront. As previously discussed, making the right choices upfront builds your culture faster, reduces costly mistakes, and greatly improves your chances of cultural success sooner rather than later.

The Leadership Selection Matrix utilizes assessment data from the six core leadership competencies and your experience and performance areas; but it does not include the data from the function, level, and business based leadership competencies. If desired, develop a similar matrix to plot function and level results for use in aligning higher performers with the higher-level positions. However, it is advisable to be less prescriptive and utilize collective judgment given the assessment information on job fit and candidate preferences to determine the best alignment for leaders who have "made the cut." Correctly positioning leaders for success is very important and all available information must be considered using a holistic approach involving the hiring manager and their hiring team.

As you utilize this matrix a candidate's starting point does matter. If they are in leadership and do not make the cut, they need to be demoted and/or removed from the organization altogether. This will most likely be difficult, but it is extremely necessary. Remember, make no exceptions; make no excuses; just make the right decision on leadership. If an internal candidate is not a leader currently and they do not make the cut for leadership, they may be just fine in their current role. If they have issues with performance or results however, they may need to improve to stay in the organization.

IT IS BETTER TO HAVE A STRONG LEADER WHO IS TECH-

NICALLY INEXPERIENCED IN LEADERSHIP THAN A TECHNICAL EXPERT WHO IS NOT A STRONG LEADER

This process may seem overly harsh in terms of judgment. It may appear to be "pigeon-holing" employees with statements like "not meant for leadership" or "remove;" but re-staffing and building leadership requires decisiveness. The process is not intended to put anyone in a box or determine the future course of their career through one assessment process. It is about your best assessment and best judgment at this one point in time. It is about where you will invest your time and efforts right now. All employees will have a chance, and be encouraged to learn and develop their skills. All leaders will focus on developing their employees based on their performance and interests; but right here and now, you are building a world-class leadership team and you want only the best.

Removing (demoting) employees from leadership and/or removing (severing) them from the company may seem ruthless. It is a hard choice and decision to make because it involves people. In the vast array of things that companies do that are ruthless or heartless like across-the-board cost cuts, layoffs or outsourcing; this decision is no harder or more ruthless, but the benefits are much greater. These decisions yield benefits that will allow you to build a positive culture. The benefits of the other "hard" things may reduce cost in the short term, but end up increasing costs and reducing opportunities because if done poorly they negatively impact culture and employee engagement. They may save money, but they don't build culture or position your organization for future success. The difficult decisions you and your leaders will have to make during this process will create significant organizational value. They will allow you to improve and build your culture while creating a work environment that attracts and engages employees. This is the time for the tough choices made fairly and executed with respect, but made definitively and without compromise.

This is about aggressive leadership selection, from the top down. The first and best attempt to start with the best leaders you can find. If you begin with your team, your direct reports, and then work with them to fill their leadership positions, you will educate the organization on how to select leaders; how to be aggressive in leadership selection; and how to utilize your selection process and information. This is effectively how you will communicate this process to your organization and to your leadership, by example. Your leadership both administers the process for their team and has participated in the process for their position. Your leadership has been successful in the process so they will more readily accept it and sell it to employees.

As you reselect leadership from top to bottom, it is important to go level by level allowing each level to fill the positions that will comprise their direct reports, their team. In terms of an estimated timetable, plan for one month per level and work to do slightly better. For a typical organization, this process will take three to five months. This is about aggressive leadership selection—not aggressive in terms of speed or decision making, but aggressively making the right decisions even if it means promoting an untested leader or removing a long-standing manager who lacks leadership ability.

BE AGGRESSIVE ABOUT YOUR LEADERSHIP SELECTION; DO NOT COMPROMISE YOUR PROCESS.... THIS IS THE TIME FOR THE TOUGH CHOICES MADE FAIRLY AND EXECUTED WITH RESPECT, BUT MADE DEFINITIVELY AND WITHOUT COMPROMISE

Your selection process isn't perfect and even if you execute it perfectly, you will have some leaders in positions that will need to be changed out because they are not getting the right results in the right ways. While not perfect, your selection process will significantly decrease the number of bad hires by providing you the advantage of finding many more of the right leaders and putting them in roles in which they will succeed.

As you move through your process, your influence as CEO must be present. In addition to being aggressive about getting the right leaders in the right positions, you must prevent compromise of the process. Some leaders will desperately want to compromise the process. As soon as leaders think that they are a better judge and predicator of success than the selection process and the data it provides, they will begin to make choices about positions that will increase your number of bad leadership hiring decisions. If this occurs, you will end up with as many bad calls as good ones and you will have shifted the odds away from your favor, negating the advantage your selection process is designed to bring you. In their book, *Execution, The Discipline of Getting Things Done,* Larry Bossidy (former Chairman and CEO of Honeywell) and Ram Charan underscore the value of managing the quality of your people, particularly leaders.

> "Given the many things that businesses can't control, from the uncertain state of the economy to the unpredictable actions of competitors, you'd think companies would pay careful attention to the one thing they can control—the quality of their people, especially those in leadership pool. An organization's human beings are its most reliable resource for generating results year after year. Their judgments, experiences, and capabilities make the difference between success and failure. Yet the same leaders who exclaim that "people are our most important assets" usually do not think very hard about choosing the right people for the right jobs."[7]

Your selection process provides you the advantage of selecting the right leaders the first time and minimizing costly personnel mistakes. Reselect and realign all your leadership positions in the organization from the top down. As you do so, recognize that leadership can't be created. You have to find it, select it, and position it for success. Be aggressive about your leadership selection and do not compromise your process.

Utilize your selection processes to identify leaders that make the cut for proficiency in the six core leadership competencies. Then utilize the position and company customized competencies, personality preferences and job fit, as well as experience and performance to align those leaders into positions across the company. This is the time for the tough choices made fairly and executed with respect, but made definitively and without compromise. Do not make excuses or exceptions for previous leaders who do not make the cut in the six core competencies. Regardless of their other qualifications, move them out of leadership and/or out of the organization. Keep and select only the best.

STEP 5—BUILD STAFF AND CROSS FUNCTIONAL TEAMS

Step 5: Define leaders and their direct reports as teams with shared goals and a clear understanding of team member roles and expectations. Deliberately define through discussion and collaboration all the cross-functional, permanent, or long-standing teams (committees) and special project teams. Acknowledge these teams through a formal team charter developed by the team leaders and team members. Develop organizational awareness of the teams, team accountabilities, and shared responsibilities through multiple lines of communication.

As you reselect and restaff your leadership from the top down, the first task of your new leadership will be to define and build their team. As we've discussed building their team goes far beyond filling their positions and naming their leaders. It entails identifying the team; developing and discussing a team charter; and acknowledging the team throughout the organization. As leaders work through a team charter, they will discuss and define team goals, purpose, vision, key stakeholders, recognition, scope, timing, measurements and team member experience, perspectives (diversity), roles and expectations. Most importantly they will also begin to lead by facilitating the team and involving team members in active discussion during the first team meeting.

In Step 5 you will define and build the staff and cross-functional teams that will be immediately active across your organization. This will allow your leaders to begin to define team member roles and expectations as well as start to establish awareness and understanding of who is working to accomplish what and what the organizational inter-dependencies will be for each team.

The timeline for Step 5 has a start date, (it will slightly lag Step 4, the reselection of your leaders) but it has no real end date. It has no end date because you never truly finish building your team, promoting teamwork, and fostering a positive team environment. However, getting a team defined by beginning to build a foundation of understanding and trust is a key activity that you and your leaders must focus on immediately.

The single best exercise a leader can do to kick off and define a new team is to conduct a team forming session. A team forming session is a fairly lengthy working session with a very straightforward agenda containing the following items:

Team Forming Session Agenda

I. New Team Acceleration Process
II. Team Charter Development
III. Sponsor Check-in
IV. Team Socialization Activity
V. Meeting Review/Debrief

This agenda may seem brief, but it actually will involve a tremendous amount of discussion and exchange amongst the team members. Once completed, the team will have covered a tremendous amount of ground in terms of information and understanding; greatly accelerated the typical timeline for team formation; and begun to set a tone for team interactions and outcomes.

I. New Team Acceleration Process

The new team acceleration process is an exercise to accelerate interpersonal relationships between the team leader and team members as well as relationships amongst the team members themselves. It is intended to establish clarity around expectations, styles, and preferences; and to answer the typically unasked questions. It involves four questions:

- What do we know about the team leader?
- What do we want to know about him/her?
- What do we want them to know about us?
- What do we need from them to be successful?

The exercise involves the team members collectively working through these questions with the team leader absent from the room. Once they are finished discussing and recording their responses to these four questions, the team leader returns and works through their questions/responses and provides their responses and reactions. This two-way exchange provides an opportunity for additional dialog, discussion, and additional clarifying questions. These four questions will significantly accelerate the team leader/team relationship and the relationships between the team members themselves. It provides team members a chance to share things about themselves with the entire team, learn things about their team members (sharing diversity), and begins to establish expectations for each team member. When this simple exercise is conducted properly, it breaks down the natural "getting to know someone barriers" very quickly and sets an immediate tone for open communication, trust, and teamwork.

II. Team Charter Development

Developing a team charter and defining the team itself will be the most intensive part of your initial team forming session. It will require significant time and energy; yet it will still not be completely finalized by the end of the meeting. The discussion, debate, and resulting understanding the team will experience are critical and will accelerate the completion of the team charter.

GET TEAMS STARTED BY LAYING DOWN A FOUNDATION OF UNDERSTANDING USING A TEAM ACCELERATION PROCESS AND TEAM CHARTER

As you would expect, a team charter is built on the core attributes of teamwork (Effective Team Leadership, Clear Understanding of Roles and Expectations, Shared Vision and Goals, Team Member Diversity, and Reward and Recognition). The team charter provides the opportunity for the team to work together with their leader to define details, develop understanding as well as revise and update the specifics of the charter. An example format for a **team charter** is shown below.

TEAM CHARTER	
TEAM NAME/SUBJECT: Quality Improvement Team	**DATE:**
TEAM LEADER: Sue Jones (Unit Manager)	**TEAM SPONSOR:** Chuck Wren (Plant Manager)
TEAM MEMBERS: Phil Johnson Brad Fisher Karen Benson Rod Derton Jerry Preston	**TEAM MEMBER ROLES AND EXPECTATIONS:** Provide process analysis Serve as safety consultant Provide insight on production line methods Assist with quality control and measures Material and inventory coordination
KEY STAKEHOLDERS: Line Employees Production Manager Customer Service department Supply Chain and Quality Control	**TEAM SUPPORT MEMBERS:** Ralph Penton (Finance/Business Analyst) Gary Austin (Employee Relations)
CLEARLY WRITTEN OPPORTUNITY OR PROBLEM STATEMENT (WHY DOES THIS TEAM EXIST?): An opportunity exists to reduce the number of product defects on assembly line #5 and improve cost efficiency and customer satisfaction.	
TEAM VISION AND GOAL: The product defects on assembly line #5 have been analyzed and corrected resulting in improvements that can be shared across the company to further realize improved cost efficiency and customer satisfaction.	
IN SCOPE (WHAT THINGS CAN THIS TEAM ADDRESS?): Processes, performance, equipment, tools and methods	
OUT OF SCOPE (WHAT IS OFF LIMITS FOR THIS TEAM?): Organizational Structure, disciplinary actions for performance, material selection, product design	
EXPECTED OUTCOMES (WHAT ARE THE DELIVERABLES?): Process Map Analysis of defects Recommendation for improvement Go forward measures	
TEAM MEMBERSHIP PERSPECTIVES (EXPERIENCE, BACKGROUNDS, STRENGTHS) Process design, business analysis, line experience, materials, quality control practices, metrics design, employee health and safety	
TEAM MEMBERSHIP PERSPECTIVE BLINDSPOTS (WHERE IS THE TEAM LACKING IN EXPERIENCE, BACKGROUND?) Finance, sales and marketing, product design and engineering, customer service and consumer perspectives	
MEASURING RESULTS (HOW WILL RESULTS BE MEASURED?) Reduction in number of defects, maintain current level of productivity/output	
KEY TIMELINES AND DATES (WHAT ARE THE MILESTONES, CHECKPOINTS AND CRITICAL PATH ITEMS?) Process Map – 1 week Defect analyses – 3 weeks Recommendations – 8 weeks	
RECOGNITION AND REWARD (HOW WILL THE TEAM ACHIEVE RECOGNITION, WHAT ARE THE POSSIBLE REWARDS?) Bonus Incentives, organization recognition	

The team charter is a living and flexible document for team discussion and the development of the team charter must be reiterative. As you work through the process of developing a team charter, it will be necessary and helpful to circle back and update areas to keep them aligned with each other. The team leader and team sponsor will complete a first draft of the charter. This provides the team with a starting point and gives them something to react to initially. Plan to work through the team charter two or three times, most likely at different meetings. As each leader sits down to develop the team charter and then subsequently works through it with team members, they should consider the following.

Team Name/Subject

Defining a team name, typically by the subject or function that the team will focus on, is important to give the team an identity and to establish your organizational terminology around "teams" and "leaders." You no longer have supervisors and the people that work for them. You have team leaders and their teams, team members and their teammates. To have effective teamwork infused into your culture and to build a positive culture that is driven by teams, you have to recognize them and make them aware that they are a team. Establishing the team name begins the expectation for the group of employees to work, act, and perform like a team.

Team Leader and Sponsor

Identifying the team leader and their role upfront is important for the same reason as establishing a team name. It is the beginning of the team's identity and the expectation for teamwork. You can't have an effective team without a team leader so the team leader role must be established immediately. The team leader has the responsibility for the team. They must perform specific actions to lead, build, support, and guide the team. A team sponsor is less visible and interacts less than the team leader; but also plays a key role. The team sponsor is typically the person the team leader works for or has been commissioned by, who controls the resources and has the authority to implement most or all of the team recommendations. The team sponsor and team leader have the ultimate responsibility for answering questions from the team, approving the team charter and revisions, and ultimately the team recommendations and solutions.

Team Members and their Roles and Expectations

A significant amount of time must be spent with the team members simply being introduced and getting to know one another. Who are the team members, what are their roles on the team, and what expectations do the other team members have of them? This is a great exercise to do in an open forum as it draws out opinions, raises key questions, and eliminates confusion later because it minimizes gaps in expectations for team members. This is an area you will to circle back to and revise as needed after you've defined additional team charter items such as opportunity/problem statement, goals, and measurements.

Key Stakeholders

Who are the key stakeholders that will be most interested and impacted by your team's actions, performance, and results? The team must spend time carefully considering their list of key stakeholders and potential stakeholder issues. A simple exercise the team must conduct is creating a list of stakeholders, estimating their current level of acceptance or resistance, and attempting to identify their concerns or issues. Your key stakeholders will greatly impact the team's success and, if managed properly, improve the ease of team operation and implementation.

A stakeholder is defined as anyone that has an interest in the team outcomes and shares the results or is impacted by the team actions, recommendations, or results. Any employee, team, or functional area that falls under this definition is critical because they can support, impede, or accept the team's efforts and progress. Key stakeholders can be tremendous allies or impenetrable barriers for your team if they are not included, involved, and given a chance to influence. Ensuring that stakeholders are informed, involved, and accepting of team recommendations or direction will not happen naturally. Remember 50% of resistance comes from not asking the opinions of others. Always consider your stakeholders' points of view and give them opportunities to be included and influence. Never underestimate the level of passion a stakeholder may have around acceptance issues and never assume the technical solution will suffice in building stakeholder acceptance (they are both important, $2A * Q = E$). At times they may disagree and you may have to adjust to accommodate them, but it is always time better spent upfront rather than on the backend. Ultimately the team must manage stakeholders so that they achieve "critical mass" in terms of acceptance and support.

Team Support Members

Who are the people that are not part of your team, but you know you will need them or depend on them for a critical component of your team's effort? You may not need them all the time and therefore they are not a part of the team, but you know there is a critical part of your team's effort where you will need them as a resource. These are the team support members. They are honorary team members who need not commit to the team full time, yet they need to be very effective doing their part for the team when the time comes. It is very important to identify team support members so you can reach out to them and confirm them as a dependable resource. This will prevent the team's work from being halted by a critical need that none of the team members can provide.

Clearly Written Opportunity or Problem Statement

Why does this team exist? What is the reason it was formed? A clearly written opportunity or problem statement defines for the team why it was formed, its purpose. The opportunity or problem statement must be clear and concise. It must state the opportunity that exists to improve, or what the problem to be solved is without speculating on or determining the solution or direction. It should not include questions, nor should it attempt to assess the reason for, or assign responsibility to, the problem or shortfall. Examples of well-written opportunity/problem statements:

- An opportunity exists to reduce the number of product defects on assembly line #5 and improve cost efficiency and customer satisfaction.
- The roles, responsibilities, and training for product testing and design are not clear and consistent across the company. This has resulted in reduced levels of internal customer service and production delays.
- Turnover in operations area five has increased from 3% to 15% over the last year, negatively impacting services levels and training costs.

Examples of poorly written opportunity/problem statements:

- Why is the number of product defects on assembly line #5 the highest in the plant? They also lack the proper maintenance procedures. {Poorly written because it asks questions and draws a conclusion about the solution.}
- The product testing and design department is not doing its job; several other departments are frustrated because they can't get the internal services they need to meet their deadlines. {Poorly written because it assesses blame to individuals, rather than focusing on the issue.}
- Turnover in operations area five has increased from 3% to 15% over the last year because of recent process changes. New processes must be established to improve morale. {Poorly written because it because it draws conclusions and provides a solution}

For long-standing teams like staff teams, it may be understood that the opportunity will be ongoing. For example, they will continually be working to improve customer service and optimize efficiency. This is an item that requires significant thought and consideration. Some questions a team may want to consider as they develop the opportunity/problem statement are:

- What information or data do we have that makes us believe we have an opportunity or a problem?
- What benefits will the team, its stakeholder, and the company realize from our efforts?
- What are the key processes involved with our opportunity/problem?
- What missed opportunity, problem, or shortfall would occur if this team did not exist?

A team will not be effective if there is confusion around the opportunity/problem statement. An opportunity/problem statement must in fact be worked on until the team leader believes to a high degree of confidence that all the team members understand, agree on, and can commit to it.

Team Vision and Goals

A team vision and goals that is shared by all team members is critical to team success. This is the opportunity to dream with a vision and be realistic with goals. A great quote by Joel Barker sums this up nicely, *"Action without vision merely passes time, Vision without action is merely a dream, Action with vision can change the world."* Vision and goals are tied closely to your opportunity/problem statement in that they define for the team the "end-state" of its efforts or what has been achieved after the problem has been solved or the opportunity realized. It must not attempt to describe "how to get there" or the "solution;" but what has been achieved and what the world looks like after the team put forth its best efforts.

A team vision allows the team to shape the future and provide a description of an end-state that they can easily relate to, identify with, and define as success. It also provides additional support for the opportunity/problem statement by adding further clarification as to why the team exists and why it is important they work towards their defined goals. Some example team vision and goals statements that accompany the previously stated opportunity/problem statement examples:

- The product defects on assembly line #5 have been analyzed and corrected resulting in improvements that can be shared across the company to further realize improved cost efficiency and customer satisfaction.
- The roles, responsibilities, and training for product testing and design are clear and consistent across the company and the level of internal customer service for the department is extremely high.
- Turnover in operations area five is at an all time low. It is considered a terrific place to work and a model for the rest of the company.

Again for long standing teams, this may be a vision that continues indefinitely as it may focus on continually improving an ongoing service or function. The team leader must assure all the team members share the vision and that every team member is on board and working together towards the same end. It is also a time to carefully set the team goals to assure they are ambitious, achievable, and acceptable to the team. A team must believe the goals are achievable. A team will not be effective if they are not unified in their vision and shared goals so make the effort to get everyone's input and get it right.

In Scope and Out of Scope Areas

Defining the areas that are "in scope" and "out of scope" for a team is a tremendous time saving exercise because it creates accepted boundaries and realistic expectations for the team. It is natural and beneficial to think broadly when working to solve a problem or capture an opportunity; but all projects run the risk of expanding their scope beyond their resources, budget, deadline, or what is desired and/or expected of them by their sponsors and stakeholders. Limiting the team's scope prevents the team from overreaching its boundaries or resources and protects the team from outsiders adding to or increasing their scope beyond what they can realistically accomplish.

Changing the team's scope mid-process can threaten the team's chance of success and must be considered carefully and thoroughly. If the scope change outpaces the team's resources or timeline, it could jeopardize the original project goals.

Likewise if a team oversteps what its sponsors and stakeholders expect it to do, the team may find itself investing time, money, and energy into an effort that will not be fully supported and/or realistic to achieve. Establishing the team's scope will also prevent any individuals from pushing their own agenda upon the team. This is often a natural and not necessarily malicious occurrence. Everyone has their own preferences and ideas; so determining a solid scope is important to achieving balance and a shared understanding. Have the team ask themselves the questions, "What areas can the team get involved in, what issues or items can they address, and what actions can they take?" as well as "What areas, items, issues, or actions are off limits to the team?" After they complete the list of what is "in scope" and "out of scope," they must review each item with their team leader, sponsor, and where applicable stakeholders, to assure their agreement as well as the availability of resources to accomplish the team goals.

Expected Outcomes

Defining expected outcomes in terms of actual deliverables provides an opportunity for the team to understand in greater detail the team's expected work efforts. The expected outcomes will be a list of tangible items the team will produce that are still high level and expected to evolve over time. This will prove very valuable in building the team's understanding of their work and planning for their overall resource and time requirements.

Team Membership Perspectives and Blind Spots

Discussing, defining, and understanding your team member perspectives and blind spots is an open discussion about the diversity of the team. It's an opportunity to delve further into the individual team members' backgrounds, experiences, skills, and unique perspectives. It's an opportunity to identify, understand, and value where those perspectives are unique and where the team members share them. This allows the team to identify upfront where they have similar ideas, perceptions, and preferences and where their opinions may differ. This type of discussion will help build trust as the team self-discloses their ideas and various positions. It's the first foray into what will be positive conflict, disagreement, and discussion. The sooner team members can understand and predict where each other may be coming from on different issues and ideas, the sooner they can get past the natural concerns and angst associated with conflict and focus on the key issues.

The second part of the discussion, once the team has thoroughly reviewed backgrounds, experiences, skills and perspectives, is to challenge them to identify team blind spots. Where are they lacking in perspective, in experiences, in backgrounds or diversity? This can be tricky as it may be asking them to identify what they don't know or see in themselves. This part of the process will tie back to key stakeholders and key support members. Consider the viewpoints of your key stakeholders, what perspectives will or can they provide? What additional support members can be identified to help the team in terms of additional diversity of background or experience?

This exercise can also create an opportunity for the team members to solicit input from the rest of the organization outside the team structure on team blind spots. Asking this question will only improve the support for the team and demonstrate their sensitivity to the issue of differing perspectives and concerns. Identifying team member perspectives and blind spots is a very introspective and valuable exercise. Armed with the awareness of potential blind spots, this may be an exercise that the team chooses to repeat at different times throughout its existence.

Measurements and Results

What are the key measurements for the team, how will they be measured, and what are the specific results the team will achieve? Team discussion around results and how they will and can be measured is a terrific way to assure that the goals are realistic and achievable. It also sets appropriate expectations with the team, establishes shared accountability and buy-in for the results, and sets appropriate organizational expectations of the team. Formally publishing and communicating the team measurements and goals with the rest of the organization is important for this very reason. The team wants to be successful and be viewed as successful by the organization if they achieve their goals. Sharing measurements and desired results will help the team accomplish that success and build organizational awareness of the team's achievements.

Key Timelines and Dates

What is the team's timeline for realizing its goals, what are the critical dates for deliverables and completing key tasks? Just like measurements and goals, having the team discuss and define a high-level timeline is a terrific way to assure it is realistic, achievable, and accepted by the team. It establishes accountability and expectations for the team and the organization. It also allows the team to consider if they have adequate resources to achieve the goals in the desired or required timeframe. Lastly, the team must review and confirm timelines and critical dates with team sponsors and stakeholders to set their expectations and obtain their agreement.

Recognition and Rewards

How will this team achieve recognition and what will be the potential rewards for achievement? While on the surface this exercise may seem self-serving for the team, it is actually as important as all the other items on the team charter. It forces the team to consider what will be recognized about their work that will link back to goals, vision, and the opportunity and/or problem the team is working to address. It forces the team to think about how to get positive "internal press" through recognition. As we have discussed before, acceptance has twice the impact as the technical solution. Building acceptance, understanding, and organizational momentum for a team's efforts is important to the team success; and part of it is done through active recognition of the team's progress and achievement.

Recognition is a form of reward; but reward can also apply more broadly and include compensation, advancement, incentives, and non-monetary "perks." When teams consider the potential rewards and recognition, they must review if the form and delivery of the reward and/or recognition will have the desired impact. Will it be more than just money? Will it tie back to key behaviors and results and will it give employees the incentive to act like owners? If you can effectively hit on each of these points, you will be effective in your reward and recognition efforts. The team doesn't have the ability to determine their reward, but a discussion of how they can be rewarded can be valuable for understanding the value of the team's work to the organization. It also provides an opportunity for the sponsor to share thoughts and ideas on rewards and recognition and link them directly to the benefits the team will realize for the company.

III. Sponsor Check-in

Once you have made the first pass through your team charter, you will want to meet and review your work with the team sponsor(s). Use this as an opportunity to probe, confirm, ask questions, and challenge every aspect of the team charter. Most importantly, capture any unanswered questions or follow up items required to further solidify your work on the charter.

IV. Team Socialization Activity

Plan a team socialization activity as part of your first team forming session. Although it may sound like a fancy term for a party, it isn't. Plan time for the team to socialize with each other in a comfortable and preferably neutral (from the team's perspective) setting. The activity may or may not occur at the meeting. It could in fact occur before or after the meeting. Whether it is over lunch, dinner, or other event to share non-work aspects (hobbies, interests, etc.), provide time for the team members to get to know each other and connect. This isn't intended to be "nice" by giving some free time or a free lunch; it is a necessary part of accelerating relationships. Team members do not need to be best friends, but they must know each other well enough to have positive and trusting work relationships.

V. Meeting Review/Debrief

Lastly, plan to review and debrief the team forming session. Ask teams members to share their thoughts on everything from the content of the meeting to the comfort level of the meeting location and facilities. Ask them to identify what went really well; what didn't go well; and what they would do different next time. This can be done in an open format or, depending on the team leader's perception of the team's comfort level, anonymously. A simple approach is to hand every team member three cards colored red, yellow, and green and ask them to put positives on the green card, concerns on the yellow, and problems on the red card.

Regardless of the format used, this closing exercise is important for many reasons. It allows the team leader to get a read on how all the team members feel, their likes, dislikes or lingering concerns. It also establishes that everyone has, and will continue to have, an equal voice on the team. Most importantly, it allows the team leader to leverage (or repeat) the positives; address the negatives; and, where appropriate, make improvements. As the team leader ends the first team forming session, they must emphasis the team's accomplishments; thank them for their work; and close on a positive note.

***

Armed with your team forming session agenda and team charter, you can begin establishing teams across your company. Every leader is a team leader and every employee is a team member, so defining the staff teams is simple. Every leader has a team of their direct reports. These are the teams you and your leaders must focus on first, because they are the teams that will last the longest. They will exist until the organization structure is changed and they will function each and every day. They will run "full-time" and do 95% of the work in your company. The value of effective teamwork is tremendous. This value is amplified if every leader builds a successful team and every employee is part of an effective team.

Lead by example; define your new staff as a team and conduct a team forming session with them. Work through the team charter start to finish and set the tone for what your leaders will do with their teams, and so on down the organizational line. Once completed, you and your leadership will have set an expectation for teamwork and a strong first example of your leadership. It is the first step for every leader in their effort to build a successful team. Once all the leaders throughout the organization have established their immediate team, they will be ready to identify the other teams throughout the company.

THE VALUE OF EFFECTIVE TEAMWORK IS TREMENDOUS. THIS VALUE IS AMPLIFIED WHEN EVERY LEADER BUILDS A SUCCESSFUL TEAM AND EVERY EMPLOYEE IS PART OF AN EFFECTIVE TEAM

Once all the staff teams have been assembled and organized and after they have reviewed and fully developed their team charters, you must challenge the organization to identify the natural cross-functional and long-standing teams (committees). I use the term "natural" cross-functional teams because you do not want to prompt the organization to create them or force them to identify a certain number. You want bring the pre-existing teams to the surface and so you can create awareness and acknowledge their existence. The more matrix-based your organization, the more cross-functional teams you will likely identify. Places to look for cross-functional teams include around processes, product lines, services, or issues that require input or participation from many individuals, teams, or functions. This definition may include every process or service in your company so focus on the key processes that require the occasional tune-up, modification, or problem related debrief. Cross-functional teams may also be present around financial reviews, annual investment allocations, crisis management, external communications, and seasonal processes.

Like staff-based teams, your cross-functional teams will be long standing and most likely continuous in nature. They typically will not run full time like your staff based teams; but they will more likely pull together when needed. For this reason, organizational understanding and acknowledgement of cross-functional teams is very important. It is important because organizations and employees change frequently so the members of your cross-functional teams will also. Unlike staff teams that are up and running all the time or special projects teams that come together and stay together until they have completed the project, cross-functional teams meet more sporadically. If they are not well establish, they will only remain strong and well organized if the organizational relationships holding them together are strong and consistent, and because organizations and employees change roles that puts the long-term stability of these teams at risk. This can create situations where organizations end up starting over from scratch when team members leave and others fill their place. That is why it is important that these teams are purposefully identified and their team charters developed and integrated into your organization's knowledge base.

Challenge your organization to identify and acknowledge the cross-functional teams in your organization. Create a comprehensive list; discuss the list with your leadership team; add any missing teams; and eliminate any that seem too trivial based on consensus of the leadership. After the entire organization has established their immediate team and they have completed the mental exercise of identifying the other critical cross-functional teams throughout the company, they will be ready to assign team leadership and team membership, develop charters, and acknowledge those teams.

All organizations establish short duration, special project teams to tackle problems and capture opportunities. When doing so, have your leadership follow the same approach of using a team forming session to launch their teams and establish their team charter.

Use the results of the team forming sessions, the development of team charters, and your leadership team to create a communication plan to inform employees of your progress and share the results of your team establishment efforts. Establish a standard format for sharing the team charters so the organization becomes familiar with the content and the information. As you do this, you'll find that the information in the team charters will create interest and discussion; and most importantly, energy and excitement. The team charters will also provide you and your leaders with a solid head start for creating individual roles and performance expectations documents for each employee. Likewise, the charters will capture to a large degree what your leaders and their employees believe their company is all about. Capturing a sense of the collective vision and goals sections of all the charters will assist you and your leadership in developing, firming up, adjusting, or linking to your overall vision, strategy, and goals for your company.

The value of effective teamwork is tremendous. This value is amplified when every leader builds a successful team and every employee is part of an effective team. Define leaders and their direct reports as teams with shared goals and a clear understanding of team member roles and expectations. Then deliberately define through discussion and collaboration, all the natural cross-functional teams, permanent or long-standing teams (committees), and specials project teams. Acknowledge these teams through a formal team forming sessions and team charters developed by the team leaders and team members. Develop organizational awareness of the teams, team accountabilities, and shared responsibilities through multiple lines of communication. Most of all, lead by example and use teamwork to lead. Define your team, share your team charter, and set the pace for teamwork within your company. As your leaders follow your example they will establish a great foundation for teamwork.

STEP 6—COMMUNICATE, COMMUNICATE, COMMUNICATE (YOUR MISSION, VISION, STRATEGY, AND GOALS!)

Step 6: Communicate your mission, vision, strategy, and goals widely, deeply, and repetitively across your company. Conduct formal and informal forums at every level in the organization to discuss, clarify, and build understanding. After initial communication, at every opportunity discuss them and reinforce them with all employee groups. Assure they are visible in individual employee expectations and performance discussions, reward and recognition efforts, company communications, and the workplace.

Communicate, communicate, communicate your mission, vision, strategy, and goals. Why say the word communicate three times? In reality, saying it only three times isn't enough. We need to fill the page with the word "communicate" to visually depict how much you need to communicate these topics. When it comes to mission, vision, strategy, and goals, you need to communicate them clearly the first time and re-communicate them every future opportunity you get. Once you think everyone has heard it, understands it, and doesn't need to hear it anymore, communicate it again. You need to be a broken record.

Leaders and employees must come to EXPECT you to talk about your mission, vision, strategy, and goals and be surprised when you don't. Don't stop communicating your mission and vision, sharing your strategy, and focusing on your goals as they change and evolve year to year. Communicating them, keeping them in front of employees and on the minds of every leader, will be part of your annual "cultural" processes and part of your daily leadership actions.

Step 6 is not about how to develop and define a mission, vision, strategy, or organizational goals; it is about integrating and institutionalizing them into your organization. It is about making sure employees understand and believe in them. Your positive culture is your business advantage. Having the significant majority of your employees engaged, energized, and excited about their job means they will deliver results even in the absence of a shared mission, vision, strategy, or goal. Now, imagine all of those employees working together towards a shared mission and vision and striving to realize common goals associated with a well-understood strategy. This is the reason you are reselecting leadership. This is the reason you are building a positive culture. It is the big payoff and it will differentiate your company from the competition. In prosperity and disparity, a positive culture with strong leadership and an engaged workforce united in a common vision will prevail and succeed. It will pull you through the worst of times and increase your lead in the best of times.

Effective communication is the lifeblood of a positive culture. An organization and its culture will thrive, be sustained, and be nourished by effective communication; or it will be weakened, reduced, and limited by a lack of it. Effective communication enables employees to understand your mission, vision, goals, and strategies. This allows employees and teams to communicate ideas, problems, challenges, and solutions that will help you achieve those goals, implement the strategies, and realize your vision. Jack Welch, considered by many to be one of the best CEO's of his time, led General Electric with a core focus on communication. He said:

> "The only way to change people's minds is with consistency. Once you get the ideas you keep refining them and improving them, the more simple your idea is defined, the better it is. You communicate, communicate and then you communicate some more. Consistency, simplicity, and repetition is what it's all about".

As with all your endeavors, you must include, engage, and tap into leadership and employee ideas to improve your results. Your mission, vision, strategy, and goals are no different. Make the broad strokes and set the overall direction and tone. Then, allow the organization to react, provide feedback and influence via minor adjustments and modifications. This approach will build understanding, increase employee acceptance, and improve the effectiveness of your communication. Don't be afraid to "pilot" your mission, vision, and strategy with a test group of employees. Specifically, present the information as preliminary and in a format that allows you to capture employee feedback. It will not only help you consider potential changes or improvements, but also provide direction on how best to present and share the final product to optimize employee understanding and acceptance.

IN PROSPERITY AND DISPARITY, A POSITIVE CULTURE WITH STRONG LEADERSHIP AND AN ENGAGED WORKFORCE UNITED IN A COMMON VISION WILL PREVAIL AND SUCCEED

We won't discuss in detail how to create your mission and vision, but here are a few guidelines for consideration. Your mission and vision must be simple, clear, and short. It is tempting to write multiple paragraphs and fill a page with everything you wish your company to be, but those statements are too lengthy and complex to be meaningful on a daily basis. If you work hard enough you can boil your description down to one sentence that captures the essence of your vision.

Mission and vision must be extremely clear to everyone. Clarity comes from common everyday words (nothing that needs to be looked up in a dictionary or explained) phrased such that the meaning can only be interpreted one way. Also, don't feel that they need to be grandiose to be meaningful and inspiring. Simple and clear has mass appeal and it has staying power. Lastly, keep it short—no more than a sentence, but preferable a phrase. If you must write a page worth of vision, you must also be able to sum it up in one simple clear phrase. Think about companies whose "tagline" you can easily remember and the vision associated with them. They are simple, clear, and short.

- Wal-Mart—"To give ordinary folk the chance to buy the same thing as rich people."
- Mary Kay Cosmetics—"To give unlimited opportunity to women."
- 3M—"To solve unsolved problems innovatively"
- Merck—"To preserve and improve human life."
- Walt Disney—"To make people happy."
- General Electric—"We bring good things to life"

Whether you consider these a mission, vision, or part of a company brand, each are simple, clear, and short which makes them memorable, meaningful, easy to communicate, and ultimately, very effective. If you create a simple, clear, and short mission and vision, and communicate them effectively; every employee in your company will be able to articulate them without even having to think about it. If you do it right, your customers and investors will also understand and remember your mission and vision. Then you not only have a vision, you have an effective brand.

Your strategy will be more detailed than your mission and vision. For communication purposes, you'll want to present your strategy as a handful of discussable bullet points. In this format, leaders and employees can discuss each of the bullets, their value, and how to help the company achieve them. Strategy isn't just for your executives; it is for every employee. Employees are keenly aware of when strategy is lacking. They know when the ship is drifting aimlessly; and when it is, they will yearn for stronger direction and to know someone is at the helm. "Just tell me where you want to go, and I'll help you get there!" is a phase I've unfortunately heard many times. Employees want to feel a part of a serious, purposeful, and strategic business. They want to be a part of a successful, winning team. All successful teams have a vision for success and a strategy on how to achieve it.

Goals must be very specific and represented by annual improvement targets, efficiency levels, or project outcomes that are both visible and measurable. Goals should be in the form of numbers whenever possible. Measurable goals must be made visible and accessible to the organization via monthly updates and progress reports that are posted and shared electronically (email, intranet) and/or hardcopy (mail, bulletin boards). Goals, in the form of targets and progress reports, must be readily available to all employees and communicated as early in the business year as possible. This allows leaders to link their team's, and individual employee's, work efforts and actions to organizational goals. Goals should be challenging and at times difficult, but always realistic. Lastly, the goals you set for the organization must link to performance assessments, compensation, and incentives. This link is your primary feedback mechanism to positively reinforce employee focus and support and achievement of organizational goals.

Once you've developed, piloted, and established your mission, vision, strategy, and goals; you are ready to "launch" them across your organization. In doing so, you'll need a solid communication plan that will communicate deeply, widely, and repetitively across your company. In terms of deeply and widely, you must reach every function and every employee. Mission, vision, strategy, and goals are applicable to everyone at every level in your organization. It will never hurt you to have every employee aware and it will always be worth the investment. From the mailroom to the boardroom, everyone plays a part, impacts cost and performance, and is a part of your organizational culture. Make sure the messages and your communications reach every bulletin board and water cooler as well as the corner of every office and workspace of your company.

Develop a standard meeting format for leadership and their teams to share and discuss mission, vision, strategy and goals. Hold both formal and informal forums at every level in the organization to discuss, clarify, and build employee understanding. Begin with your team. Model the process for them and ask them to do the same with every leader and team in the company. Assure the meetings happen within specific and aggressive timelines. Remember, timeliness of communication and information translates into importance, status, and respect. Ask for feedback and reactions; and where applicable, capture and re-communicate positive items to the organization. After initial communication, at every opportunity thereafter to discuss your mission, vision, strategy and goals, reinforce them with all employee groups and integrate them into your organizational leadership processes. Look for opportunities were employees and teams have made significant efforts or contributions and recognize them formally and communicate their achievements to the whole organization.

If your vision requires your company to be the premier customer service provider in your industry, look for examples where employees have gone above and beyond the call to resolve sensitive customer service issues. Look for customer letters and feedback indicting positive service experiences and highlight them throughout your organization by rewarding the involved employees.

If cost improvement is part of your overall strategy, seek out examples of where employees reduced cost and/or improved efficiency. Even if the amount involved is a nominal amount, reward the initiative, the focus, and the action taken by the employee to support the strategy. If every employee is looking for opportunities, the small gains will add up and the large opportunities will be uncovered.

If you have a goal of zero safety incidents, look for examples of employee actions and attitudes, safety improvements, exemplary safety records, or performance that are supporting the goals. The more recognition you and your leaders can provide, the more meaningful your mission, vision, strategy, and goals will become to your employees.

Recognition efforts such as these are a very effective way to keep communicating and keep focus on your mission, vision, strategy, and goals. Challenge yourself and your leaders to link every communication, every new initiative, and every achievement back to the support, achievement, or advancement of your mission, vision, strategy and goals.

EFFECTIVE COMMUNICATION IS THE LIFEBLOOD OF A POSITIVE CULTURE. ORGANIZATIONS AND THEIR CULTURES THRIVE, ARE SUSTAINED, AND ARE NOURISHED BY EFFECTIVE COMMUNICATION; OR WEAKENED, REDUCED, AND LIMITED BY A LACK OF IT

Mission, vision, strategy, and goals are worthless if they are not visible and integrated into your company's cultural processes. Assure they are visible in individual employee work expectations and performance discussions, reward and recognition efforts, company communications, and the workplace. A formal effort must be undertaken every year to communicate and/or reaffirm mission, vision, strategy and goals. In the book, *Nuts,* Kevin and Jackie Freiberg share the business practices and philosophy of Southwest Airlines. Constant communication is one of the leadership practices they use to develop and maintain their highly effective culture.

> "One of the reasons Southwest has been so successful in getting people to internalize and embrace the company's principals and priorities is constant communication. Rather than having the mission statement in one place—the lobby—Southwest displays it everywhere in the system to serve as a performance standard and a consistent reminder of what is important for all employees. Like an old bulldog that playfully grabs your pants leg and refused to let go, the airline tenaciously looks for ways to communicate its mission, vision, values, and philosophy to employees over and over again."[8]

In terms of changes, mission and vision may be the most longstanding and consistent. Strategy will be similar, but adjusted more frequently depending on industry and market conditions. Goals will more likely change or be adjusted annually.

At the beginning of the year, leaders will setup team and individual employee work expectations, initiatives, and projects to support the organizational strategies and goals. In turn, these will be linked to rewards, recognition efforts, annual performance reviews, and incentives. You and your leadership must also link your vision, appropriate strategy points, and goals into all company communications, both internal and external. Lastly, make your mission, vision, strategies, and goals visible in the workplace via company intra-nets, bulletin boards, and publications.

FROM THE MAILROOM TO THE BOARDROOM, EVERYONE PLAYS A PART, IMPACTS COST AND PERFORMANCE, AND IS A PART OF YOUR ORGANIZATIONAL CULTURE

As the CEO, you are the ultimate champion of this communication campaign; but your leaders, as in all things, will have the greatest organizational impact. This is an area where your communication leadership competency will pay off. Leaders who are strong communicators will organize their communications by clarifying purpose and importance; strongly emphasizing key points; and integrating mission, vision, strategy, and goal messages. Leaders are the key to seeking input during these communications, checking understanding, and adjusting accordingly to optimize the message and information.

Communicate your mission, vision, strategy, and goals widely, deeply and repetitively across your company. Effective communication is the lifeblood of a positive culture. It enables employees to understand your mission, vision, goals, and strategies. Hold formal and informal forums at every level in the organization to discuss, clarify, and build understanding. Communicate clearly the first time and re-communicate at every opportunity following. Once you think everyone has heard it, understands it, and doesn't need to hear it anymore; communicate it again.

Keep your mission, vision, strategy, and goals visible to employees and on the minds of every leader. Make this focus part of your annual "cultural" processes and part of your leadership actions every day. In prosperity and disparity, a positive culture with strong leadership and an engaged workforce united in a common mission and vision will prevail and succeed.

STEP 7—DEVELOP TEAMWORK AND TEAMBUILDING

Step 7: Educate and coach your employees on teamwork and team building. This will not only develop your organization's ability to work in teams. It will appropriately set organizational expectations for teamwork and communicate that it is a skill and a competency that is highly valued and will be rewarded. Institutionalize the training and refresh it annually. Debrief and review team performance and results annually.

Invest time and energy into educating and coaching your employees on teamwork and team building. A positive culture is driven by teamwork and focused on employees. In order to be driven by teamwork, your organization must understand teamwork and be proficient in using it to achieve goals and drive your company's actions. As discussed in Step 5, you are creating an organization where every employee is a team member and every leader is a team leader. Given these needs and expectations, you must provide the organization with resources to understand, grow, and develop teamwork. Providing resources to train and improve employees also demonstrates your strong focus on them and their individual development.

This education effort will not only develop your organization's ability to work in teams, it will appropriately set organizational expectations for teamwork and communicate that it is a skill and a competency that is highly valued. Formal education and training for leadership is an absolute necessity to set the tone for teamwork across the organization. It communicates that you and your leaders expect teamwork to drive your culture and deliver your results; and that you are willing to invest time, energy, and resources in making your organization great at it. As more employees become involved in developing their teaming skills, teamwork will become an ingrained part of your culture.

TEAMWORK AND TEAMBUILDING EDUCATION WILL DEVELOP YOUR EMPLOYEES' ABILITY TO WORK IN TEAMS AND ESTABLISH APPROPRIATE ORGANIZATIONAL EXPECTATIONS FOR TEAMWORK

To educate employees on effective teams and teamwork, there are significant resources you can tap into to develop and administer training. Whether you develop training in-house and/or utilize a consultant, you should customize and expand your teamwork training process to suit your company's needs; and, at a minimum, include the following base subject matter.

Building a Successful Team

This training will be developed from the leader's perspective as well as the team member's perspective and cover the base leadership skills and actions required to build a team. It will also be available as part your leadership training as it is one of the six core leadership competencies. Building a successful team is not a secret recipe to be shared only with leaders. When team members understand what a team leader is trying to accomplish in terms of team leadership, they will help build the team more quickly and more readily support the team leader's efforts. Given that a positive culture is driven by teamwork and every employee is a team member, this class is required for every employee.

Team Leadership

This training will have several of the same components as the building a successful team competency class; but it will also include additional tools for team leadership such as coaching team members, team dynamics, positive conflict, resolving disruptive conflict, team planning and organization, and team leader decision-making. It is required for all leaders as all leaders are team leaders and for employees who will be leading special project teams.

Creating a Team Charter

It may seem overkill to focus training on the creation of one document; but so much can be learned and accomplished by a team in the process of creating an effective team charter, it is an absolute must. A solid team charter is a foundational document for a team. It focuses the team on key activities and outcomes in addition to helping answer questions and resolving issues that could otherwise become roadblocks. Reviewing and discussing each of the segments of the team charter and teaching leaders how to construct an effective team charter is critical o building a successful team. This is a requirement for all team leaders.

Collaboration and Stakeholder Analysis

Working collaboratively as an individual or as team is a very challenging competency to master because it involves a delicate balance of keeping key stakeholders informed of appropriate information in adition to moving forward and taking action within an acceptable timeframe. This is further complicated by the fact that you cannot always effectively identify all your stakeholders, their issues, or their reactions. This training will prove critical to understanding the importance of managing internal and external stakeholders as well as provide guidance on how to collaborate with them for successful outcomes. Recommend this for all team leaders.

Facilitation Skills and Meeting Planning

Facilitation and meeting planning skills are important tactical tools for team leaders and team facilitators. These skills focus on team efficiencies and optimizing the talents and input of all the team members. Being able to effectively plan a meeting and facilitate the team members through that meeting plan while drawing out key points, concerns, and ideas from all the team members will greatly influence the productivity and output of your teams. In some situations, team leaders will facilitate. In others, a separate facilitator can be used (the latter approach allows the team leader to focus and participate more as a team member). This is a requirement for all team leaders and team facilitators.

Team Member Diversity

Diversity is often a misunderstood and avoided topic. It tends to make people uncomfortable and focus on issues of the "haves" and "have nots", fairness and exclusion. While these are no doubt real and concerning situations, developing training on team member diversity allows you to develop positive perceptions of this very important topic as you build understanding of the value of leveraging diversity. It must focus on diversity of thought, inclusion of all team member perceptions and ideas, and how to leverage different perceptions, thoughts, and experiences to achieve the best possible outcomes and results. Given that a positive culture is fueled by diversity and focused on employees, this training is required for every employee.

***

Teamwork training will provide a solid foundation and a terrific learning opportunity for your organization. As discussed, it will also be used to realize training objectives in areas other than teamwork such as leadership, diversity, communications, etc. Leadership and team leaders must invest time every year in taking and/or refreshing this training. Additionally, all employees must be trained in building a successful team and team diversity as part of their orientation to your company and your culture.

BUILDING A SUCCESSFUL TEAM IS NOT A SECRET RECIPE TO BE SHARED ONLY WITH LEADERS, EDUCATE EVERY EMPLOYEE ON TEAMWORK AND TEAMBUILDING

It is suggested that you develop and establish your teamwork training in two to three months. Development and implementation of your teamwork training and education efforts will be reiterative as you improve and refresh it over time; but work to establish the initial training program within this time frame. At this point, you will have already selected your leaders and performed your team identification processes (Step 6). The organization has been functioning in teams, developing team charters, and getting a feel for their team's unique team dynamics and has their team leader's leadership style. This is the point when leadership will begin to get hungry for training, coaching, and improvement in the area of teamwork and team building.

Develop a communication plan to introduce your teamwork training process to the organization. A portion of the training will be required for all employees so communicating it and introducing it is a very important step. It is also a tremendous opportunity to build and influence your culture. It represents a significant corporate commitment to developing employees and sends a terrific message. You and your leadership team must make the most of this positive news and nail down all the key messages you want the organization to hear and understand.

In terms of ongoing coaching and development, each team leader must establish a routine of gathering feedback from the team members on team performance, individual team member's performance, and the team leader's performance. This can be accomplished by debriefing team successes, improvements, and mistakes. These processes must be ingrained into every team—both special projects and long standing, staff based teams.

Establishing a process of evaluating what went well, what didn't go well, and what team members recommend be changed or done differently will provide many improvement and coaching opportunities as well as uncover best practices that will be shared and used to refresh your training. Assuring that the organization systematically generates, captures, and acts on this data will help develop your culture around teamwork and establish expectations for openness and trust around improvement opportunities.

Lastly, this step is focused on providing training around teamwork and team building because it is critical to quickly establishing effective teams at every level in your organization. It is not meant to imply that this is the only training you will need, but understand that it is foundational in nature. It must be in place at this time to support and influence your positive culture. In addition to the teamwork training effort, a company that is focused on employees and their development will have much broader training programs in the areas of job skills, leadership competencies, diversity, communications, ethics, etc. You will need to develop and provide comprehensive training that is structured to focus on employees, your positive culture, and the unique needs of your business.

Educate and coach your employees on teamwork and team building to develop your organization's ability to work in teams. Lead by example and set appropriate organizational expectations for teamwork across your company. Invest time and energy into educating and coaching your employees. Create a teamwork training process that includes classes on building a successful team, team leadership, creating a team charter, collaboration and stakeholder analysis, facilitation skills, meeting planning, and team diversity. Establish the expectation for routine gathering of feedback from the team members on team performance, individual team member's performance, and the team leader's performance. Capture best practices and lessons learned; refresh training content annually; and institutionalize your teamwork training process with an unwavering level of commitment. Your teamwork and team building training is foundational. Put it in place after establishing teams to support and influence your positive culture.

STEP 8—CREATE DEVELOPMENT PLANS FOR LEADERSHIP

Step 8: Identify and create development plans for every leader in the organization. Make the development process an ongoing effort and a point of formal communication between leader and employee. Promote open and full disclosure of development efforts. Make the development focus situational and applicable to upcoming challenges and work initiatives. Leaders develop leaders. All your leaders must model this commitment and effort to development.

A positive culture is focused on employees, human assets. Human assets are the most versatile, creative, and important assets of any company. Human assets must be developed and maintained like all other assets. The organization must invest time, money, and energy into continually growing and improving them. This is a critical step in building a positive culture that is focused on its employees.

Personal development plans can save significant time and energy for the organization. If you do it right, development will not be extra effort. Development is doing the right coaching and supporting of employees at the right time. It is doing the things that need to be done regardless of any formal development effort. This is why formal development efforts are beneficial to the employee, their leader, and the organization when they focus on the right development opportunity and have a sound process to work through the development effort.

Formal development not only improves and supports ongoing performance; it is a tremendous time and energy saver for leadership and the organization. For example, consider an employee that is challenged by, and therefore needs to improve upon, building trust. If this is the employee's primary area of needed improvement, several situations will arise throughout the work year that will require coaching and attention from their leader. Making this the key developmental focus between the employee and their leader creates an opportunity for ongoing coaching and openness around improvement. It allows the leader to quickly address and support the employee in an area that requires their attention regardless of having a formal development plan. In this way, a formal development plan that is focused on the right development opportunity saves each employee and their leader both time and energy over the course of the work year. In the book, *The Human Capital Edge: 21 People Management Practices Your Company Must Implement (or Avoid) to Maintain Shareholder Value,* Bruce N. Pfau and Ira T. Kay document their findings on executives' viewpoints regarding development at strongly performing companies.

> "Top executives believe creating a "culture for learning and innovation" is the key leadership behavior involved in mobilizing people. Getting employees on board, committed, and moving in the same direction is the most vital objective for top executives in today's knowledge-based economy. To keep executives focused on that one goal, the most successful companies have instituted leadership development programs."[9]

Personal development as a process can be described in many ways and formats. Regardless of your chosen development theory, format, or approach, it will have a much better chance of success if it is simple, straightforward, and easily understood by the organization as a whole. With this in mind, I recommend you describe and implement the process in four basic steps:

Discovery

Discovery is the part of the process where the actual development focus, the competency, and/or behavior to be developed is discovered and identified. While there will be several potential opportunities for development, the challenge is to define the one that will most benefit the employee at the current time given their role, expected work issues, and challenges.

Acceptance

Once the development focus has been discovered and identified, the employee must achieve acceptance of the opportunity. They must take the time to consider, affirm, and recognize that there is truly a development opportunity for them and that improving in this area will be beneficial and valuable for them.

Plan Development

A personal development plan provides the primary working document for development. The format for the plan includes a definition of the development opportunity, why it is important, required timing, goals and objectives, strengths to leverage, barriers to overcome, strategies and key actions to improve, and the resources required. The creation of the plan plays a key role in the discovery, acceptance, and implementation parts of the process.

Plan Implementation

Plan implementation is the process of actually working the personal development plan. It involves capturing situational opportunities as well as planned training and learning, active participation between the individual and their leader, and assessing and measuring progress towards the goal.

***

As with other steps of the Blueprint, you will implement in levels; lead by example; and educate leadership from the top down on how the process will look and feel. Once again, you, the CEO, need to go first. Work with your Human Resources Vice President, your staff, and/or an outside executive coach to create a personal development plan for yourself.

If you have the courage and you really want to make a significant statement through a huge example, go through the leadership competencies assessment portion of your leadership selection process. Share the results and formulate your personal development plan around those results. This will be an incredibly powerful example for your leaders and it will quickly make the entire organization comfortable with the process. Regardless of how you develop your own personal development plan, you, the CEO must go first.

EVERY LEADER MUST HAVE A DEVELOPMENT PLAN; EVERY LEADER MUST PARTICIPATE IN THE DEVELOPMENT OF OTHERS

Establish your "leadership based" personal development plan for the year. A "leadership based" development plan will focus on developing the "how," in developing your leadership. Do not build it around a goal or a performance objective; but, focus on making it competency and behavior based. Also, make sure it is a behavior that you are visibly going to work to get better at. Share this with your staff and with the rest of the organization. Ask for their support and participation in your plan. As you begin to discuss development, share past development efforts you've undertaken and how you have benefited from them. Sharing this with your staff and inviting them to help you demonstrates the tone of openness you want every leader to have with their own development.

Your example establishes several important points. First and foremost, that it is acceptable, important, and required that every leader have a development plan. It also establishes the expectation for every leader to invest in personal development and the development of each employee on their team. It sends a message that development does not mean you are broken, have a problem, or are fatally flawed as a leader. It communicates that every leader, even the CEO, has improvement opportunities and that everyone can continue to learn and improve for the benefit of themselves and the organization.

LEADERS DEVELOP LEADERS; ALL OF YOUR LEADERS MUST MODEL THIS COMMITMENT

Now you are ready to begin this process with your staff. Before you begin, it is important to know that each one of these steps is critically important to a successful development experience. The process of development will center on time spent between the leader and their employee working the process together. It will involve meeting both formally and opportunistically to think deeply about, strategize on, and work the development process.

<u>Discovery</u>

To begin the process of **discovery**, schedule an initial meeting with each of your employees and set the tone upfront that the purpose of the meeting is to create a development plan. Reiterate that personal development is a process that you have begun for yourself and a process that all of their peers and all leaders will undergo as well. It is important to establish that this process is an opportunity to improve, not a disciplinary action. Share the Personal Development Plan form as well as your personal development plan as an example of a completed plan. Your willingness to be open and share your plan will set the appropriate tone and expectation for the initial meeting. Remember that discovery is the part of the process where the actual development focus, the competency and/or behavior to be developed is discovered and identified. The challenge is to discover the opportunity that will most benefit the employee at the current time given their role, expected work issues, and challenges.

Begin the meeting by sharing your thoughts and ideas on development overall—its importance, what it means, and the value it brings to individuals and to the organization. Reinforce that a positive culture is focused on employees and that developing employees is one of the company's core leadership competencies. Explain that the purpose of the meeting is to work towards the creation of a development plan for them and to begin their development process. It is important to note that this is the beginning of creating a plan. Often the most meaningful part of the process is first discovering and then accepting the development opportunity. This is the case because very often the actual effort of improving, or executing the development plan, is easier than discovering and accepting what needs to be developed. Once employees achieve awareness and acceptance, modifying the actual behavior may in some cases be the easier part of the development process.

During the discovery phase, there are two development concepts that often prove helpful. The first concept is situational development; the second is opposing competency strengths and weaknesses.

Situational development entails considering your current role in upcoming challenges or projects for the year and assessing the development focus that will most benefit you given your current or expected work situation. For example, a leader that has recently been promoted may have been a solid communicator in his former role; but now finds he needs to improve communication skills because the diversity of his audiences has changed, the communication frequency has increased, and the messages and situations have grown more complex. This in no way suggests that communication is a weakness for this leader. Rather, it recognizes that strong communication skills at the team leader's present level may only be satisfactory communication skills at the Vice President level. Situational development is not only valuable to the employee because it allows them to address needs at the key moment in their career; but, it also provides a format to address and consider development needs in a non-threatening way.

The second development concept is opposing competency strengths and weaknesses. Often an individual's primary strength will result in a natural opposing weakness, a potential development opportunity. Our primary strength is what has allowed us to achieve and succeed throughout our scholastic and professional careers so we naturally leverage that strength and seldom work to balance or put it in check. Each of the following examples is a potential opposing strength and weakness:

- Drive for Results and Working Collaboratively
- Strategic Thinking and Managing and Measuring Work
- Gaining Commitment and Decision Making

- Patience and Drive for Results
- Analysis and Dealing with Ambiguity

An employee who is known for their patience or for being balanced and measured, may not drive hard enough for results. Conversely, someone who is terrific at driving for results may at times be seen as impatient. Both of these competencies are valuable as strengths, but there are business situations where the opposing weakness can be problematic.

<u>Example</u>

Joe is great at driving for results. He consistently gets things accomplished on time every time. However, the weakness that opposes his strength is that he often doesn't take the time to collaborate with peers and key stakeholders. Joe's leader frequently gets pulled into issues where stakeholders have concerns and are preventing Joe from moving forward because he did not work with them upfront. This is a perfect example of where a formal development plan focused on working collaboratively would significant help Joe develop that skill, save time for him in his work efforts, and save time for his leader. In the absence of a formal development plan, Joe's leader still gets pulled into issues as a result of Joe's improvement need; but rather than investing time and energy in a positive way to help Joe build a new skill and improve, they are troubleshooting the results and not working to remedy the cause.

Share the concepts of situational development as well as opposing competency strengths and weaknesses during your first meeting with employees to help discover their most opportunistic development focus. Ask employees to prepare for the meeting by thinking ahead of time about some potential development opportunities and let them know that you will do the same. You may be surprised that you both may quickly converge on a common development theme. Also, ask them to consider leadership based development opportunities that focus on developing the "how," of developing their leadership. During the meeting, discuss and consider the following questions with each employee:

- What situations have changed for you that will require more or an improved performance of a specific skill or competency?
- What is your greatest competency strength?
- What competency naturally opposes that strength and is it a perceived development opportunity or need for you?
- What additional performance or perception information would be helpful?
- Who else could we seek development input from (peers, staff, friends, or family)?
- Do we both see the development focus we are considering as a beneficial opportunity?

Seeking additional input from coworkers, friends, and family is also valuable in discovering and/or confirming a potential development opportunity. In collecting that data, the employee can take several different approaches. They can directly solicit input and feedback; they can assemble a quick survey and distribute it so it can be completed anonymously; or they can opt for a more extensive and standardized assessment tool (such as a 360-feedback assessment).

During the first meeting to discuss development, you and your employee will capture your collective thoughts and ideas on potential development opportunities, but not finalize the development focus. It is important to provide time for reflection on the initial discussion and thoughts on potential development opportunities. In fact, based on additional information as well as input and feedback from others, the process of discovery can take several meetings. Finalizing the description of a development focus should not occur until both you and the employee are comfortable with it.

<u>Acceptance</u>

The process of **acceptance** may appear straightforward, but seldom is because it requires a great deal of self-awareness. Even the employees who are very receptive to development must put effort into this part of the development process. Once the development focus has been discovered and identified, employees must achieve acceptance by recognizing it is a real development opportunity and that improving it will be beneficial and valuable for them. While the employee may generally agree on the development focus, they may still not buy-in 100%. Often employees will allow themselves to be guided by their leader and be quick to agree on a suggested development focus, but do not truly see the improvement opportunity in themselves. One way to build acceptance is to ask the employee to seek confirmation from their closest coworkers—the people that know them best. Ask them if they observe behaviors and/or can provide examples that verify the development focus opportunity that is under consideration. A more real time approach to building acceptance is to discuss and agree that both leader and employee will actively look for situations and opportunities that verify the development focus. Everyone is different and some employees will need to begin to see or feel the value before they can fully accept.

The acceptance part of the process can come early coinciding with discovery or much later, reaching far into plan development or even plan execution. Regardless of the eventual timing, it is important to note that acceptance must be realized fully before final completion of the plan execution. If an employee never truly accepts their development focus as a need and an opportunity, they will never fully commit to developing and capturing the benefits associated with new skills and behaviors.

Acceptance should be openly discussed; but even then, there may be no sure way short of internal honesty and high self-awareness to fully assure that acceptance has been achieved. Employees can fool themselves into thinking that they accept and buy into the development opportunity, but not truly believe in it deep down. In most cases, sharing the overall process of development and the individual steps and their importance will lead to honest discussion and eventual acceptance.

Plan Development

The next phase of the process, **plan development,** begins after the development focus has been decided upon. A personal development plan is the primary working document for development. The suggested format for the plan (see below) includes a definition of the development opportunity, why it is important, required timing, goals and objectives, strengths to leverage, barriers to overcome, strategy and key actions to improve, and the resources needed. The creation of the plan plays a key role in every other part of the process (discovery, acceptance and implementation). The following provides guidance on completing each section of the **personal developmental plan.**

<table>
<tr><td>Personal Development Plan</td><td>Name:</td><td>Date:</td></tr>
<tr>
<td>Focus: What have I targeted for development?

Coaching for success (as it relates/links to aligning performance for success).</td>
<td>Why: Why is this important for me to focus on at this time?

This is a key opportunity to establish a new approach to execution, tracking, and evaluating performance with a newly formed department. It is an opportunity and a need to grow my leaders and my team. I believe this team is a tremendous organizational asset with some amount of untapped potential.</td>
<td>Timing: What is my desired and/or required timeline for improvement?

I am currently completing my annual operating plan and defining the annual goals and initiatives for my team, I intend to improve my skills in this area and be in position to leverage my new skills heavily from mid-year to year-end to coach my team to success.</td>
</tr>
</table>

<table>
<tr>
<td>Goals and Objectives: How will I define and measure success? What specific behaviors and actions will I demonstrate to realize different outcomes?

• A well-defined operating plan that measures performance against goals.
• Regular and timely progress reviews (as defined by leaders) that are honest, objective, and identifies development opportunities
• Complete, concise, and clear individual performance expectations for team
• Combined and cooperative actions across the organizations with key stakeholders</td>
<td>Event Driven Opportunities: What situations, people, or events signal that right now is an opportunity to put new behaviors into action?

• Missed target dates and process delays
• Disconnects with key stakeholders on expectations and roles/responsibilities
• Disagreement on key priorities and organizational direction</td>
</tr>
<tr>
<td>Strengths: What personal strengths will I leverage to achieve my development goals and objectives?

• Leadership style (willingness to understand and take risks)
• Experienced and strong leaders
• Strategic/tactical mindset</td>
<td>Barriers: What potential barriers will I face in realizing my goals and objectives, and how will I overcome them?

• Relative unfamiliarity with certain functions of organization
• Unexpected organizational distractions
• Different cultures across leadership team
• Geography and travel</td>
</tr>
<tr>
<td>Strategy and Actions: How will I achieve my objectives? What specific actions will I take?

• Routine progress review meeting with my leader and HR support person
• Identify and interview an internal resource who is known to be very strong at coaching
• Develop a strategy to identify and create coaching opportunities
• Identify one external resource (training, conference, book) on coaching</td>
<td>Resources: Who are the people, what are the tools, and how much time will I need for each action?

• Time commitment from me, my leader and my HR partner
• Time and participation from coaching mentor
• Time, support, ideas and feedback from my leader, HR partner
• Time and funding for external resource</td>
</tr>
</table>

Focus

This is where you will describe the leadership area of focus that will be targeted for development. The description must be clear and concise; and at most, three short sentences. The development focus must be behavior based and competency focused. It can, but does not need to be, a specific leadership competency. The development focus may also be a component or subpart of a competency or skill. Most importantly, it must be worded and described such that it is meaningful and clear to both the employee and their leader. As previously discussed, identifying the right development focus will save time and effort and bring tremendous value to the employee, their leader, and the organization. Take as much time as needed to get it right.

Why

This section defines the value or benefit of the chosen development focus. It also defines why the development focus is important to the employee at this particular time. Include in the description any recent or upcoming challenges or situations in which the new skills will be needed. Be concise and very specific in terms of what benefits the employee will realize once the development effort has been completed. Go deeper than just being better in the development focus. Identify the benefits in terms of productivity, job performance, morale, working environment, personal satisfaction, reduced frustration, etc. This section is important to get right because it will support and accelerate the process of buy-in and acceptance.

Timing

It is important to define either a required or a desired timeline for completing the development plan. Developing a timeline establishes expectations for actions as well as measurement of progress. The timeline may need to coincide with a business need or opportunity, and therefore be defined and planned accordingly. If this is not the case, define a reasonable amount of time to work the development effort. One year is a good standard to use, knowing that the development timeline could always be adjusted based on need or progress. An important point to emphasize is that development actions, new behaviors, tactics, and skills can be helpful and positively impact work life throughout the entire process and timeline. The development plan and implementation doesn't necessarily need to be fully completed to begin delivering benefits to the employee.

Goals and Objectives

In goals and objectives you will describe a lofty vision of a future state where the development focus has become an easily deployable skill that allows the employee to deal successfully with previously challenging situations. It will describe this vision in terms of behaviors and actions that the employee will be able to utilize and the positive resulting outcomes once the development effort is completed. In doing this, you will also define measures that can be used to judge progress towards goals.

Event Driven Opportunities

This section is very important in that it helps build insight and self-awareness of the specific situations and opportunities when the development focus will be valuable and utilized. Defining the situations, people, or events that signal an opportunity to practice the development focus will create a proactive advantage for the employee as they move forward with implementing their development plan. Awareness of these situations, the cues that signal that different actions and behaviors are required, is often half the challenge of working a development plan. Conversely, missing these signals and opportunities will be a disadvantage and perhaps a significant barrier to development.

Strengths

Create a list of the employee's top three strengths and then consider how they can be used to realize developmental goals and objectives. Consider which strengths can be leveraged and how they will be helpful. If the development focus opposes a strength of the employee (opposing strength/weakness), then their particular strength may not be one that they can leverage; but in most cases, other strengths can be used in some fashion to build new skills. This approach will help the employee by allowing them to use skills or strengths that are familiar and well practiced to further their development effort. Leveraging strengths to develop and build new skills is a positive and beneficial approach to development.

Barriers

Create a list of the realistic barriers that the employee will face during the development process. Understanding these barriers upfront and considering how best to overcome and/or neutralize them can greatly improve the flow of the development process, set appropriate expectations, and minimize possible frustration for the employee. Understanding the natural obstacles that will occur during development and developing strategies to manage through those obstacles will greatly benefit the employee throughout the development process.

Strategy and Actions

This is the section where the employee will document specific actions they will take to help them achieve their development goals and objectives. While effort to add actions to this section will be made at the beginning of process, expect to modify and further develop it throughout implementation. One required action item is the routine progress meeting with the employee's leader and Human Resources support person. These meetings will be the cornerstones of the plan and implementation part of the process. Other actions that are often considered include training, reading specific topic books, meeting with peers or a mentor, planning and identifying situations in which the new behavior or skills can be practiced, and capturing and reviewing skill-based opportunities and situations.

Resources

Defining the resources needed to implement your development strategy and actions is important so both the employee and their leader can assure they are realistic and available. The employee must consider who the individuals are that they will rely on for assistance and council, how much time will they need for specific activities, training, etc., and what tools will be utilized in the implementation effort. One required resource is a time commitment from both the employee and their leader to work the implementation plan together. Define the needed resources, confirm their availability, and adjust strategy and actions as needed.

***

To complete the plan development process for your team, work with each employee to complete and develop a personal development plan. After one or two working sessions, the plan should be 80%—90% complete. It is important to establish that it is acceptable and expected to revisit and revise the plan as needed, particularly in terms of strategy, actions and resources.

Plan Implementation

The next phase of the process is **plan implementation**, actually working the personal development plan to success. Few things will be as valuable and as fulfilling for you, your employees, and your team as this single exercise. It will help you and your leaders uncover and address the most pressing and challenging people and team issues that you will come across in your daily work efforts.

The one single, most important part of the plan execution will be the formal and informal progress check-ins and the accompanying open dialog between you, the employee, and your Human Resources support person. Look for real time opportunities and examples that can be integrated in the development process. This is where situations and opportunities are explored and debriefed, new strategies discussed and conceived, and true understanding of the challenges and how best to overcome them are realized. It is where leaders develop leaders and themselves in the process. Lastly, it will cement the fact that you and the organization are focused on employees and are willing to investing time in them and in their success!

OPTIMAL DEVELOPMENTAL EFFORTS TAKE ADVANTAGE OF REAL TIME WORK SITUATIONS, CHALLENGES AND NEEDS

If you successfully complete this process start to finish, you will experience its tremendous value. No one who completes this process and does it right will ever ask, "Do I really have time for this…isn't this just a nice thing I do when I can fit it into my work schedule?" If you do it right, the value and benefits will be obvious. It will help you and your employees more successfully navigate terrain that would otherwise absorb tremendous organizational time and energy.

FEW THINGS WILL BE AS VALUABLE AND AS FULFILLING FOR YOU, YOUR EMPLOYEES, AND YOUR TEAM AS THE FORMAL PROCESS OF EMPLOYEE DEVELOPMENT

***

Identifying and creating personal development plans for all leadership must be completed before Step 9, Reassess Leadership for Results, Vision and Acceptance. Step 9 requires the organization to know its leadership, to have completed this development effort, and to have taken measure of both progress and performance. In Step 9 you will once again be making some very crucial and difficult decisions about leadership so you must execute Step 8, Create Development Plans for Leadership, very well.

Plan to begin Step 8 with a one or two month lag from beginning Step 7, Develop Teamwork and Teambuilding. The effort of leadership development will go hand-in-hand with your teamwork training process. While development isn't training, the two efforts will be linked, overlapping in some important areas and supportive in focus. It is important to establish that the developmental process isn't training. It is development. It isn't classes or books. It is a one-on-one leader and employee work effort and it is often done in real time. The best developmental efforts take advantage of real time work situations, challenges, and needs.

You, the CEO, and your staff must all have a development plan in place as the most visible leadership team in your company. Once you do, you'll be ready to develop communications; share your personal development plans and past developmental experiences; and begin to spread the process throughout the leadership ranks of the company.

Building understanding and acceptance of the development process will at first be a big challenge. All too often the top leaders at companies do not like to have development plans. They feel they are above them and don't have time for them. Again, this is a very dangerous point of potential compromise. Make sure it is one in which you do not lose ground. Every leader must have a personal development plan every year. In the book, *The Human Capital Edge: 21 People Management Practices Your Company Must Implement (or Avoid) to Maintain Shareholder Value,* Bruce N. Pfau and Ira T. Kay documented the strong link between highly admired companies and their commitment to employee development.

> "In general, the study found that highly admired companies make it a point to compute their "investment per employee" and ensure that they are at the high end of the averages for their industry. They also turn much of their leadership's focus on career development. Executives in many of these companies are held personally accountable for successful development of top managers. These leaders are expected to take a primary role in transferring and expanding the organization's knowledge base, not only through formal instruction, but also through individual coaching and mentoring."[10]

In their book, *Execution, The Discipline of Getting Things Done,* Larry Bossidy and Ram Charan describe the necessity of a robust "people process" to assess and develop employees, and the key role of leadership in executing those processes.

> "When we where putting these processes into place at Allied Signal, one guy—a pretty good guy—said to me at a meeting, "You know, I've got to go through this people ritual again this year." I said. "That's the dumbest comment I've ever heard, because you tell the world how little you know about your job. If you really feel that way, you've got to do something else, because you are not going to get good at this, you can't be successful. "I didn't say it in front of everybody, but I thought to myself, that just tells me maybe I've got the wrong guy."[II]

Leaders will always have development needs and opportunities. Their employees will always have development needs and opportunities. They must lead by example so they must be skilled at and understand the entire development process in order to execute it with their team and support it across the organization. They must understand and capture the value of development.

Identify and create leadership based development plans for every leader in your organization. Make the development process an ongoing effort and point of formal communication between leader and employee. Promote open and full disclosure of development efforts. Make the development focus situational and applicable to upcoming challenges and work initiatives. The process of development should include discovery, acceptance, plan development, and implementation. The best developmental experiences take advantage of real time work situations and needs.

Leaders develop leaders and all of your leaders must model this commitment. Every leader must have a development plan and every leader must participate in the development of others. You (the CEO) and your executive staff must be the model for development as a team. Few things will be as valuable and as fulfilling for you, your employees, and your team as the formal process of employee development.

STEP 9—REASSESS LEADERSHIP FOR RESULTS, VISION, AND ACCEPTANCE (MAKE **CHANGES!**)

Step 9: Reassess leadership for results, acceptance, and buy-in of your mission, vision, and culture. Assess "how" they lead and do things as well as "what" they do. Make the difficult changes and remove the leaders that do not get the performance results and/or do not share the cultural values. In removing the leaders that do not share the cultural values and do not do things the right ways, you are removing the individuals that will erode your culture and what you've worked to build.

Leaders must get results and they must get them in the right way, the way that will build and maintain a positive culture. You will now evaluate and redefine "making the cut" for leadership in your organization. The new leadership cut is based on the "how" and the "what", (2H*W=P), where the "how" is twice as important as the "what" in terms of overall leadership performance.

Leaders must get results and they must believe in the value of leadership and culture. They must do the right things as managers in the right way as leaders. If they don't, your company will not achieve the results you need nor build the positive culture you wish to create. Without a positive culture, you will not achieve the level of employee engagement you need to create your competitive advantage and excel in your industry. Remember how it all fits together to achieve effective team solutions in addition to strong individual and company performance:

$$2A * Q = E$$
$$2H * W = P$$
$$2C * S = P$$

Leadership building **acceptance,** being great at the **"how"** and creating a positive **culture,** combined with strong **technical solutions, "what"** employees do everyday, and sound **business strategy** will result in **effective Solutions**, strong **individual Performance** and optimal **company performance.**

Step 9 is about reassessing your leadership choices, making the needed adjustments, and taking the appropriate corrective actions. It is about reaffirming decisions and addressing the imperfections of Step 4 when you initially reselected and realigned your leadership. This time you are doing it with more accurate and greater amounts of information. You now have the advantage of actual "in position" observed actions, behaviors, and measured results to factor into your assessment.

In Step 4 you utilized a process to develop the best assessment information and predictors of candidate success to select your leadership. As discussed, it is a solid process that greatly improves the quality of your leadership selection decisions; but, it is not perfect. There will always be adjustments that will come after you have observed actual performance. Now is the time to make those adjustments. I've seen great leaders propelled by their strong leaders; and I've seen them hurt by the "wrong" leaders they failed to remove. Great leaders leverage great leaders and remove poor ones to achieve success.

Step 9 is part of an annual assessment process for your leadership. If you do it fairly, consistently, and thoughtfully, it will not be an annual bloodletting full of fear, severances, and demotions. Rather, it will be a time when leadership adjustments and changes are made that are needed, expected, and understood by the majority of employees. Leadership performance and results are always visible to the overall organization. Likewise, leadership acceptance, buy-in, and support of the company's mission, vision, leadership philosophy, and culture is equally, if not even more, visible to employees. The collective organization knows who has bought-in, who is part of the team, and who is delivering the results. Even more often, they know who isn't and who needs to be removed from leadership.

GREAT LEADERS LEVERAGE GREAT LEADERS FOR SUCCESS AND REMOVE THE POOR ONES

Executing Step 9 requires leadership to consistently manage performance and requires a commitment to coaching, training, and leadership development. These efforts will provide leaders with every opportunity to succeed; and, in some situations, confirm if a leader needs to be in a different leadership role, in a role as an individual contributor, or needs to be removed from the organization.

As previously discussed, the business world today is focused almost solely on results with an all too often Machiavellian approach where the results justify the means employed to deliver them. Not only can this approach potentially get a company into ethical hot water; but, ultimately, it will not lead to a positive culture and the high level of employee engagement required for success.

Leaders who do not buy into your mission, vision, or leadership philosophy as well as a positive culture and to the importance of "how" things are accomplished, must be removed, even if they get the business results. If you keep them as leaders they will, by their very example and existence in your company, undercut your leadership and cultural efforts. Leaders and employees know who the best performers are. They also know who the best leaders are and the leaders who are neither will be very apparent to them. They will watch to see what is done to address these leaders and judge you and form their opinions on the organizational culture based on these actions. If you fail to address these damaging leadership issues, you will send a very negative message about performance management, your culture, and your commitment to your ideals.

In their book, *Execution, The Discipline of Getting Things Done,* Larry Bossidy and Ram Charan affirm the importance of assessing "how" leaders get things done and the significant damage they can do when getting things done in the wrong ways.

> "One of the many things mechanical evaluations miss is *how* candidates performed in meeting their commitments—whether they did so in ways that strengthened their organization and people capability as a whole or weakened it. How leaders meet their commitments is at least as important as whether they meet them and is often more important. Meeting them the wrong way can do enormous damage to the organization."[12]

> "A leader who achieves his numbers at the expense of the organization can do a great deal of damage. We know of executives who had to be removed because their negative behavior prevented their teams from working together effectively and drained energy form the entire organization. It's not hard to identify the person who is wrong for a job because of his behavior. But it's better to make sure such a person doesn't rise to a critical job in the first place. Early feedback on behavior can have a major impact on your competitiveness."[13]

Reassess your leadership for results, acceptance, and buy-in of your mission, vision, and culture. Use performance reviews in addition to development effort information and insights to assess both the "how" and the "what" for every leader. Once again, you will have to make very difficult changes and remove the leaders that do not get the performance results and/or do not share the vision. In doing so, you are removing the leaders that will erode your culture and what you've worked so hard to build.

THIS IS THE TIME FOR THE TOUGH CHOICES MADE FAIRLY AND EXECUTED WITH RESPECT, BUT MADE DEFINITIVELY AND WITHOUT COMPROMISE

Performance Results

Begin by assessing performance in terms of getting results and doing the right things from a business/managerial perspective. Consider each leader's performance results and what was expected of them over the past year. Then put them into one of the following three categories.

Almost Always—Leader consistently delivers in the area of performance results. They almost always exceed expectations by doing the right things and making the right decisions to deliver results. They excel in the "what" part of getting things done. In a leadership role they are a visible and easily identified model for performance results.

Sometimes—Leader is inconsistent in their ability to perform well and deliver results. They sometimes meet expectations, but it is questionable as to whether they will consistently do the right things and make the right decisions needed to deliver positive results every time. In terms of performance, expected successes may also be followed by unexpected shortfalls. They may be in a stretch role where the challenges of their role outpace their current level of ability. They may not have the skills to function at a leadership level or they may need more time and experience to develop in their current role.

Almost Never—Leader consistently under-delivers in the area of performance. They almost never meet expectations. There is little confidence or expectation that they will do the right things and make the right decisions to deliver results. In a leadership role they are a visible and easily identified under-performer.

Leadership Shares the Cultural Values

Now assess each leader in terms of sharing the values of the organization. Do they buy-in, support, maintain, and actively work to create a positive culture? Do they support and believe in the company mission, vision, and leadership philosophy? Are they successfully executing on the "how" part of getting things done? Consider these questions and assess each leader in terms of sharing the cultural values and put them into one of the following three categories.

Almost Always—Leader's actions consistently demonstrate that they share the cultural values and actively work to build a positive culture. They almost always exceed expectations in terms of leadership. There is no doubt that they share the cultural values; buy-into the mission, vision, and leadership philosophy; and are actively engaged in building and maintaining the culture. The leader excels in the "how" part of getting things done. In a leadership role, they are a visible and easily identified model for leadership and sharing the cultural values.

Sometimes—Leader is inconsistent in their actions. They sometimes meet expectations for sharing the cultural values, but it is questionable as to whether they truly share the cultural values or if they will consistently act deliberately to build a positive culture. Their level of "buy-in" and support for the mission, vision and leadership model is undetermined. In a leadership role, they are viewed as questionable—an unknown in terms of truly sharing the cultural values and performing the "how."

Almost Never—Leader's actions consistently demonstrates that they do not share the cultural values and are not working to build a positive culture. They almost never meet expectations for leadership and sharing the cultural values. There is no question that they do not "buy-in" or focus on the "how" part of getting things done. In a leadership role, they are visible and easily identified as not sharing the cultural values, supporting, or buying-in to the organizational direction and culture.

***

This second assessment (the "how") is clearly the more challenging of the two. Performance results are typically much easier to measure (budgets, earnings, productivity customer satisfaction, sales, etc.). How results were achieved and if a leader believes and buys into culture can be more difficult to measure; but your coaching and development processes will provide information for you to make the assessment. The type of information to consider is direct discussions, information from the candidate, and noted resisting actions and/or inaction at key times.

One of the best ways to assess if a leader shares the cultural values is to ask them. This may seem too straightforward; but more often than not, leaders will tell you what they think, how they feel, and how much they buy-in or believe in the culture. Routinely query your leaders for feedback and their opinion on leadership and cultural efforts. The leaders that truly do not believe or buy-in will tell you if you listen to them carefully.

Look for resisting actions in leaders, situations where they subtly or even visible resist cultural improvement activities and efforts. This may be evident in terms of resisting actions or simply inaction by not executing on these activities. Evaluate where a leader places priorities. Are they consistently giving leadership and cultural activities less attention or lower priority? If so, they are sending a signal about their perception of value. They are communicating that they do not understand the value of these culture-building activities.

The other reason that assessing if leadership shares the cultural values can be challenging is that believing and buying-in is often not an all or nothing state. It is important for leaders to always question and consider. You need to be careful that active questioning isn't being misinterpreted as a lack of sharing the values. Many leaders who actively question will support, help push, and mold positive cultural changes.

It is unrealistic to think everyone can immediately believe and buy-in fully to techniques and concepts they have never before experienced. Many leaders will become more convinced as they see the affects of what leadership is doing in terms of positive culture and employee engagement. This is a natural and expected part of the process. During your first year, you may expect to have a significant portion of leaders in the "sometimes" category; but over time, these percentages will and must change for the better.

Reassessment and Actions

To make your reassessment of leadership, you will use your assessment of performance results (the "what") and sharing the cultural values (the "how"). To illustrate how to evaluate these two areas together, we will utilize a **leadership evaluation matrix.**

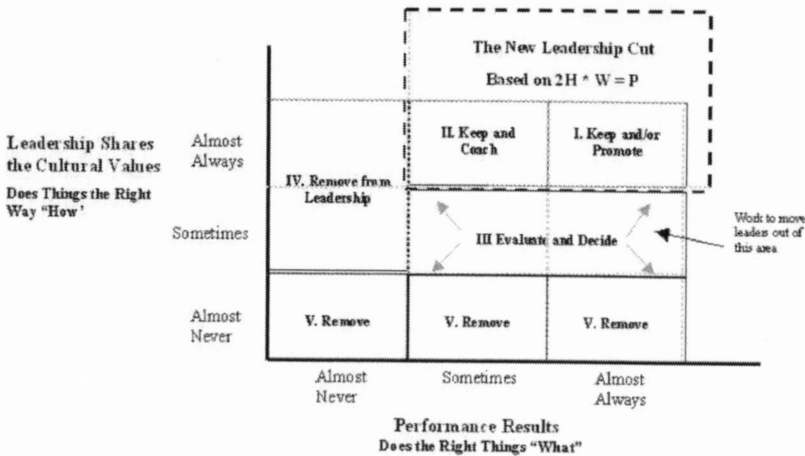

The vertical axis shows the rating for sharing the cultural values; the horizontal axis shows the rating for performance results. Similar approaches are used by many companies to assess employees on both "what" they do to, and "how" they achieve results. This matrix allows you to evaluate a leader's overall performance consistently and categorize the results into five distinct outcomes.

Next we'll discuss the five distinct assessment outcomes you will experience during leadership reassessment and the associated resulting actions you must take based on those outcomes.

I. Keep and/or Promote

Leaders that consistently demonstrate that they share the cultural values and deliver the performance results are your top leaders. They excel at both the "what" and the "how." These are the leaders you must strongly focus on regarding retention and succession as well as look for opportunities to grow and promote them. They not only have the leadership skills and the performance results; but, they consistently demonstrate the ability to skillful execute in both areas. They are the leadership models for your organization.

II. Keep and Coach for Results

Leaders that consistently demonstrate that they share the cultural values and "sometimes" deliver the performance results are worth keeping and coaching. Ultimately, they must deliver the results; but their belief, buy-in, and support of the culture and leadership example makes them a key resource. Even though their performance results need to improve, they are doing things in the right way. They are helping you build and maintain a positive culture. It is better to have a strong leader who is technically capable, yet inexperienced than a technical expert who is not a strong leader. For this reason, these are the leaders you must invest time in developing.

They are strong leaders and are too valuable for you to not work to keep them in a leadership role even through they are not currently achieving the performance results you require. They must be nurtured and given the opportunity to gain more experience to improve their performance results. It is possible they are not in the right role at this time and can perform better if aligned to a position that better suits their present skills and abilities. If, over time, they do not improve and achieve the required results; you will need to move them into a less challenging leadership role or potentially into a role as an individual contributor. If the situation is managed tactfully and respectfully you will at the very least still have a valued employee who is supportive and engaged. At the very best, you will have coached them to improve performance results and they can be moved into the "Keep and/or Promote" category as a top performing leader excelling at both the "what" and the "how."

III. Evaluate and Decide

Leaders that "sometimes" share the cultural values; and either "sometimes" or "almost always" deliver performance results are in the category of "Evaluate and Decide." Ultimately, a leader either shares the cultural values or they don't. If a leader only accepts some of the values some of the time, then they are not truly on-board with the organizational direction or culture. Leaders that have been placed in the "sometimes" rating of sharing the cultural values must be evaluated over a defined period of time and moved into either the "almost never" or "almost always" category. In the longer term, there is no in-between; there can be no "sometimes" in the long-term.

In terms of results, these leaders need to move out of the "sometimes" rating and into the "almost always" rating. If they can deliver results sometimes, it means they either need time to develop; gain experience and mature through coaching and support; or they have topped out and need a less challenging role or assignment. Reassigning a leader can be a difficult choice, but there is nothing wrong with positioning leaders for success. It is often best for both the leader and the organization. In the long term, if the leader cannot get results in their current role with the organization; neither the leader nor the organization will be satisfied.

Significant time and consideration will be spent on the leaders in the category of "evaluate and decide." Leaders that fall into either rating—"sometimes" shares the cultural values and "sometimes" gets results or "sometimes" shares the cultural values and "almost always" get results, have the opportunity to move up and become a model leader. They ultimately need to move out of the "sometimes" rating. If, after a full year, the same leaders show up in "evaluate and decide," then you haven't decided. You are either avoiding the tough decision to move them and/or not investing enough time and effort into coaching, supporting, and developing them. The challenge with these leaders is that you must move them out of "Evaluate and Decide." No leader should be there for more than 18 months. Make a determination of whether or not they share the cultural values and move them accordingly into making the new leadership cut or out of leadership.

IV. Remove from Leadership

Leaders that "almost never" achieve performance results and "almost always" or "sometimes" share the values must be removed from leadership. Even if they share the values and have strong leadership skills, they must be removed from leadership because they are not achieving the performance results you need. If they believe and support the values and culture, but they are simply not able to deliver results in a leadership role, an intermediate step would be to evaluate if they could be moved into a less challenging leadership role. If this can be accomplished, you can leverage their strong leadership and ability to build culture in a role where they can be successful. If ultimately they cannot deliver the performance results in a leadership role, they must be moved out of leadership and into an individual contributor role. They are worth keeping in your organization because they are a supportive and engaged employee.

V. Remove

Leaders that "almost never" share the cultural values must be removed from the organization. Not just from a leadership role, but from the organization, even if they deliver results. Leaders that "almost never" share the cultural values and "almost never" or only "sometimes" deliver results are easier to remove than those that get results; but the problem is the same. If they don't share the cultural values, you cannot have them in your organization.

Leaders that "almost always" achieve the results and "almost never" share the cultural values must be removed from leadership and from the organizational. These are the toughest decisions to make because it is always hard to remove a leader that delivers results. However, the critical issue is that if they get the results in the wrong ways or if they do not share the cultural values and excel at the "how," they will undermine and erode your culture. They are the most damaging leaders you have in your organization. Their success in delivering results, regardless of how they deliver them, sets a negative example for all other leaders. Even if you were to keep these leaders, their ability to deliver the results in the long-term is doubtful and limited by their approach to getting them.

If you have a leader that unquestionably does not share the cultural values, you must remove them from your organization no matter what results they deliver. These will be some of the hardest leadership decisions that you will make; but, this is where your commitment to your vision and your culture must prevail.

***

Once again, this is where your leadership resolve and commitment to a positive culture will be tested. You must remove the leaders that are not building and maintaining a positive culture regardless of all other considerations, including performance results. While this may seem ruthless, in the business world it pales in comparison to the typical actions companies take with employees that are associated with outsourcing, downsizing, and cost cutting. It is much less ruthless than the all too often failures to address performance because of previous relationships, conflict avoidance, flawed individual opinions, and unwillingness to admit a mistake was made when placing the leader.

Under-performance is often left undressed for these reasons and as a result of general unwillingness to make the hard decisions and take on the difficult employee issues. These problems exist even at the highest levels in organizations. Employees who are performing well will always feel the negative impact of under-performing employees that are left addressed by leadership. This negative impact is often further amplified because of the belief that senior leadership is unwilling to make the tough decisions, admit a mistake, or compromise a personal relationship for the betterment of the organization.

In their book, *Execution, The Discipline of Getting Things Done,* Larry Bossidy and Ram Charan identify this common business situation and the dire results it can have for a company.

> "Most people know someone in their organization who doesn't perform well, yet manages to keep his job year after year. The usual reason, we find, is that the person's leader doesn't have the emotional fortitude to confront him and take decisive action. Such failures can do considerable damage to a business. If the non performer is high enough in the organization, he can destroy it."[14]

Why is it business leaders can so easily outsource or downsize entire functions or departments full of employees regardless of their performance with the rationale that it is in the best interest of the company? Yet, they consistently fail to manage the poor performance of the very damaging few. Great companies manage leadership as well as purposefully and rigorously manage performance. In Jim Collin's book, *Good to Great,* this was one of the culture disciplines identified in all of the "great" companies they researched.

> " When you know you need to make a people change, act….. Letting the wrong people hang around is unfair to all the right people, as they inevitably find themselves compensating for the inadequacies of the wrong people. Worse, it can drive away the best people. Strong performers are intrinsically motivated by performance, and when they see their efforts impeded by carrying extra weight, they eventually become frustrated……. the good-to-great leaders did not pursue an expedient "try a lot of people and keep who works" model of management. Instead, they adopted the following approach: "lets take the time to make rigorous A+ selections right up front. If we get it right, we'll do everything we can to try to keep them on board for a long time. If we make a mistake, then we'll confront that fact so we can get on with our work and they can get on with their lives"[15]

The process of leadership reassessment and adjustment is contemplative, based on data and observed results and actions. These difficult decisions truly are impartial and justified by comparison, unlike the majority of personnel decisions in the business world today. It is a much greater disservice to employees and shareholders NOT to address poor performance, both from a results and cultural perspective. You will have measured and reviewed leadership results and actions for well over a year; but when the assessment results are in and the conclusions are evident, you (the CEO) must commit the organization to making the right and difficult decisions. You must commit for your culture and for your bottom line. In the book, *The Human Capital Edge: 21 People Management Practices Your Company Must Implement (or Avoid) to Maintain Shareholder Value,* Bruce N. Pfau and Ira T. Kay document the positive effect on company performance resulting from both coaching improvement and removing poor performers.

> "Successful companies are strong at helping poor performers improve, and they are worth 0.7% more on the stock market as a result..... successful companies use clear goal setting, management coaching, frequent performance discussions, poor bonuses and salary increases, and shifting to new roles.
>
> Companies that terminate employees who perform unacceptably are worth 0.6% more. The low productivity of poor performers is just the beginning of their effect on coworkers' productivity and morale, and the message their continued presence sends about management. There is another important dimension to failing to terminate poor performers. If these poor performers are in management positions, their negative impact on management development, morale, and productivity is leveraged due to their position in the hierarchy."[16]

Never underestimate the impact of having the wrong leader in a job. The wrong leader will always do much more harm than good. Don't use the excuse of needing that person for their experience and expertise or not having a suitable replacement. It is better to have a vacancy than to have a wrong leader in place in your organization doing the wrong things. A wrong leader diminishes everyone's belief in your culture and your leadership. That situation alone, will call into question you and your leadership's intentions simply by your unwillingness to address the problem. You will always have to work harder to manage the issues, problems, and shortcomings associated with the wrong leader in the wrong role.

IT'S BETTER TO HAVE A VACANCY THAN TO HAVE THE WRONG LEADER IN PLACE

The new leadership cut is based on the "how" and the "what," (2H*W=P), where the "how" is twice as important as the "what" in terms of overall leadership performance. Significant time and consideration must be spent on the leaders in the category of "evaluate and decide." These are the leaders that are not clearly the best in terms of both performance results and sharing the cultural values, but they are clearly not the worst. They are either diamonds in the rough that will become solid leaders or they will eventually prove unable to make the new leadership cut. Your challenge, and the rest of leaderships' challenge, is to correctly evaluate, influence, determine, and decide which way they will ultimately turn out.

Deficiencies in the "what," the results, is the easier of the two issues to coach and develop. Teaching skills will always be easier than changing attitudes. Set appropriate expectations for improvement; devote both time and resource to assisting, coaching and supporting achievement of those goals. Also, evaluate if a lower level or different leadership role will be a better fit for that employee. Give them every opportunity to improve and get the performance results the organization requires.

Deficiencies in the "how," sharing the cultural values, is the more difficult area to assess, coach, and develop. To coach and develop sharing the cultural values, you'll need to have dialogue about issues, about values, and about where cultural building activities deliver benefits and results. Ultimately, the employee must have both these leadership skills and choose to use them. Your leaders' personal development plans will focus on developing and enhancing key leadership skills; but the choice to use them, believe, and buy-in to the culture must come from the leader.

When assessing your leaders for sharing the cultural values, there will be one additional and very important challenge you must manage. It is the challenge of identifying your leaders that are your active "culture pushers?" These leaders are vocal, actively questioning, participating, and discussing positive cultural decisions and direction. You must take extreme care in your leadership assessment not to confuse these leaders with the leaders that are not fully sharing the cultural values. Do not confuse active discussion, questioning, and participation with discontent or disagreement with the organizational culture or direction.

In many ways, this challenge is about balancing diversity of thought with having everyone on the same page, sharing the same mission, vision, leadership philosophy, and culture. While you will work very hard to establish shared understanding and acceptance in these areas, you will also encourage news ideas, positive conflict, debate, and creativity. It's important to remember that a positive culture is fueled by diversity and that leveraging diversity is a core leadership competency that strong teams are built upon. The last thing you want to do is misinterpret diversity of thought, active questioning, and positive conflict as not sharing the cultural values. These are all important actions to be strongly encouraged. Your "culture pushing" leaders will often be out in front in terms of sharing and engaging in positive discussion and/or debate over important leadership and cultural issues. The organization needs them to press, push, mold, and influence your positive culture over time. These leaders will be the true owners, builders, and architects of your culture as it grows and matures year in and year out. The leaders who are culture pushers will help you adjust, fine tune, and keep your positive culture on the right track.

IDENTIFY YOUR LEADERS THAT ARE THE POSITIVE "CULTURE PUSHERS" AND DO NOT CONFUSE THEM WITH LEADERS WHO MAY NOT SHARE THE CULTURAL VALUES

In assessing leadership sharing the cultural values, do not make the mistake of putting your visible and questioning leaders into the "sometimes" shares the cultural values category just because they are vocal. You need to truly look at the issues and actions to determine if they are supportive and positive. Active questioning of ideas and actions with the intent of building and maintaining a positive culture is very important. Inaction or resisting action around positive culture building activity is very different. In some cases, your least vocal employees may be the ones that resist and share the cultural values the least through inaction and non-participation. As you work through leadership assessment in terms of sharing the cultural values, keep this key concept in front of you. Ask the questions and look for leaders that actively push the culture in a positive direction versus a negative direction (or no pushing at all).

Reassess your leadership for results, acceptance, and buy-in of your mission, vision, and culture. Make the new leadership cut based on the "how" and the 'what," (2H*W=P), with the understanding that the "how" is twice as important as the "what" in terms of overall leadership performance. Spend significant time and consideration on the leaders in the category of "evaluate and decide." Assess "how" they lead as well as "what" they do and invest in coaching, developing, and positioning them for success.

Identify your leaders who are positive "culture pushers" and do not confuse them with leaders who do not share the values. Complete your assessment and make the difficult changes by removing the leaders that do not get the performance results and/or do not share the cultural values. Don't make excuses to avoid making the needed changes. It is better for the organization to have a vacant leadership position than to have the wrong leader in place doing the wrong things and compromising your culture. Consider role changes, coaching, and development to better position leaders for success and remove those leaders that do not share the cultural values, regardless of performance results.

Great leaders leverage great leaders for greater success and remove the poor leaders from their organization. In doing this, you are removing the leaders that do not share your cultural values and will erode the positive culture you've worked to build. Be a great leader by making the difficult, valuable, and correct leadership decisions.

STEP 10—ESTABLISH ANNUAL PROCESSES TO SOLIDIFY AND DEVELOP A POSITIVE CULTURE

Step 10: You must establish, institutionalize, and perfect the processes and activities that will solidify and further develop your culture. These processes and activities include but are not limited to: standard leadership selection processes, standard development processes, culture surveys, performance measures, communication processes, education for leadership on leadership, education for employees on teamwork, performance reviews, and reward and recognition programs. Use these processes to establish an annual culture calendar.

In step 10 you will define, implement, institutionalize, and perfect the culture forming processes and activities that will solidify and further develop your culture. To truly have a positive culture, it must be strategically maintained and thoughtfully planned. Positive cultures are not self-sustaining. Cultures will take hold and influence your company in many ways and almost always have lasting power; but without thoughtful guidance and planning, the naturally occurring issues and situations will mutate the culture in a direction that is counter to what you want and need it to be. It may sound defeatist; but the reality is, if left unattended, cultures will deteriorate. A positive culture will not happen naturally because there are simply too many variables in terms of business pressures, external influences, employee viewpoints, and preferences.

Positive cultures are not self-sustaining and therefore must be strategically maintained and thoughtfully planned. To address this need, establish a culture calendar for your organization that includes annual processes to build, measure, adjust, and maintain your positive culture. Your culture calendar should be developed with the following objectives in mind:

Culture Calendar Objectives

- Communicate and reinforce your mission, vision, leadership philosophy, and desired culture
- Communicate your annual and multi-year goals and strategies
- Engage and involve employees in efforts and plans to meet goals and execute strategies
- Establish clear expectations and measures for employees, teams, and the company as a whole

- Measure employee engagement and the progress of your culture building efforts
- Develop action plans to further build and maintain your culture and address areas of concern
- Develop leaders and employees, invest in your human assets
- Reassess and adjust leadership as needed
- Connect all of these processes in a supportive and meaningful way
- Build, measure, maintain, and improve your positive culture!

Creating your culture calendar involves repeating Step 6 through Step 9 of the Blueprint while integrating your annual goals, strategies, and measurements into the process. The following is a recommended starting point for a **cultural calendar** for your company. It is based on the assumption that your fiscal year follows the calendar year. The start of the calendar is based on this assumption to coincide with the development of annual goals and strategies as well as reporting of company achievements, earnings, and incentive/recognition programs. Your culture calendar must be similar in timing and include the same key actions to meet the objectives. The calendar visually depicts suggested start and end times for each activity. The dotted lines indicate linkages and dependencies between the activities.

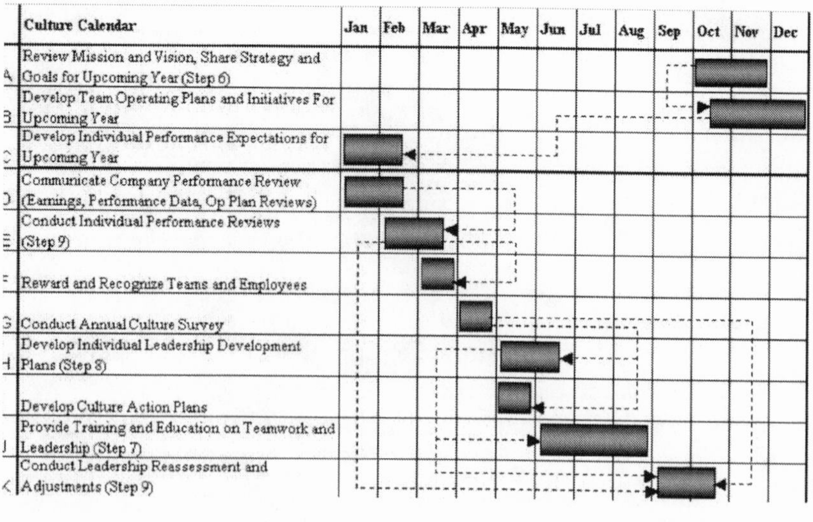

	Culture Calendar	Jan	Feb	Mar	Apr	May	Jun	Jul	Aug	Sep	Oct	Nov	Dec
A	Review Mission and Vision, Share Strategy and Goals for Upcoming Year (Step 6)												
B	Develop Team Operating Plans and Initiatives For Upcoming Year												
C	Develop Individual Performance Expectations for Upcoming Year												
D	Communicate Company Performance Review (Earnings, Performance Data, Op Plan Reviews)												
E	Conduct Individual Performance Reviews (Step 9)												
F	Reward and Recognize Teams and Employees												
G	Conduct Annual Culture Survey												
H	Develop Individual Leadership Development Plans (Step 8)												
	Develop Culture Action Plans												
J	Provide Training and Education on Teamwork and Leadership (Step 7)												
K	Conduct Leadership Reassessment and Adjustments (Step 9)												

The following provides a description of each event on the culture calendar, its purpose, timing considerations, and key linkages and dependencies.

A. Review Mission, Vision, Share Strategy and Goals

This is the kickoff of your upcoming year. It's a communication effort that will include reviewing your company's mission and vision, sharing your desired goals for the upcoming year, discussing the importance of those goals, and sharing the high level strategies to achieve those goals. It is a time for leadership to engage every employee in discussing and planning how to achieve company goals. This is the time to share desired performance data, financials, and projections. This is where leaders not only communicate your goals and their importance, but also recruit every employee by asking for their support and best ideas on how to accomplish those goals. This action precedes asking leaders, teams, and every employee to develop formal team operating plans to accomplish your goals. These interactive meetings must occur over a period of a month in an open forum that generates positive discussions and ideas.

B. Develop Team Operating Plans and Initiatives

After launching your communication effort on mission, vision, strategy and goals, the organization can begin developing plans to realize those goals. After hearing the message, as soon thereafter as possible, your leaders and their teams must begin working to identify initiatives and develop team operating plans. This is how leaders will tap into their engaged employees and leverage the diversity of their teams to capture new ideas and opportunities. This is the time for teams to work together to be creative and innovative about how to achieve the goals and execute the strategies that have been established for the upcoming year. Ask them to create challenging, yet achievable, team operating plans. Assure that leaders communicate and collaborate across the organization with other teams to coordinate plans and projects. Creation of team operating plans will define team performance goals that will be used to create individual performance expectations. The process of developing team operation plans will slightly lag the communication of your strategy and goals for the upcoming year. Leadership teams must work the plans to completion and approval in two months.

C. Develop Individual Performance Expectations

Each teams' operating plans will be utilized by their leaders to develop individual performance expectations. Individual performance expectations must clearly and concisely document the goals, strategies, and measurements that will be used to evaluate and measure each employee's performance at year-end. The expectations must define an employee's specific contributions to plans, projects, and initiatives <u>in addition to</u> including the primary responsibilities of their job function. The creation of the document provides an opportunity for each employee to discuss and clarify with their leader what is expected of them for the coming year and to assure that the goals and expectations are reasonable given available resources.

Every employee including you (the CEO) must have individual performance expectations. Each employee will want to link their goals and expectations to their leader's performance expectations as well as to the overall team operating plan. Establishing individual performance expectations is a critical component of managing performance, developing employees, and recognizing and rewarding them appropriately. It is an opportunity to link organization goals with individual work efforts; to link team operating plans and initiatives to individual work efforts and contributions. Individual performance expectations engage each employee by making their job and their work contributions important and meaningful by linking them to the overall goals and long-term success of the company. Establish **individual performance expectations** in four to six weeks. Manage, review, and update them via a check-in process at least twice prior to year-end individual performance reviews.

INDIVIDUAL PERFORMANCE EXPEXTATIONS	**NAME:**	**DATE:**
GOALS AND STRATEGIES What needs to be accomplished?	**EXPECTATIONS, INITIATIVES OR JOB FUNCTION** What will I do to contribute to realizing the goals execute the strategy?	**MEASUREMENTS** How will I measure success?
1. Safe working environment	Achieve personal safety goal of zero accidents and injuries: Realize team safety goal Implement all training and programs	Safety Statistics Safety Statistics Training Records
2. Employee focus, communication and culture	Complete individual performance expectations Complete individual performance expectations for each employee Hold timely/frequent performance reviews with direct reports, provide more "direct" feedback on performance Implement culture survey and related actions plans Ensure positive labor relations through union avoidance and management	Completed on-time Completed on-time Document reviews and outcomes Culture survey results Culture survey results #Grievances Maintain union free status
3. Personal and team development	Establish and implement a personal development plan Establish and implement development plans and training for each employee	Completed plan and observed improvement by leader
4. High performance teams and cross functional relationships	Implement team forming meetings and activities, provide and attend needed training Partner with HR and communications on culture issues and plans Improve partnership/relations with the following functions……	Performance results and culture survey Feedback from partners on level of involvement and collaboration Feedback from partners on level of involvement and collaboration
5. Effective financial performance and cost management	Deliver On-target O&M and capital budgets Renegotiate expiring external service provider contracts Improve cost per unit by 3%	Budget reports Terms of new contracts Internal cost per unit measures
6. Technology improvements	Successfully implement transition to new cost accounting system Execute key technology projects on-time and on-budget	On-time implementation, level of successful utilization On-time implementation, budget results and open implementation issues/bugs

D. Communicate Company Performance Review

At the completion of your fiscal year, you will in effect have a performance review for your company. You will close your books, develop information to create your annual report, and communicate earnings and overall performance to your shareholders. In parallel with this effort, you and your leaders must make an equal effort to communicate internally to employees on company performance. In addition to the information developed for shareholders, assure that processes are in place to develop the necessary year-end performance data and results to effectively measure and communicate not only the company's performance, but also team operating plan achievements and individual performance. This communication effort provides you (the CEO) and your leadership with a great opportunity to recognize employees and teams, create excitement around accomplishments, and provide leaders with the data they need to conduct their individual performance reviews. Complete this information gathering process during the first four weeks of the year; then use the next two weeks for internal and external communication efforts.

E. Conduct Individual Performance Reviews

Every leader must conduct individual performance reviews with each of their employees. They will use the individual performance expectations that were developed at the beginning of the year and the year-end results data for the company, teams, and each individual. The reviews are opportunities to reinforce the positives, coach the negatives, take measure of overall performance, and determine appropriate level of recognition and reward for each employee. This effort is the cornerstone of performance management, the last step in the annual process of establishing expectations, checking in on progress, and assessing overall results and performance. As previously mentioned, performance management must occur throughout the year and conclude with a year-end review. Complete all performance reviews in a four to six week timeframe.

F. Reward and Recognize Teams and Employees

Reward and recognition is a process that must take place year round, timed such that significant and meaningful efforts or successes that surpass expectations are recognized and rewarded as soon as practical. Additionally, your annual process of granting salary increases and adjustments as well as paying out performance incentives must be well understood, documented, and executed. Each year, as the company takes measure of its performance, the performance of teams and individual employees, formal salary increases, incentives (bonuses) and other rewards and recognition must be strongly linked to the performance results.

This very important action must be well timed and optimized in terms of cultural benefits, employee focus, and fairness. Employees will watch this process very carefully. The integrity of the process must be sound. It must be executed on time and with a high degree of correctness. Never miss the opportunity to tie these annual monetary rewards directly back to performance results and sharing the cultural values for leaders and all employees. The annual reward and recognition process must ideally occur in parallel with, and at the completion of, individual performance reviews. It should be completed within four weeks and at most slightly lag (two weeks) the individual performance review process.

G. Conduction Annual Culture Survey

Conducting an annual culture survey is an absolute must! It is your culture report card—a chance to measure first-hand the progress you and leadership are making in your efforts to build a positive culture and achieve a high level of employee engagement. It is an opportunity to demonstrate that you are committed to the values and ideals you have asked employees to embrace and that you are committed to changing and to achieving a positive culture. A culture survey builds trust by promoting open communication and discussion of cultural issues, progress, and concerns. It builds trust by allowing leadership to visibly act to change and improve culture based on survey results and feedback.

Develop the survey such that results can be summarized at the company, department, and function level; but most importantly, at the team level. This will allow each leader to measure themselves and their team as well as establish appropriate culture forming action plans and teams to improve future survey results. It also allows each leader to identify the necessary leadership actions they must take to improve culture and their team. These actions can also link to and be incorporated into the leader's personal development plan.

Structure the survey responses such that employees must answer "strongly agree," "agree," "disagree," or "strongly disagree" for each question. Do not provide noncommittal response options such as "neutral" or "no opinion." Employees must then make a conscious decision and choice about answering each culture-forming question. Also carefully track your percentage of employee participation in your survey; participation itself is a measure of your cultural progress. You must design a culture survey that is focused on measuring employee engagement, the core attributes of a positive culture, teamwork, mission, vision, and your leadership competency model. Some of these areas will be unique to your company so design your own customized survey ranging from 15 to 25 questions. The following **culture survey** provides a list of core questions common to measuring a positive culture and employee engagement that you will want to include.

	Culture Survey	Strongly Agree	Agree	Disagree	Strongly Disagree
1	I feel respected as an individual regardless of differences in background, race, age, gender, values, perspective, experience or interests				
2	My company promotes a safe, healthy and respectful work environment				
3	The sharing of experiences and ideas, input and participation is encouraged from all team members and effectively leveraged to optimize team performance and results				
4	My leader, and others at work, cares about me as a person				
5	I feel involved and informed and my ideas, opinions and feedback are valued				
6	I clearly understand what is expected of me				
7	I have the information, materials and equipment I need to effectively and efficiently do my job				
8	I have the opportunity to do what I do best every day				
9	Leaders, teams and employees are held accountable for their performance				
10	In the last six months, my leader has talked to me about my progress and provided me timely and constructive feedback about my performance				
11	This last year, I have had opportunities at work to learn, grow and improve my skills				
12	In the last seven days, I have received recognition or praise for doing good work				
13	People in my team are effectively recognized and rewarded for their performance and improvement efforts				
14	There is a real sense of teamwork and trust among my coworkers				
15	My team operates with open and honest communication				
16	Efforts among my team and other company teams units are effectively coordinated				
17	The company mission and vision makes me feel my job is important				
18	Leadership is committed to building and maintaining a positive culture				

If 80% to 90% of your employees agree with these 18 questions, you have a tremendously high level of employee engagement and a very positive culture. Begin your annual culture survey immediately following your annual reward and recognition program (salary increases and incentives) and complete it within a month.

H. Develop Individual Leadership Development Plans

The process and purpose of creating individual development plans was described in detail in Step 8. This is a required annual process for all leaders that must also include non-leader team members as much as is practical. Development plans will be created using observed behaviors and situations, feedback from the annual culture survey, and individual performance review results. Create them for all leaders within four to six weeks after the completion of the annual culture survey and communication of the results.

I. Develop Culture Action Plans

Each leader in your organization must create culture action plans that focus on the most needed and lowest rated area on their team's culture survey. This effort will not only serve to further create culture and guide it in the desired direction, it strongly demonstrates to all employees that their feedback has been heard; and as a result, actions will be taken to improve.

As with all initiatives, each leader must involve and engage their employees (their team) in identifying, creating, and implementing the culture action plan. The owners of the action plan are the leader and the leader's entire team. Making them a true owner of the action plan commits them to engaging in and improving the specified area and the overall culture. These efforts will further shape and drive your positive culture in the right direction and the efforts will be reflected in your annual culture survey results. Culture actions plans will be created in parallel with leadership development plans. Put them in place for all leaders and their teams within four weeks after the completion of the annual culture survey.

J. Provide Training and Education on Teamwork and Leadership

Providing training and education on leadership and teamwork supports employee development needs by continuing to build skills and abilities among leaders and team members (all employees). Step 7 of the Blueprint describes how to start up new teams and the process that can be performed annually to sustain them. Leaders must conduct teambuilding exercises and focus on their team and teamwork regardless of the maturity of the team. This effort will keep the teamwork and the team "new," further strengthening and growing the team.

Training classes and schedules must be planned and communicated every year so leaders and employees can integrate the formal training classes into their development and education efforts. Providing this training, communicating its availability during the three months following the creation of individual development plans, and implementing culture action plans, creates a positive expectation for leaders and employees to prioritize time for training. It strongly demonstrates your cultural commit to focus on employees.

K. Conduct Leadership Reassessment and Adjustments

Leadership reassessment and adjustment, Step 9 of the Blueprint, is an annual process of utilizing performance results, development efforts, culture survey results, and observed leadership behaviors to reassess every leader in your organization for both "what " they do and "how" they do it. Performing this process every year is critical to improving your culture and building your company's leadership. Making the needed adjustments, repositioning leaders into more suitable roles, coaching them for improvement, or removing them from leadership and/or the organization is one of the most significant culture forming processes your company must employ.

Every leader and "how" they lead impacts and amplifies your vision, leadership philosophy, and culture. You must assure that leaders are leading, doing the right things at the right times and in the right ways. Leadership is everything. Leadership builds culture. This process is how you put the right leaders in the right places. This is how you assure you have the best leaders in your company. Reassess your leadership and make the necessary changes in the six weeks prior to the start of your communication and planning processes for the next year.

POSITIVE CULTURES ARE NOT SELF-SUSTAINING. THEY MUST BE STRATEGICALLY MAINTAINED AND THOUGHTFULLY PLANNED

***

In addition to developing your culture calendar, there are standard processes, policies, and models that will be important foundational aspects of your positive culture. Like our culture calendar processes, the organization must have a solid understanding of them and confidence that they will be followed and utilized. Without going into great detail, here are six significant areas for consideration:

Leadership Competency Model—In Step 2 of the Blueprint you created and communicated a leadership competency model for your company. This model is the cornerstone of your leadership philosophy and a critical component of leadership selection, training, development, and assessment.

Assure that this model is visible to employees and reinforced and communicated periodically.

Front-Line Competency Model—Apply the leadership competency model concept to every position in your company. Every employee will contribute to, impact and shape your company culture. Attitude, energy and skill based competencies are valuable and important for every position in your company. Each new hire is an opportunity to fill your company full of the best and brightest employees, ones that are great at both the "how" and the "what". Assure that this model is also visible to employees and reinforced and communicated periodically.

Leadership (and Individual Contributor) Selection Process—In Step 3 of the Blueprint, you created and defined your leadership selection process. Like your leadership competency model, this process is critical to finding, selecting, and positioning the best possible leaders for success in your company. First and foremost, assure that the process is always followed with no exceptions allowed. Any deviation from the process not only increases your chance of placing the wrong leader in the wrong role, it also undermines your culture, commitment, and employee trust you are working to build. Assure that this process is visible to employees, reinforced, communicated periodically, and that any modifications or changes are very clearly explained.

Standard Communication Processes, Methods, and Tools—Establishing standards, processes, methods, and tools for formal, planned, and expected communications will greatly assist leaders in their communication efforts. Consistent, reliable, and predictable communication processes will allow leaders to leverage their communications skills and more successfully meet employees' expectations for communications.

Compensation/Market Review—The one area we have not spent time discussing is employee compensation. The reason for this is because salary is typically not the biggest motivator for employees. Respect in the workplace, meaningful work, personal satisfaction, and culture are actually more meaningful and influential when it comes to choosing a career and/or staying with a company. A positive culture is a bigger motivator than compensation. In the book, *Good to Great,* Jim Collins confirmed this of the "great" companies they identified and researched.

> "We found no systematic pattern linking executive compensation to the process of going from good to great. The evidence

> simply does not support the idea that the specific structure of executive compensation act as a key lever in taking a company from good to great..... Yes, compensation and incentives are important, but for very different reasons in good-to-great companies. The purpose of a compensation system should not be to get the right behaviors from the wrong people, but to get the right people on the bus in the first place, and to keep them there..... If you have the right executives on the bus, they will do everything within their power to build a great company, not because of what they will "get" for it, but because they simply cannot imagine settling for anything less."[17]

If you create a positive culture, everyone will want to work for you and you can even get by with underpaying employees and still retain them. Of course, that isn't the recommended or optimal approach. You always want to compensate them fairly. Once each year, you should perform a reasonable compensation and market review for all your jobs to assure you are compensating all employees fairly. Fair compensation and a positive culture will guarantee you a tremendous amount of employee satisfaction and a very high level of retention. Having a standard process to assure fair compensation will build goodwill and trust among all employees.

Human Resources/Employee Relations Policies—Again, establishing reasonable, progressive, and fair policies around all Human Resource issues will greatly benefit employees and your culture. Make sure they are flexible, consistent, reasonable, fair, and supportive of the attributes of a positive culture.

***

Every step in your cultural calendar involves communication. In fact, 80% to 90% of the execution of each step will be communication. Communication in terms of sharing and discussing information, listening and gathering feedback, and following up as needed on key questions and suggestions. Working through your cultural calendar each year provides you and your leadership with a tremendous number of communication and leadership opportunities. Take advantage of every opportunity and optimize them in terms of building and maintaining your positive culture.

Evolve your culture calendar so it becomes "how" your company gets things done and "how" it succeeds. As you work through your culture calendar each year, allow the natural process of debriefing each activity to occur. Gather feedback and suggestions and carefully consider where to adjust and modify your execution of each step until it is perfectly executed and strongly integrated with all your processes.

EVERY STEP IN YOUR CULTURE CALENDAR INVOLVES COMMUNICATION; EXECUTING THE PROCESSES IS 80% TO 90% COMMUNICATION

Think of your cultural calendar as the high level game plan for integrating the "what" and the "how" for your company. It is combining the business goals and strategies with a leadership and cultural philosophy on how to achieve them. It is building and improving your culture and at the same time positioning the company, teams, and employees for continued and accelerating levels of performance and success.

Establish, institutionalize, and perfect the processes that will solidify and further develop your culture by creating a culture calendar. Use the processes to measure your culture in terms of employee engagement and positive attributes so leadership can take deliberate culture forming actions that guide, direct, adjust, and transform your culture. Use them to communicate and set appropriate expectations and goals at the employee, team, and company levels. As you do so, reinforce your positive culture model, your leadership competency model, and your focus on teamwork.

Positive cultures are not self-sustaining. They must be strategically maintained and thoughtfully planned. The activities in the culture calendar will allow leadership to steer your company in a direction that will ensure a high level of employee engagement and a commitment to your mission, vision, annual goals and strategies. As you work through these processes year in and year out, allow them to evolve and adjust or tweak them in terms of timing and execution. Remember that every step in the culture calendar requires communication; the process is 80% to 90% communication. Optimize the effectiveness of your culture calendar processes. Maintain their original objective and improve their outcomes. Evolve your culture calendar. It must become "how" your company gets things done and "how" it succeeds.

CHAPTER VI

Construction Timetable (Lets Start Building!)

Now that we have a Blueprint, a step-by-step guide on how to construct a positive company culture, what is your timeline for construction? Assuming you are ready to take the first big step, Commit at the Very Top, you will need to establish a timeline for constructing your culture and implemented the 10 Steps.

It is recommended that you begin as soon as practical and plan for a 12-month implementation of the 10 steps. It is important to realize upfront that building and maintaining your culture will be a reiterative process. Steps 1-5 get you started, steps 6-10 help you build, maintain and improve. You will repeat Steps 6-10 in the form of your culture calendar, every year. As you do so, you will be continuing your construction efforts (building, maintaining and improving your positive culture) each successive year.

The effort to manage and influence your culture will not end. Instead, it will become the norm—simply "how you lead" your company. You will arrive at a point in time where you have realized a high level of employee engagement (80%—90%) and are reaping the tremendous benefits of a highly engaged and motivated employee base. This will require multiple reiterations of your culture calendar. The good news is you will immediately begin to positively influence and change your culture the very first day you take the first step and begin construction. Just be prepared. Building leadership takes time; building teams takes time; communicating and changing employee perceptions takes time. As with any significant change or effort, expect struggles, setbacks, and restarts; but never wavier from your vision. You <u>will</u> see progress and your culture <u>will</u> start to feel different immediately. Perhaps it will be slow at first, but it will gain momentum as you work through the 10 Steps for the first time.

When will your culture feel positive, when will the level of employee engagement start to rise significantly? The answer is a function of your starting point, how well you and your leadership execute the 10 Steps of the Blueprint. Your starting point might slow you down a little, but not much. Even the most negative cultures will quickly start to change when the person at the top of the organization decides to change the culture and select the right leaders. It is why leadership is everything. The right leaders can start to create positive culture and instantly increase employee engagement.

The following details a **timeline for executing the 10 Steps of the Blueprint.** It provides the recommended implementation times (shown in weeks) for executing each step and identifies timing overlaps, dependencies, and linkages. One full year is typical for moving though the 10 Steps and completing a cycle of a culture calendar.

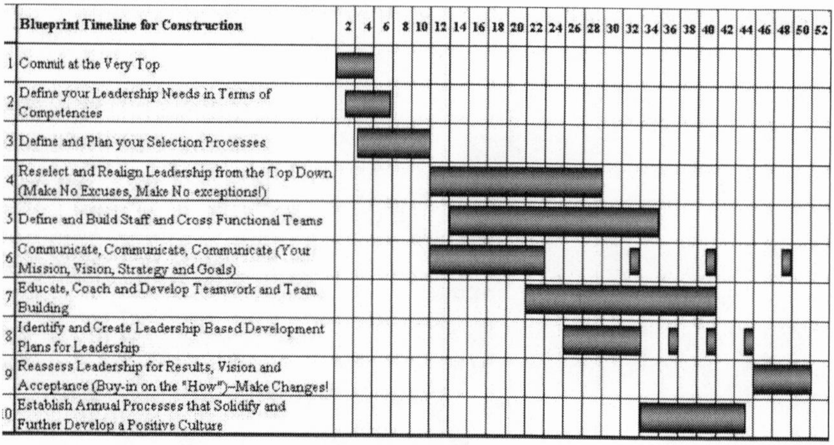

	Blueprint Timeline for Construction	2	4	6	8	10	12	14	16	18	20	22	24	26	28	30	32	34	36	38	40	42	44	46	48	50	52
1	Commit at the Very Top																										
2	Define your Leadership Needs in Terms of Competencies																										
3	Define and Plan your Selection Processes																										
4	Reselect and Realign Leadership from the Top Down (Make No Excuses, Make No exceptions!)																										
5	Define and Build Staff and Cross Functional Teams																										
6	Communicate, Communicate, Communicate (Your Mission, Vision, Strategy and Goals)																										
7	Educate, Coach and Develop Teamwork and Team Building																										
8	Identify and Create Leadership Based Development Plans for Leadership																										
9	Reassess Leadership for Results, Vision and Acceptance (Buy-in on the "How")–Make Changes!																										
10	Establish Annual Processes that Solidify and Further Develop a Positive Culture																										

Step 1—Commit at the Very Top

Execution Time: 4 Weeks

Prerequisites: CEO commitment, determination and self-awareness

Committing at the very top to the CEO's Blueprint, to making the right decisions about people and leadership, and to a new leadership and management philosophy starts the very day you (the CEO) decide to change your culture. Discuss, share, and socialize your commitment with your direct staff and key Human Resources and Communications personal over a period of four weeks. Assuming that some of them are the right kind of leaders, you will want to work to build their understanding and commitment as quickly as you can since they will comprise your initial change team.

Step 2—Define Leadership Needs in Terms of Competencies

Execution Time: 4-6 Weeks

Prerequisites: Begun Step 1

Defining your leadership needs and creating your leadership competency model will begin as soon as you have created a first draft and recruited your initial change team to review, consider, and react to your proposed model. The entire process of creating the leadership competency model, communicating it to the organization, and gathering feedback and input will take four to six weeks, lagging slightly behind the start of Step 1.

Step 3—Define a Leadership Selection Process

Execution Time: 6-8 Weeks

Prerequisites: Begun Step 2

Begin defining your selection process after you have communicated the concepts of your leadership competency model. Your leadership competency model need not be complete, but the framework and the fact that the model content will be critical to leadership selection must be well understood. The process of selection can be very time consuming so the design of the selection process is critical. Plan to use a full six to eight weeks designing an efficient process and communicating and building understanding of how the process will work.

Employee level of understanding will impact the outcome of selection itself and will be the first major culture forming communication you will undertake. For this reason, significant time must be spent on communication, education, and checking for understanding. Communication and education of your leadership competency model and selection process must be fully completed prior to the start of Step 4.

Step 4—Reselect and Realign Leadership

Execution Time: 3-5 Months

Prerequisites: Completed Steps 1-3

You will begin the process of reselecting and realigning leadership from the top down after completing and communicating your new leadership competency model and selection process. In reselecting leadership you must start at the top of the organization and move down, level by level, allowing each leader to fill the positions that will comprise their direct reports (their team). Plan for one month per level in your organization to complete this step. For a reasonably flat organization this will take three to five months.

Remember, this is aggressive leadership selection in terms of making the right decisions, not aggressive in terms of speed or decision-making. Making the right decisions is much more important than making quick decisions. Always hold out for the right leadership even if you leave some positions unfilled after the first pass. It is better to have a vacancy than the wrong leader in a position.

Step 5—Build Staff and Cross Functional Teams

Execution Time: 4-6 Months

Prerequisites: Begun Step 5

As you reselect your leadership from the top down, the first task of new leadership is to build their team. The timeline for building staff and cross-functional teams will lag slightly behind leadership reselection and realignment. As soon as a new leader's team has been selected and is in place, they will begin the process of team building.

Staff teams will be in place first; cross-functional team building will be delayed until most of the leadership reselection is completed. Team building has no real end date because the organization never truly finishes building teams, promoting teamwork and fostering positive team environments. However, a first pass of defining and building all staff and cross functional teams in your company must be completed over four to six months. While this may seem like a long time, remember that the cross-functional team identification and building will naturally need to occur later in the process.

Step 6—Communicate, Communicate, Communicate

Execution Time: 3-4 Months

Prerequisites: Complete Steps 1-3

Communicating your mission, vision, strategy, and goals can begin as soon as you start to share your leadership competency model and selection process with the organization. However, if your mission, vision, strategy and goals have not yet been solidified, start time on this step is flexible and can begin later on in the process. Step 6 is part of your culture calendar and must be coordinated with kicking off planning efforts for the upcoming year.

In terms of timing and execution, this effort must initially look and feel like an active campaign for two to three months. Share the information and key messages in several different formats and mediums to generate feedback and discussion across the organization. Then transition the effort into periodic and opportunistic communications that continually reinforce and link them back to company actions, initiatives, and results.

Step 7—Develop Teamwork and Teambuilding

Execution Time: 4-5 Months

Prerequisites: 50% Completion of Step 5

Begin to develop your teamwork and team building training programs once you are at least halfway through your team definition and building efforts (Step 5). Develop the training program and the associated communications over two to three months. This effort represents your first investment of time and energy into educating and coaching your employees on teamwork and team building.

Begin communications and offering the training resources after Steps 4 and 5 are well underway and most leaders have their teams in place. Offer the training over the course of two to three months and use it to affirm and create an organization where every employee is a team member and every leader is a team leader. This timing will strongly support and reinforce Step 5, the defining and building of teams company-wide.

Step 8—Create Development Plans for Leadership

Execution Time: 6-8 Weeks

Prerequisites: Begun Step 7

Begin to identify and create leadership based development plans for leaders with a one or two month lag from the start of Step 7. While development isn't training, the two efforts will be linked, overlapping in some important areas and supportive in focus. Identifying development focus and creating a personal development plan for each leader will be a unique and individual timeline. Selecting the optimal development focus and successfully navigating the development process is more important than the actual timeline itself. As timing guidance for leaders, they should be asked to have development plans in place within two months; and then routinely follow up with their leader and Human Resources support person to further develop and work through the overall development process.

Step 9—Reassess Leadership for Results, Vision, and Acceptance

Execution Time: 4-6 Weeks

Prerequisites: Steps 1-8

You will begin the process of reassessing and reselecting your leadership four months after you have finished filling your leadership positions. This may seem too soon to be reassessing leadership as they will have only been in their new roles four to seven months; but it is in fact the perfect time. You will have seen your new leadership team in action and you will have asked them to execute several culture forming activities in quick succession. You will have very recent and applicable performance information and observations to compare to interview and assessment results.

Complete your leadership reassessment and measure leaders in terms of getting the results and getting them in the right way. Complete this assessment and make any needed changes within four to six weeks. This may seem to be a short period of time for the assessment; but you will have all the information you need, the necessary changes will be evident, and for obvious reasons this is a process you want to execute quickly and respectfully. You must efficiently assess, decide, and act where necessary to improve leadership.

Step 10—Establish Annual Processes to Solidify and Develop a Positive Culture

Execution Time: 2-3 Months

Prerequisites: Steps 1-8

Step 10, establishing annual process that solidify and further establish a positive culture, includes creating and communicating a culture calendar; planning how to integrate your calendar into your annual processes; and assuring the key supporting processes are in place. Timing for this step is dependent on what time of the year you began construction using the CEO's Blueprint and the start and end of your normal fiscal year. You will need two to three months to develop and communicate the culture calendar and plan to kick off the start of the calendar while the communication is still fresh to the organization. For example, if you began the Blueprint in January and your fiscal year begins in January, begin creating your culture calendar after creating leadership development plans. Complete it over three months and plan to launch it in the fall, in time for the upcoming year.

***

Plan your timeline for construction. Assure that your plan takes into consideration the critical links and interdependencies between the steps when establishing your proposed timeline. Plan for approximately 12 months to execute the 10 Steps of the CEO's Blueprint. Establish a

brisk, yet flexible timeline, to assure that each step is fully completed and the desired outcomes achieved. Resist the temptation to compress the timeline for each step. Do not underestimate the effort or communication required to execute each step fully. Stay focused on the fact that 80% to 90% of the execution of each step will be communication. Communication in terms of sharing and discussing information, listening and gathering feedback, and following up as needed on key questions and suggestions. Carefully plan your timeline for construction; get your leadership involved and engaged; and start building culture!

CHAPTER VII

Human Resources and Communications (Culture and Leadership Support Teams)

Every leader, employee, department, and function will play a role in creating and maintaining your positive culture. Collectively, your employees are your cultural construction and maintenance workers. They are always on the job, constructing, maintaining, and occasionally repairing your positive culture. Two functions in particular exist for the sole purpose of assisting the organization in creating and maintaining a positive culture, your Human Resources and Communications functions. They are your culture and leadership support group. They support all culture forming efforts as the engineers and architects for your culture. They provide the materials, processes, and formats that are used to construct, maintain, and repair culture. They provide the "technical support" for leaders in their utilization and implementation.

Execution of the CEO's Blueprint's initial 10 Steps and the annual Culture Calendar activities require that specific skills and abilities be present in your Human Resources and Communications functions. For this reason, it is very important to identify the key deliverables and the supporting actions they must perform while clearly understanding the internal skills that these employees must possess to support leaders' culture forming efforts. Human Resources and Communications employees are critical to the successful execution of the CEO's Blueprint. The following illustrates some of their **key deliverables and supporting actions** needed to successfully execute the 10 steps of the CEO's Blueprint.

Step	The Blueprint	Human Resources	Communications
1	Commit at the Very Top	• Strategies for communicating and engaging various employee groups	• Message content and development • Communication plan for introducing the start of the culture forming process to direct reports and the entire organization
2	Define your Leadership Needs in Terms of Competencies	• Facilitate construction of leadership competency model • Administer and maintain leadership competency model and leadership competencies	• Message content and development • Communication plan for sharing leadership competency model
3	Define and Plan your Selection Processes	• Develop, administer and maintain and standard selection process • Partner in selection of all positions	• Message content and development • Communication plan for sharing selection process
4	Reselect and Realign Leadership from the Top Down (Make No Excuses, Make No exceptions!)	• Partner in the selection process for all leadership positions	• Communication plan for announcing new leadership • Communication plan for dealing with unsuccessful candidates
5	Define and Build Staff and Cross Functional Teams	• Coach and support team dynamics and development	• Communication plan and internal reporting of progress and events
6	Communicate, Communicate, Communicate (Your Mission, Vision, Strategy and Goals)	• Strategies for communicating and engaging various employee and stakeholders groups	• Message content and development • Internal and external communication plan
7	Educate, Coach and Develop Teamwork and Team Building	• Coach and support team dynamics and development • Training development and participation	• Communication plan for training content and schedule
8	Identify and Create Leadership Based Development Plans for Leadership	• Partner in the development process for all leadership	• Communication plan and internal reporting of progress and events
9	Reassess Leadership for Results, Vision and Acceptance (Buy-in on the "How") – Make Changes!	• Partner in the reassessment process for all leadership positions • Strategize and consult on realignment and reassessments	• Communication plan for announcing new leadership • Communication plan for dealing with changes
10	Establish Annual Processes that Solidify and Further Develop a Positive Culture	• Develop, administer and maintain the culture calendar, culture survey, individual performance expectations process, standard employee relations policies, compensation/market review, etc.	• Communication plans for each item in the culture calendar • Communications support for any updates to stand processes or policies

This list only touches on the higher level deliverables and support actions these functions will provide. The sum total of deliverables and supporting actions that Human Resources and Communications will provide throughout the implementation of the CEO's Blueprint are vital. You simply cannot succeed without them. The initial effort they put forth in helping leadership execute the CEO's Blueprint for the first time will pale in comparison to the impact of the continual role they will play in building and maintaining a positive culture. Carefully consider these key deliverables and support actions when developing and staffing your Human Resources and Communications functions.

Human Resource and Communications personnel not only need to have the skills and expertise to support your culture forming efforts; they also must be utilized, and utilized correctly, by all your leadership. Human Resources and Communications personnel must be integrated into every leader's team. They must be consulted on key culture impacting decisions, communications, and employee issues. They will assist in coaching and developing leaders as well as their employees. As they do so, they link leaders and functions across the company together and insure common decisions, standard practices, and shared leadership approaches that align with your cultural philosophy and leadership model. Leadership must include, collaborate, involve and partner with them each and every day to insure that they are connecting and guiding culture-forming efforts.

As you execute the CEO's Blueprint, your Human Resources will be the ultimate internal consultant on employee and team issues. They are the experts on managing your most important assets, your employees. Leadership is everything because leaders build culture and engage employees. Finding, assessing, developing, and coaching the right leaders and employees is "how "you focus on employees and build your most important asset. Leaders need support to do these things and do them well. They need experience, expertise, and balanced viewpoints to address and work successfully through important and often complex employee issues. As Human Resources supports leaders in developing, coaching, and focusing on employees, they must clearly understand the company's mission, vision, strategy, and goals as well as your blueprint for a positive culture. They must understand them in order to integrate them into employee-related decisions and policies that shape and form your positive culture.

As you execute the CEO's Blueprint, you will communicate internally more than ever before in terms of frequency, volume, and deliberate culture forming content. This level of communication will not decrease. It will become part of your culture and it must continue because communication is the lifeblood of an organization. Effective communication by your leadership is crucial. Your company culture will thrive, be sustained, and be nourished by effective communication.

Your Communications personnel must be able to support and assist leaders in developing content, materials, and formats for communications. They must coach and support leaders to be effective communicators. In doing so, they must understand your mission, vision, strategy, goals, and your culture so they can integrate and reinforce the key messages and components into every internal and external communication. Every leader must have a partner in communications. Their partner will help them effectively communicate to enable employees to understand the company's mission, vision, strategy and goals; allow them to capture employee's ideas and solutions; and to listen to and address their issues and concerns. They must help leaders be both deliberate with planned communications and dynamic when key communication opportunities present themselves.

Human Resources and Communications employees are critical to executing the CEO's Blueprint and executing it well. The very nature of their roles positions them to strongly influence your culture and your leaders. You must have the right leaders in every role in your organization. Human Resources and Communications must have the right leaders in the right roles as soon as possible. This means that in terms of sharing the cultural values and reassessing leadership, you must have less patience for grooming this group of leaders. They as a leadership team, must "get there" much sooner than the rest of the organization. You simply cannot afford to have any leaders in these functions that do not clearly and strongly share and model your cultural values.

Every leader must have a key partner in Human Resources and Communications as part of their team—working with and supporting them on communication issues, employee issues, employee relations, employee development, and supporting actions that build a positive culture. They are the experts in their field. Every leader must use them; rely on them; and let them fulfill their important role of making leaders better every day. Human Resources and Communications are your culture and leadership support group. Make certain these functions have the skills and unquestionably share the cultural values; then deeply integrate them into every aspect of your culture forming efforts.

CHAPTER VIII

The Right Leaders (The Best Insurance)

Although we covered the importance of the right leaders in creating culture in great detail, I want to further emphasize their tremendous importance as the best insurance against culture killers. Culture killers are the actions, situations, and mindsets that can kill a positive culture or prevent you from ever creating one. The culture killers are the antithesis of the core attributes of a positive culture, the six core leadership competencies, and the core attributes of teamwork. If you wanted to create a negative culture survey, you would use the culture killers to construct your questions. The following is a quick review of the top 10 culture killers, the things to avoid at all cost; the things that the right leaders will prevent from occurring.

1—Lack of Commitment at the Very Top

If the CEO and his staff are not committed to creating and maintaining a positive culture it cannot and will not evolve. It takes too much work, too many difficult leadership decisions, and continuous, deliberate actions to create a positive culture. Without a commitment to do these things, a positive culture cannot exist.

One year, in an attempt to establish direction and vision, our executives created a list of ten corporate goals and objectives. After the initial communication the goals and objectives were completely absent from meetings, communications, business strategy, and decisions. They were not referenced, reinforced, or utilized by the executives. As a result, they quickly evaporated from the organization's consciousness. The CEO and his team were visibly uncommitted to the goals and objectives so the organization quickly disregarded them as valuable influences and began focusing on the actions of the CEO and his team to understand what they <u>really</u> cared about.

This is all about you (the CEO) being the right leader; and it is an all or nothing deal. Without your commitment, it simply will not happen. In this case your commitment and your leadership's commitment are the best insurance. To avoid this culture killer you must commit, make the right choices about leadership, and remove leaders who are not committed to the cause. You (the CEO) must model commitment and send the message to leadership, "get committed or get out!"

2—The Wrong Leaders

Your leaders are everything when it comes to creating and maintaining a positive culture. Having the wrong leader or leaders in place will do a lot of cultural damage in a very short time. Through wrong actions or inaction, they will eat away at or fail to create your positive culture. It is better for the company to have no leader or a vacancy than have the wrong leader in a position.

I have seen the wrong leaders in action. These are the leaders who do not deliver the performance results and/or do not share the cultural values. The effect these leaders had on their immediate area of influence hurt the organization in terms of performance; and the effect they had on the culture around them was much more damaging. They served as a negative role model for other wrong leaders and created frustration and doubt among the right leaders. The right leaders expected and needed the organization to remove the wrong leaders. Delaying that decision negatively impacted our leadership. Once addressed, it reinforced our positive culture.

Once again this is on you, the CEO and each and every other leader in your company. The process of leadership selection and alignment, performance reviews, leadership development, and leadership reassessment is all about having the right leaders in the right positions. Avoid this culture killer by involving yourself deeply in leadership selection and reassessment by demanding that the right leaders remove the wrong leaders; and strongly supporting them in their efforts!

3—Ineffective Communication

Ineffective communication in the form of poor communication or lack of communication will stop your culture-forming efforts dead in their tracks. If you can't communicate, you can't build trust, gain commitment, build teams, leverage diversity, or develop employees. If you communicate ineffectively, you will create distrust, confusion, and disrespect.

The one situation I would always dread as a leader is when one of my employees would ask, "what is going on with this decision, what was our team's involvement, and how come we didn't get told about it at the same time as everyone else?" I dreaded these situations because it meant that I, my peers, and/or leadership as a whole did not communicate timely and effectively. The issue itself may or may not have impacted the employee or the team; but regardless, the real concern was one of equal access to information and inclusion. The best recovery in these situations is to follow up quickly, provide as much information as possible, and if appropriate acknowledge the communication failure.

Every leader must be able to communicate and communicate well. That is why it is one of the six core leadership competencies. Assuring that each leader has these skills through the selection and development processes; and that each utilizes and involves their communication partner for support and execution is vital. As an organization, make sure your leaders seize every formal and informal opportunity to communicate on key messages, concerns, and culture. This includes listening, gathering feedback, and responding. To avoid this culture killer, make sure you have the right leaders and that they practice, plan, and become great at communicating!

4—Distrust

Distrust of your organization by your employees will lead to adversity at every turn. Distrust breeds distrust so it will quickly spread to distrust of leadership, company initiatives, policies, plans..... virtually everything. Distrust means employees will use every means possible to throw up roadblocks on the things you are working to accomplish; regardless of if it will truly impact them negatively or not. In a distrusting organization, employees' perceptions will always be negative. Because you the management have more information and more power, employees will always be skeptical of your motives. If you are unionized, distrust will result in grievances; if you are non-unionized, distrust will result in unionization.

I have seen unions routinely reject the company-wide annual incentive payouts for their members. It was actually a check offered by the company to each employee; but because it was not part of the union contract, the union chose to not accept it on behalf of the membership. They distrust the company and believe that the practice of annual incentives which are based on performance results will degrade their future base salary increases. This is a clear example where leaders have failed to create trust. Distrust actually resulted in lower compensation for employees by their own choice and a loss of the positive impact incentive pay can have on employee performance for the company.

Every leader must be able to build trust. Trust in themselves, trust in leadership, and trust in the company. Trust enables effective teamwork; and more importantly, it eliminates the resistance and churn associated with distrust. This is why building trust is one of the six core leadership competencies. To avoid this culture killer, make sure you have the right leaders to build and maintain trust, day in and day out, one employee at a time!

5—Ignoring the Benefits of Diversity

Diversity of ideas is a major business advantage; no company today can afford to ignore the benefits of a diverse workforce. From an employee morale and engagement perspective, capturing the benefits of diversity is crucial. No one wants to work in an environment where they feel isolated or where their ideas and input are ignored and/or disrespected. The perception of favoritism or simply the lack of respect as a result of race, sex, or religion will be disastrous. It is a label that can get attached quickly; spread throughout the organization like a cancer; and proves daunting to overcome. Leveraging diversity brings great value while ignoring it brings great problems.

During a large employee meeting, an employee asked a CEO about his plans and thoughts on the value of diversity. Instead of taking the opportunity to underscore the value of diversity, the CEO stated that an individual in the company would look at establishing a program but nothing more ever came of it. That answer become burned into the mind of every employee and was seen as a complete disregard for diversity and the value it offers.

Every leader must be able to leverage the diversity of their team and optimize the benefits of a diverse team. Leveraging diversity is one of the six core leadership competencies because it delivers better results and builds a strong culture AND it means your leaders will understand, appreciate, and be aware of diversity issues. To avoid this culture killer, it takes the right leaders at every level dealing with individual employees and leading teams to effectively leverage organizational diversity and capture the benefits it has to offer!

6—Failing at Teamwork

Teamwork is a key attribute of a positive culture because positive cultures are driven by teamwork. When you fail at teamwork, you are left with a group of people who do not work together, respect, or trust each other. Failing at teamwork is at best limiting when you end up having a committee instead of a team; and at worst, debilitating when you have active infighting and opposition. A failed team will not realize the best outcomes nor optimize the value of each person. This greatly limits what this "team" can accomplish and as a result they will fall short in terms of performance. This will cause the "team" to become more dysfunctional, creating distrust of team member motives. The "team" will actually become a barrier to achievement and a drag on culture. Employees will not be engaged or excited if they are a part of a dysfunctional or failing team. Wherever you find a failing team, you will also find a struggling leader.

One of the worst teams I ever experienced resulted from a lack of team leadership. Our COO, the team leader, did not engage the team members or work to create a team. We did not establish a meaningful team charter and therefore never established clarity of roles, expectations, or a shared vision and goals. Despite his failure to do the necessary things to establish the team, he actually wanted us to be a team. The result was a collection of peers who agreed to disagree, avoided all positive conflict, only worked together when it satisfied individual interests and achieved absolutely nothing of substance. For those of us that valued teamwork, it was a frustrating, discouraging, and demoralizing team experience.

Every leader must be able to build a successful team. Building a successful team is one of the six core leadership competencies because it ties together trust, communication, and diversity. It is how your organization drives towards and achieves results. To avoid this culture killer, find the right leaders. They will build successful teams and a positive culture in the process!

7—Failing to Gain Employee Commitment

No organization is less efficient than one without employee commitment. You can set quotas and crack the whip; but ultimately, you will not get one additional ounce of effort more than the minimum if employees do not believe and are not committed. The worst thing you can do is to give an employee a job. No one is committed to a job. A job is just a task that requires completion. Instead, give your employees a profession, an occupation full of meaningful work linked to a vision and connected to a successful team. Remember, uncommitted employees will let you fail; committed employees will do everything they can to help you succeed. You need them to be committed, to give their extra effort, and to capture their best ideas for improving your business.

The previous example in which our executives created ten corporate goals and objectives to establish a shared vision and direction is a great example of failing to gain employee commitment. In this example the executives themselves are the employees and the CEO failed to gain their commitment to the goals and objectives. They didn't choose to ignore them nor even necessarily disagree with them, but they never became committed to them. Why? Because they didn't believe and/or understand the value they could bring to the organization. They were not convinced that strongly reinforcing and utilizing the goals and objectives would bring them or the company success. They never openly opposed them; but through their lack of commitment, they allowed them to slowly slide away into the annals of forgotten corporate ideas and slogans.

Every leader must be able to effectively gain commitment on mission, vision, strategy, and goals as well as commitment on day-to-day items, issues, policies, and changes. Gaining commitment is one of the six core leadership competencies because leaders who cannot do it effectively are not leaders. They are supervisors—a word to be avoided. Gaining commitment each and every day is a huge component of employee engagement. The right leaders understand that gaining commitment is not about ruling by committee. It is about helping employees understand, asking for their input, and gaining their support on key business issues, strategies, and goals. To avoid this culture killer, find the right leaders because they gain employee commitment along with the extra employee efforts and ideas it brings!

8—Ignoring your Human Assets

Employees are assets. Like all other assets you need to acquire, build, develop, and maintain them. If you let an office building deteriorate and waste away, never investing time or energy into maintaining or improving it, employees will notice. The inaction communicates that the asset is not worth the investment to maintain or improve it. This example holds true for employees. Whether it is buildings or employees, inaction in terms of investing time or money communicates a low perceived value. You need to focus on employees, develop them, and invest in them through training, education, new skills, new opportunities, and new career paths. A positive culture is focused on employees and if it is not, employees will notice.

My employer once made a policy decision to eliminate their relatively low cost employee tuition reimbursement plan. This action significantly impacted employee morale. Even though the program only directly effected a small population of employees, it sent a crystal clear message to all employees that the company was not willing to invest in its human assets.

A company that does not invest in its most important assets sends a message to employees. That message is that we are not growing or building for the future because we choose not too and/or we don't understand the value of our human assets. Investing in employees, their training, skills, and continued development is an often overlooked and significant cultural mistake. Leaders have the responsibility for development, coaching, and improving your human assets. To avoid this culture killer, commit your organization to developing employees and model that commitment with your own participation; and find the right leaders because they will develop leaders, focus on employees, grow and maintain your valuable human assets!

9—Disrespect of Anyone at Anytime

Disrespect is disrespect, regardless of circumstance and regardless of the individual. You must constantly evaluate your actions and your leaders' actions to assure you are a respectful organization. Showing disrespect to anyone is a visible statement of the company's values. Regardless of the circumstance, be it dealing with the most disrespectful customer or competitor or terminating the most under-performing and disrespectful employee, you will always benefit from demonstrating respect in <u>your</u> actions. Disrespectful actions by the company imprints on all its employees because they are all part of your company and your team; and they all value respect.

During one of our expended staff meetings, my boss shared a true antidote regarding one of our union negotiators and the fact that a naked woman knocked on his hotel room door in the middle of the night. The incident had nothing to do with the on-going negotiations as the unfortunate women apparently became locked out of her hotel room. The story was met with uneasy laughter and silence. The majority of the 20 or so male and female attendees recognized the sharing of the story as inappropriate, bad judgment and disrespectful. While it was discussed after the meeting, it was never addressed or corrected. It demonstrated a lack of respect in many ways. Everyone has said or done something at one time that has offended others. The right leaders almost always avoid these situations or quickly recognize, recover, and correct them if they occur.

Leaders are always under a microscope. Their actions are always visible, noticed, reviewed and critiqued. They are most often critiqued for respect. The right leaders are aware of this and are mindful of their actions and dealings with all employees. Being respectful does not mean you can't be firm, truthful, set appropriate expectations, and measure performance. It is about respectful interactions with equal and fair treatment. Not only do leaders have to be respectful, they have to assure a respectful working environment. To avoid this culture killer, make respect a priority and be wary of disrespectful actions. Most of all, find the right leaders because they are responsible for addressing and preventing disrespect as well as modeling respect for the organization!

10—Leadership Hypocrisy, Superiority or Entitlement

It is easy for employees to resent "the boss" because they are "the boss." It can be easily construed that the boss is better, perhaps smarter, and more successful because they have been promoted; they have the "higher up" job; and/or a higher salary. Even the slightest indication of "do as I say not as I do" or "the rules do not apply to me" or "I'm entitled to something better" will compromise trust, respect, and commitment. These attitudes are unfortunately all too common and they always lead to resentment and disrespect for leaders.

Our CEO once had all the departmental leaders fly in to our corporate headquarters so he could give everyone a lecture on reducing travel expenses. We all found the missed opportunity for a cost-effective teleconference to really make his point to be sadly laughable. This example seems so painfully basic, but it demonstrates how easily top leaders can be blinded when they view themselves differently than and superior to the rest of the organization.

Ken Iverson, CEO of Nucor, whose steel company outperformed the market by more than 5 times between 1975 and 1990, wrote in his book, *Plain Talk:*

> " Inequality stills runs rampant in most business corporations. I'm referring now to hierarchical inequality which legitimizes and institutionalizes the principle "We" vs. "They"...The people at the top of the corporate hierarchy grant themselves privilege after privilege, flaunt those privileges before the men and women who do the real work, then wonder why employees are unmoved

> by management's invocations to cut cost and boost profitability...When I think of the millions of dollars spent by people at the top of the management hierarchy on efforts to motivate people who are continually put down by that hierarchy, I can only shake my head in wonder."[1]

In his Book, *Thriving on Chaos,* Tom Peters' blunt observation of the corporate world reiterates the same sad point:

> We insult employees with executive parking spots, heated, no less; with executive dining rooms; with bonuses and 'strategy meetings' in lavish settings for the top 100 officers, and their spouses even after lousy years..... How do you humiliate and demean someone and then expect him or her to care about product quality and constant improvement?"[2]

Leaders are constantly under a microscope. The right leaders are as careful in these areas (the appearance of hypocrisy, superiority or entitlement) as they are in the area of respect. The last thing they want is to project superiority or be seen as a hypocrite. They are grounded, humble, and understand that no one is better than anyone else. They consider their actions and how they could potentially be perceived and when necessary, alter them. The right leaders will specifically act to avoid any semblance of hypocrisy in their actions, any air of superiority or entitlement because they understand the damage it can do and because they share the cultural values!

***

I chose to share these negative leadership examples to strongly emphasize that the right leaders are your best insurance against the culture killers. To be fair, I have experienced ten times as many great leadership examples by the right leaders as negative ones by the wrong leaders. Unfortunately, the negative examples have much more cultural impact and do much more damage. It takes significant effort to create a positive culture and very little effort to negatively impact it. If you choose the right leaders, negative examples will be recognized as culture killers and will quickly be deemed unacceptable by your positive culture and your leadership.

These top 10 culture killers are the biggest threats to executing the CEO's Blueprint successfully and to building and maintaining a positive culture. In your quest to create a positive culture, it is critical to understand what you are trying to create, and equally important to understand what you working to avoid. Smart business people protect their investments. The last testimony to leadership, to leadership selection, and to filling your organization with the "right" leaders is that they are the best insurance against the culture killers. In fact, they are the ONLY insurance against the culture killers!

CHAPTER IX

The Litmus Test (Are you a Builder?)

So now that you know everything you need to know to construct a positive culture, the only question that remains to be answered is "are you a qualified builder?" Like I said when I started this, none of these business concepts are new. I'm not a business guru with new and revolutionary ideas on how to improve your business. What I have given you is a solid plan, a Blueprint to build a better company...a great company. It encompasses what the business world already knows about organizational development, leadership, employee engagement, and company culture. It provides you with the format to combine all these tried and true concepts into a structure that will remake your company's culture. The revolutionary idea is this...you can create a positive culture, it will translate into extraordinary business performance and results if, and only if, you commit to making the effort bigger than yourself.

I hate to say it; but so much of this is all about you, the CEO. I hate to say it because your ego is already big enough because you're the CEO. The ironic part of this test is that it is about being so good, so visionary, and so great a leader that you put your ego aside. The question is "are you a qualified builder, are you ready to take the first step and commit?" If you don't, I can assure you no one else will.

Why do companies hire consultants, pay them huge fees to mine the organization for existing ideas, and implement the changes employees have been talking about for several years? It is because those companies have failed to manage their culture, to create a positive culture. They are unable to overcome the turf issues and cultural barriers so they can successfully lead employees through change. They failed to manage their biggest challenges, leadership and culture. Instead, they hide behind their project, their consultant, and the large dollar investment they made for the consultant to edict change. Afterwards, they wonder why it did not deliver the results as conceived. The answer is that regardless of the changes they made, they still don't have a positive culture and they still don't have a high level of employee engagement. Of course, consultants can be extremely useful in providing needed expertise and added resources at key times; but if you are using them to implement ideas you already have and to accomplish things you failed to accomplish, you must look deep to self-assess your company and ask why you hired them. If you are honest with yourself, you'll discover the true issues you are trying to overcome are cultural and your failure is lack of leadership.

All too often companies find new yet uncreative ways to cycle through and repackage downsizing, restructuring, outsourcing, and strategic mergers year after year. It is the all too familiar corporate playbook to deliver short-term benefits that lead to a long-term downward spiral. If this is all you do, it may not mean ultimate ruin for your company; but it will mean mediocrity. You will never be great.

These things can benefit a company if implemented at the right time in the right way and for the right reasons. However, a continuous cycle of these business activities is not sustainable. It is not true growth and it isn't being the thought leader in your industry. Building a positive culture and creating a high level of employee engagement is growth. It is creative. It will allow you to do the typical things better than everyone else and position you to do the difficult things much better than everyone else.

Remember creating positive is not about creating a feel-good, fluffy, soft-stuff organization that is too weak, too slow, and too worried about everything to deliver results. This is about having a very aggressive, hard-line business that can do all the hard things, make the cost cuts, execute the changes, address the difficult issues, and make the tough decisions that all companies must routinely make. It is about doing all those things, the very difficult things in the "right way" by being great at the "how."

If you do the right things, even the difficult things, in the "right way" you will not only execute and get the results; but you'll also have your employees and your whole organization behind you. If you must, think of the CEO's Blueprint as the "soft-stuff" that enables you to do the "hard stuff" really, really well. Reorganizations, mergers, divestures, cost cutting, or radically changing parts of your business are the hard things that all companies frequently do, but seldom do well. It is because of culture and lack of leadership that they falter. We all know that most corporate mergers fail to realize their projected benefits because of failure to successfully merge the cultures. Why is it that the business world sees the problem and understands the solution, yet the majority of companies still fail to correct it? It is because executing the so-called "soft stuff" isn't easy. It is in fact much more challenging than the typical "hard stuff." Anyone can draw up new boxes on paper and call it a restructuring; but only the right leaders will do it effectively by leading the change, engaging employees, and improving the culture in the process. Eventually your company will face these challenges. Eventually all companies face these challenges. Will you be ready, and most importantly, will your CULTURE be ready?

This brings us to the litmus test to determine if you are in fact a qualified builder. Consider the following questions:

The Litmus Test

1. **Will you commit 100% to building and maintaining a positive culture?**
2. **Are you willing to invest the organization's time, energy, and resources to building and maintaining a positive culture?**
3. **Are you willing to permanently change your leadership style and personally model teamwork, leveraging diversity, strong communication, employee development, and leadership?**
4. **Are you willing to make the very difficult personnel decisions required to find and keep the right leaders in the right roles?**
5. **Do you believe a positive culture is a significant business advantage?**

This test is simple and straightforward. These five questions are a test of will, commitment, and understanding. If you honestly answered, "yes" to these five questions then you have passed the test. You are a qualified builder. You will succeed in implementing the CEO's Blueprint and constructing a positive culture.

If you have a positive culture; if you have strong leadership; if you have engaged employees; and if your organization is great at "how" they do things; you will be able to execute any strategy and do the most difficult things businesses do. All you have to do is believe that leadership and culture are the most important things your company; believe they will make a difference; and do not compromise them as you follow the CEO's Blueprint. Do not compromise on having the best leadership; do

not compromise on using teams and the strength of diversity; and above all, do not compromise as you build and create your culture. If you believe, don't compromise, and follow the CEO's Blueprint; I promise you and your leaders will be challenged everyday to do the hard things, but it will pay dividends in all facets of your business. If you want to build a great company compete for the best culture, compete for the best people, and compete for the best leaders.

There exists limitless opportunities in every industry. Where there is an open mind, there will always be a frontier.
Charles F. Kettering

CULTURAL ORGANIZATIONAL MODEL AND LEADERSHIP PHILOSOPHY

Appendix A

Core Belief: A positive company culture, strong leadership, and teamwork are the key ingredients to build a high level of employee engagement, deliver results, and optimize company performance.

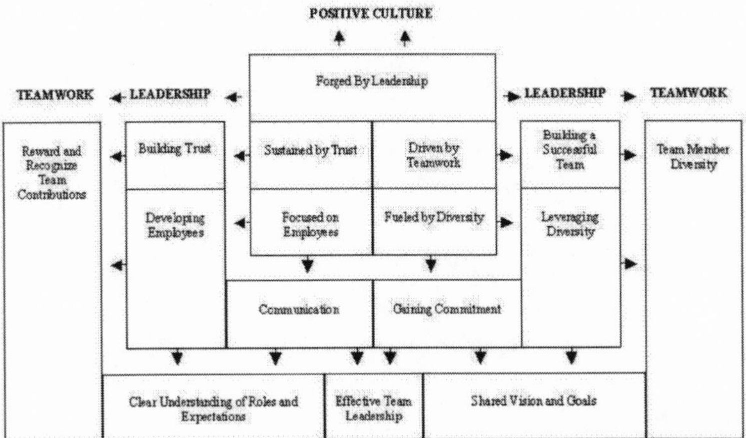

Culture: Your Culture is the foundation of your company. It defines what you do and how you do it. It is the identity for your company and your employees. Culture determines your employees' level of excitement, commitment, and engagement. A positive culture is a significant business advantage and the key to business and strategy execution. The core attributes of a positive culture are that it must be: forged by leadership, sustained by trust, driven by teamwork, fueled by diversity, and focused on employees. Creating a positive culture is the single most untapped bottom line improvement in the business world today.

Leadership: Leadership is everything. Leaders build acceptance by how they lead; and in turn, create and maintain culture. Leaders have tremendous opportunity each and every day to make your company a place where people want to work; a place where everyone wants to work. All your leaders must possess the skills to communicate, build trust, gain commitment, build a successful team, leverage the diversity of employees, and develop employees. These are the six core competencies of leadership. Leadership will build and maintain your positive culture; this is why leadership is everything.

Teamwork: Teams provide balance to decisions, leverage diversity, and optimize results. Teams, in all their forms, must exist in abundance in every part of your organization. Every employee must be a team member. Teamwork optimizes the value of diversity—diversity of thought, experience, and perception. Teamwork provides opportunity to dramatically influence culture, employee perceptions, and work environment. The core attributes of teamwork are effective team leadership, clear understanding of roles and expectations, shared vision and goals, team member diversity as well as rewarding and recognizing team contributions. Teamwork is how strong organizations execute and deliver better products, services, solutions, and results.

The CEO's Blueprint—10 Steps to Constructing Company Culture

1. Commit at the Very Top
2. Define Leadership Needs in Terms of Competencies
3. Define a Selection Processes
4. Reselect and Realign Leadership (Make No Excuses, Make No Exceptions!)
5. Build Staff and Cross Functional Teams
6. Communicate, Communicate, Communicate (Your Mission, Vision, Strategy, and Goals!)
7. Develop Teamwork and Team Building
8. Create Development Plans for Leadership
9. Reassess Leadership for Results, Vision, and Acceptance (Make Changes!)
10. Establish Annual Processes to Solidify and Develop a Positive Culture

Step I—Commit at the Very Top

Develop your understanding of the decisions you'll have to make and the leadership actions you will take; and then make a commitment to build, maintain, and develop a positive culture. Make your commitment a very visible top priority by communicating it and modeling it for your organization.

Step 2—Define Leadership Needs in Terms of Competencies

Define your leadership needs in terms of leadership competencies. Begin with the six core leadership competencies for building a positive culture and customize by level, function, and your business with an additional four to eight competencies.

Step 3—Define a Selection Processes

Define your selection process in terms of standards, steps, and timing. Develop and incorporate processes to assess the six core leadership competencies, your level and function based customized leadership competencies, personality preferences, job fit, experience, and performance.

Step 4—Reselect and Realign Leadership (Make No Excuses, Make No Exceptions!)

Reselect and realign all your leadership positions in the organization from the top down. Utilize your selection processes to identify the leaders that make the cut for proficiency in the six core leadership competencies. Then utilize the position and company customized competencies, personal preferences, job fit, experience, and performance to align those leaders into positions across the company. Do not make excuses or exceptions for previous leaders who do not make the cut in the six core competencies. Regardless of their other qualifications, move them out of leadership and/or out of the organization.

Step 5—Build Staff and Cross Functional Teams

Define leaders and their direct reports as teams with shared goals and a clear understanding of team member roles and expectations. Deliberately define through discussion and collaboration all the cross-functional, permanent, or long-standing teams (committees) and special project teams. Acknowledge these teams through a formal team charter developed by the team leaders and team members. Develop organizational awareness of the teams, team accountabilities, and shared responsibilities through multiple lines of communication.

Step 6—Communicate, Communicate, Communicate (Your Mission, Vision, Strategy, and Goals!)

Communicate your mission, vision, strategy, and goals widely, deeply, and repetitively across your company. Conduct formal and informal forums at every level in the organization to discuss, clarify, and build understanding. After initial communication, at every opportunity discuss them and reinforce them with all employee groups. Assure they are visible in individual employee expectations and performance discussions, reward and recognition efforts, company communications, and the workplace.

Step 7—Develop Teamwork and Team Building

Educate and coach your employees on teamwork and team building. This will not only develop your organization's ability to work in teams. It will appropriately set organizational expectations for teamwork and communicate that it is a skill and a competency that is highly valued and will be rewarded. Institutionalize the training and refresh it annually. Debrief and review team performance and results annually.

Step 8—Create Development Plans for Leadership

Identify and create development plans for every leader in the organization. Make the development process an ongoing effort and a point of formal communication between leader and employee. Promote open and full disclosure of development efforts. Make the development focus situational and applicable to upcoming challenges and work initiatives. Leaders develop leaders. All your leaders must model this commitment and effort to development.

Step 9—Reassess Leadership for Results, Vision, and Acceptance (Make Changes!)

Reassess leadership for results, acceptance, and buy-in of your mission, vision, and culture. Assess "how" they lead and do things as well as "what" they do. Make the difficult changes and remove the leaders that do not get the performance results and/or do not share the cultural values. In removing the leaders that do not share the values and do not do things the right ways, you are removing the individuals that will erode your culture and what you've worked to build.

Step 10—Establish Annual Processes to Solidify and Develop a Positive Culture

You must establish, institutionalize, and perfect the processes and activities that will solidify and further develop your culture. These processes and activities include but are not limited to: standard leadership selection processes, standard development processes, culture surveys, performance measures, communication processes, education for leadership on leadership, education for employees on teamwork, performance reviews, and reward and recognition programs. Use these processes to establish an annual culture calendar.

CORE ATTRIBUTES OF A POSITIVE CULTURE

Forged by Leadership

A positive culture is forged by leadership. Leadership is the key resource for building and maintaining a positive culture. How employees feel about their company and their job is most strongly influenced by their immediate "boss," the leader they work for every day. One of the biggest decisions you will make are the leaders you choose, what kind of culture you ask them to create, and how well you support them in that endeavor.

Sustained by Trust

A positive culture is sustained by trust. Like all other relationships, work relationships are built on trust. Trust between the CEO, leaders, and all employees will maintain and sustain your culture. It allows everyone to work together in an open, honest, and safe environment. It promotes communication, demonstrates respect, and eliminates wasteful efforts on hidden agendas and unproductive turf battles.

Driven by Teamwork

A positive culture is driven by teamwork. Teams are an absolute necessity in today's business world. They far outpace the smartest CEOs in terms of diversity, ideas, and results. Teamwork creates energy, builds respect among team members, sparks creativity, and provides balance for business solutions and initiatives. Teams make your decisions, collaborate, communicate, and solve your businesses problems.

Fueled by Diversity

A positive culture is fueled by diversity. Diversity of thought, diversity of experience, and diversity of perception are the fuel that fires your company's problem solving and creative furnaces. Fill your company full of smart people that think differently, have lived differently, come from different backgrounds, and have experienced different things. Diverse teams design better products, develop better plans, respond better to crisis, and create better solutions.

Focused on Employees

A positive culture is focused on employees. Focusing on employees builds a positive culture by creating a business environment where they can optimize both their personal success and the company's success. Employees are an organization's most valuable assets. Nothing is more flexible, adaptable, creative, or capable than the human mind. Creating a positive culture, means creating a high level of employee engagement. Create a positive culture by managing, focusing, and developing your human assets. The more you focus on employees, their concerns and perceptions, their work environment and their ideas, your positive culture will grow along with value of your company.

SIX CORE LEADERSHIP COMPETENCIES

Communication

Communication is the ability to clearly convey information and ideas through a variety of media to individuals or groups in a manner that engages the audience and helps them understand and retain the message. Effective communication is the lifeblood of a positive culture. An organization and its culture will thrive, be sustained, and be nourished by effective communication. Effective communication enables employees to understand your mission, vision, goals, and strategies. It allows them to communicate ideas, problems, challenges, and solutions quickly. Strong communications allows you to mine your employee base for creative ideas and opportunities as well as to optimize innovation and improvement efforts.

Building Trust

Building trust is the ability to interact with others in a way that gives them confidence in one's intentions and those of the organization. A positive culture is sustained by trust. Trust between you, your leaders, and all employees will maintain and sustain your culture. It will allow you to work together in an open, honest environment where everyone feels safe. Trust promotes two-way communication. It demonstrates respect and allows you to effectively manage and lead through your difficult business issues.

Gaining Commitment

Gaining commitment is the ability to use appropriate interpersonal styles and techniques to gain acceptance of ideas or plans and modifying one's own behavior to accommodate tasks, situations, and individuals involved. Gaining commitment is about the power of employees and understanding how powerful individual commitment and acceptance can be in the workplace. Gaining commitment is the essence of the "A," the "acceptance" in the formula **2A * Q = E**. Leaders who are able to gain the commitment of employees as individuals and groups are leveraging that part of the equation that has the most impact, acceptance.

Building a Successful Team

Building a successful team is the ability to use appropriate methods and a flexible interpersonal style to help build a cohesive team for facilitating the completion of team goals. A positive culture is driven by teamwork. Teams are an absolute necessity in business. They will always outpace individual efforts in terms of diversity, ideas, and results. Teamwork creates energy; it builds respect among team members; it sparks creativity; it provides balance for business solutions. Leaders have the responsibility to make each employee feel part of a team and to make that team successful. In doing this, they will generate results and create a positive culture in the process.

Leveraging Diversity

Leveraging diversity is the ability to recruit, develop, and retain a diverse high quality workforce in an equitable manner in addition to leading and managing an inclusive workplace that maximizes the talents of each person to achieve sound business results. A positive culture is fueled by diversity because diversity optimizes creativity, innovation as well as new ideas and approaches. Leaders must have the ability to leverage and harness this value. In doing so, they will capture benefits for the company and create an environment of respect for everyone.

Developing Employees

Developing employees is the ability to plan and support the development of individuals' skills and abilities so that they can fulfill current or future job roles and responsibilities more effectively. Development is a continual process of growth and improvement. It must be undertaken to keep pace with the constantly changing business world and the day-to-day challenges it brings. Leaders must actively focus on developing employees to optimize their abilities, prepare them for new challenges in their job, and make them feel valued and supported. These efforts will make development part of your culture and send a message to employees that they are the most valuable assets in the company.

CORE ATTRIBUTES OF TEAMWORK

Effective Team Leadership

To have an effective team, you must have effective team leadership. A team cannot achieve success, realize its goals, or have positive team dynamics without it. Every leader must have the ability to be a team leader to lead their team of direct reports each and every day. They must also be an effective team member, not only for the team they lead, but also as a member of their leader's team. An effective team leader must have the ability to build a cohesive team and facilitate the completion of team goals. Effective team leaders establish clear direction for the team in terms of purpose, importance, priorities, and measurable team goals and objectives. They must skillfully involve all team members in discussions, decisions, and actions as well as share information that is important to the team and leverage the team members' diversity all the while modeling commitment for the team itself. They must participate and guide, provide appropriate direction, and make decisions when needed without dominating or limiting discussion. They need to assess team member buy-in and acceptance, acknowledge points and opinions, and then know when to invest time and when to move past non-productive areas. Effective team leadership requires focus and practice, the development and refinement of many skills, and an understanding that at times it is more of an art than a science.

Clear Understanding of Roles and Expectations

To have an effective team, the team and each team member must have a clear understanding of roles and expectations. Establishing expectations creates team member accountably and responsibility for tasks, deliverables, and results. Clarity of individual team member roles and expectations will translate into clarity of role and expectations for the team itself. Teams and team members must have accountability for results and they must have trust. Establishing clear roles and expectations is a building block for both.

Shared Vision and Goals

An effective team has well defined goals and a clear vision that is shared by each team member. Time must be spent establishing the team vision and goals; and to quickly build acceptance and buy-in of those goals. Team members that do not share the vision and the goals will not be committed and therefore will not be part of the team. The critical word is "shared." The team members must share the vision and the goals as well as understand what the vision and the goals are, to fully commit to achieving them.

Team Member Diversity

Team member diversity is vital to optimizing team results. Diversity of experience added to background perception and thought will optimize and amplify team performance. When team building, it is important to have a keen awareness of diversity and your ability to leverage its benefits. Team members must "fit-in" when it comes to sharing vision and goals. But, they must think differently and challenge each other with different ideas thoughts and perspectives. Select team members deliberately and seek out opportunities to include different background, experiences, cultures, races, sexes, and personality types on your team; but also look past the typical "surface features" of diversity. While it is valuable to *look* diverse from a culture and employee base perspective, it is more important to *be* diverse. Regardless of what team members look like, an effective team will be comprised of team members who are diverse in experience, background, and their way of thinking. Diversity enables and creates opportunity for positive conflict, open and respectful dialog, and discussion of different and often opposing ideas. Create teams that reflect true diversity, leverage the strength of that diversity, and optimize your team's results.

Reward and Recognition of Results

Effective teams reward and recognize results—results in terms of progress, small victories, major successes, and completion of final goals. Effective reward and recognition of results provides critical feedback and positive reinforcement for the team and the team members. It is positive reinforcement for the team; helps to keep the team focused on the right things; and, when necessary, helps the team adjust focus or behavior. Teams must be focused on results so rewards and recognition help achieve that focus. Effective reward and recognition for teams builds culture by positively reinforcing teams and teamwork. Every time a team is recognized, it builds increased understanding of the value of and expectation for teamwork.

LEADERSHIP COMPETENCIES AND DEFINITIONS

Appendix B[I]

Communication: *Clearly conveying information and ideas through a variety of media to individuals or groups in a manner that engages the audience and helps them understand and retain the message.*

Oral Communication: *Makes clear and convincing oral presentations to individuals or groups; listens effectively and clarifies information as needed; facilitates an open exchange of ideas and fosters an atmosphere of open communication.*

Written Communication: *Expresses facts and ideas in writing in a clear, convincing, and organized manner.*

Informing: *Provides people with timely information they need to know to do their job, make decisions and to feel that they are an important contributor and team member.*

Listening: *Has patience to hear people out and practice attentive and active listening, able to restate opinions of others even when in disagreement.*

Gaining Commitment: *Using appropriate interpersonal styles and techniques to gain acceptance of ideas or plans and modifying one's own behavior to accommodate tasks, situations, and individuals involved.*

Building Trust: *Interacting with others in a way that gives them confidence in one's intentions and those of the organization.*

Manage Diversity: *Manages all employees equitably and deals effectively with all races, nationalities, cultures, disabilities, ages, and both sexes. Supports equal and fair treatment and opportunity for all employees.*

Leveraging Diversity: *Recruits, develops, and retains a diverse high quality workforce in an equitable manner. Leads and manages an inclusive workplace that maximizes the talents of each person to achieve sound business results. Respects, understands, values, and seeks out individual differences to achieve the vision and mission of organization. Develops and uses* *measures and rewards to hold self and others accountable for achieving results that embody the principles of diversity.*

Interpersonal Skills: *Considers and responds appropriately to the needs, feelings, and capabilities of different people in different situations; is tactful, compassionate and sensitive, and treats others with respect.*

Employee Relations: *Understands why groups of employees do what they do, able to sense group perspectives in terms of values, positions, concerns, reactions, needs and how to motivate them. Able to accurately predict how multiple employees groups will react given different situations and construct effective solutions, approaches, and communications to appropriately address those reactions.*

Developing Employees: *Planning and supporting the development of individuals' skills and abilities so that they can fulfill current or future job/role responsibilities more effectively. Co-develops development plans with employees, is aware and understands employees' career goals. Provides challenging and stretching tasks and assignments and holds frequent development discussions.*

Personal Development: *Seeks feedback and identifies the opportunity to improve and change personal, interpersonal and leadership behaviors. Works to leverage strengths and compensate for developmental needs. Understands situational development and has awareness of changing personal demands and requirements and structures development efforts in accordance with those changes.*

Continual Learning: *Grasps the essence of new information; masters new technical and business knowledge; recognizes own strengths and weaknesses; pursues self-development; seeks feedback from others and opportunities to master new knowledge.*

Coaching: *Providing timely guidance and feedback to help others strengthen specific knowledge/skill areas needed to accomplish a task or solve a problem.*

Sizing Up People: *Able to identify the strengths and limitations of people given reasonable exposure to them. Is a good judge of talent who is able to predict what individuals will do in a variety of situations.*

Self-Awareness: *Knows personal strengths, weaknesses, opportunities and limitations. Willing to recognize and learn from mistakes or shortcomings. Is receptive of constructive criticism and seeks to gain insight from others feedback.*

Personal Disclosure: *Freely shares thoughts about personal strengths and weaknesses,* *admits mistakes and shortcomings. Asks for feedback and invites active coaching from peers and direct reports. Is open about personal beliefs and feelings and is easy to get to know.*

Building a Successful Team: *Using appropriate methods and a flexible interpersonal style to help build a cohesive team; facilitating the completion of team goals.*

Motivating Others: *Empowers others and shares ownership and visibility. Invites input from each person, makes employees feel their work is important and needed. Creates a climate in which employees want to do their best, able to motivate a variety of employees and effectively assesses their interests.*

Rewarding and Recognizing: *Consistently recognizes and rewards performance through appropriate measures. Understands what motivates individual employees and groups, is able to differentiate and appropriately reward significant extraordinary efforts as well as recognize solid job performance day in and day out.*

Aligning Performance for Success: *Focusing and guiding others in accomplishing work objectives.*

Managing and Measuring Work: *Sets clear and measurable objectives and assigns responsibility for tasks and decisions. Monitors progress toward results.*

Accountability: *Assures that effective controls are developed and maintained to ensure the integrity of the organization. Holds self and others accountable for rules and responsibilities. Can be relied upon to ensure that projects within areas of specific responsibility are completed in a timely manner and within budget. Monitors and evaluates plans; focuses on results and measuring outcomes.*

Drive For Results: *Appropriately push self and other for results, very bottom line orientated. A top performer that can be counted on to consistently exceed goals.*

Planning and Organizing: *Establishing courses of action for self and others to ensure that work is completed efficiently.*

Delegating Responsibility: *Allocating decision-making authority and/or task responsibility as appropriate to others to maximize the organization's and individual's effectiveness.*

Decision Making: *Identifying and understanding issues; problems, and opportunities; comparing data from different sources to draw conclusions; using effective approaches for choosing a course of action or developing appropriate solutions; taking timely action that is consistent with available facts, constraints, and probable consequences.*

Problem Solving: *Identifies and analyzes problems; distinguishes between relevant and irrelevant information to make logical decisions; provides solutions to individual and organizational problems.*

Analysis: *Identifying and understanding issues, problems, and opportunities; comparing data from different sources to draw conclusions.*

Initiating Action: *Taking prompt action to accomplish objectives; taking action to achieve goals beyond what is required; being proactive.*

Setting Priorities: *Quickly assesses and separates the important and critical issues from the trivial ones. Creates focus on critical issues, works to remove roadblocks and determines what will help or hinder goal accomplishment.*

Time Management: *Values time and utilizes work time effectively and efficiently. Can attend to a broad range of activities and get more done in less time than others.*

Process Management: *Aptitude for figuring out processes to get the desired result; knows how to organize resources and activities and sees opportunities for integration and improvement. Able to define what to measure and how to measure it and simplify overly complex processes.*

Innovation Management: *Exhibits good judgment on which creative ideas and suggestions will work, able to facilitate effective brainstorming. Good at assessing and bringing creative ideas of others to market.*

Conflict Management: *Identifies and takes steps to prevent potential situations that could result in unpleasant confrontations. Manages and resolves conflicts and disagreements in a positive and constructive manner to minimize negative impact.*

Facilitating Change: E*ncouraging others to seek opportunities for different and innovative approaches to addressing problems and opportunities; facilitating the implementation and acceptance of change within the workplace.*

Managerial Courage: *Provides current, direct, complete and actionable feedback to others, doesn't hold back on what needs to be said and addresses people problems quickly and directly and is not afraid to take negative action when appropriate.*

Political Savvy: *Identifies the internal and external politics that impact the work of the organization. Approaches each problem or situation with a clear perception of organizational and political reality; recognizes the impact of alternative courses of action.*

Interpersonal Savvy: *Relates well to all kinds of people at all levels inside and outside of the organization. Builds constructive and effective relationships, uses diplomacy and tact, able to diffuse tense situations and build rapport.*

Working Collaboratively: *Seeks out opportunities to build effective working relationships with others, facilitates agreement and support of ideas and models partnership oriented actions. Clarifies situations through discussion and listening, develops others and own ideas and subordinates personal goals to team or organizational goals.*

Building Strategic Working Relationships: *Develops and uses collaborative relationships to facilitate the accomplishment of work goals.*

Organizational Agility: *Experienced and knowledgeable about how organizations work, understands how to accomplish things through both formal and informal channels. Understands cultural nuances and preferences.*

Dealing with Ambiguity: *Effectively copes with change, and is able to act and make decisions without having all the information, comfortably handles risk and uncertainty.*

Dealing with Paradox: *Flexible and adaptable when faced with difficult decisions, able to act in ways that appear contradictory and modify actions based on the situation.*

Influencing & Negotiating: *Persuades others; builds consensus through give and take; gains cooperation from others to obtain information and accomplish goals; facilitates win-win situations.*

Partnering: *Develops networks and builds alliances, engages in cross-functional activities; collaborates across boundaries; and finds common ground with widening range of stakeholders. Builds strategic relationships between one's area and other areas, teams, departments, or organizations to help achieve business goals and strengthen internal support bases.*

Building Customer Loyalty: *Effectively meeting customer needs; building productive customer relationships; taking responsibility for customer satisfaction and loyalty.*

Customer Service: *Balancing interests of a variety of clients; readily readjusts priorities to respond to pressing and changing client demands. Anticipates and meets the need of clients; achieves quality end-products; is committed to continuous improvement of services.*

Service Motivation: *Creates and sustains an organizational culture which encourages others to provide the quality of service essential to high performance. Enables others to acquire* *the tools and support they need to perform well. Shows a commitment to public service. Influences others toward a spirit of service and meaningful contributions.*

Vision Building: *Takes a long-term view and acts as a catalyst for organizational change; builds a shared vision with others. Influences others to translate vision into action.*

Strategic Thinking: *Formulates effective strategies consistent with the business and competitive strategy of the organization in a global economy. Examines policy issues and strategic planning with a long-term perspective. Determines objectives and sets priorities; anticipates potential threats or opportunities.*

External Awareness: *Identifies and keeps up to date on key national and international policies and economic, political and social trends that affect the organization. Understands near-term and long-range plans and determines how best to be positioned to achieve a competitive business advantage in a global economy.*

Strategic Agility: *Able to accurately anticipate future consequences and trends. Future oriented, able to create accurate visions of possibilities and likelihood's and develop them into competitive strategies and plans.*

Entrepreneurship: *Identifies opportunities to develop and market new products and services within or outside of the organization. Is willing to take risks; initiates actions that involve a deliberate risk to achieve a recognized benefit or advantage.*

Integrity & Honesty: *Instills mutual trust and confidence; creates a culture that fosters high standards of ethics; behaves in a fair and ethical manner toward others, and demonstrates a sense of corporate responsibility and commitment to public service.*

Compassion: *Sympathetic to others situations, genuinely cares about others and has concern for work and non-work programs. Demonstrates empathy and is willing to help others.*

Approachability: *Easy to approach and talk to, sensitive and patient regarding others interpersonal anxieties. Makes extra effort to put others at ease, good listener who is able to build rapport quickly.*

Perseverance: *Pursues everything with energy, drive and need to finish what was started, is seldom discouraged by resistance or setback, continues to work towards finishing and goal achievement.*

Resilience: *Deals effectively with pressure; maintains focus and intensity and remains* *optimistic and persistent, even under adversity. Recovers quickly from setbacks. Effectively balances personal life and work.*

Standing Alone: *Willing to stand up and be the only champion for an idea or position. Can be counted on in difficult situations, will not shirk individual responsibility in those situations.*

Flexibility: *Is open to change and new information; adapts behavior and work methods in response to new information, changing conditions, or unexpected obstacles. Adjust rapidly to new situations warranting attention and resolution.*

Composure: *Does not become defensive or irritated during difficult situations, cool under pressure, mature. Counted on to be a stabilizing factor during difficult times. Able to handle stress and easily deal with the unexpected.*

Humor: *Expresses a positive and constructive sense of humor, able to laugh at themselves and use humor appropriately to ease tension.*

Creativity and Innovation: *Develops new insights into situations and applies innovative solutions to make organizational improvements; creates a work environment that encourages creative thinking and innovation; designs and implements new or cutting—edge programs/processes.*

Perspective: *Able to think globally and envision future scenarios, has broad views and can discuss multiple aspects of a situation or issue. Applies broad ranging personal and business interests to situations and projects.*

Patience: *Tolerant of people and processes, follows processes and is able to listen and check oneself before acting. Waits for others to "catch up" before moving forward and works to understand information and employee perceptions before acting.*

Judgment: *Using effective approaches for choosing a course of action or developing appropriate solutions; taking action that is consistent with available facts, constraints, and probable consequences.*

Work-Life Balance: *Maintain a conscious balance between work and personal life, avoids one overwhelming the other. Knows how to attend to both aspects of life and get what they want out of both.*

INTERVIEW QUESTIONS FOR LEADERSHIP COMPETENCIES

Appendix C

Communication

1. Careful listening and effective communications go together. Tell me about a specific time when your skill in listening helped you communicate better.
2. How would you describe your verbal communication skills? Tell me about a situation in which these skills were very important for you.

Building Trust

1. Describe a situation in which you had to deal with an unhappy customer, how did you handle it?
2. Describe a work situation when you had to objectively consider the ides of others, even though they conflicted with your own.
3. Tell me about a situation in which you had to earn the trust of a coworker.
4. How do you show respect for others? Please provide an example.

Gaining Commitment

1. Describe a time when you had to make an unpopular decision and how you went about gaining acceptance of your decision.
2. In any organization there are often conflicting departmental goals. Tell me about a time when you modified your goal for another department's benefit, and a time when you stuck with your goal and asked another department to modify its goal.
3. Tell me about a time when you collaborated interdepartmentally with others to determine courses of action to achieve mutual goals.
4. Describe the techniques you have used to successfully gain the commitment of others.

Building a Successful Team

1. Tell me about a time when you were part of a team. If it was

a successful team experience, please explain why. If not, what could have been done to improve the team?

2. Tell me about a time when you were part of a team. Describe what you did to help clarify team members' roles and responsibilities, team goals and measurements.
3. Describe the techniques you have used to encourage team member participation and draw out the ideas and contributions of all team members.

Leveraging Diversity

1. Describe an occasion when you decided to involve others in making a decision compared to another occasion with you decided not to involve others? What factors guided your approach?
2. Describe a situation in which you intentionally adapted your behavior/approach around other people's styles.
3. Tell me about a time when you involved direct reports or team members in decisions affecting their work. What kinds of decisions did you involve them in? How satisfied/dissatisfied were you with that, and why?
4. At times we are all required to deal with difficult people. An even more demanding factor is to be of service to a difficult person. When have you been successful with this type of person at work?

Developing Employees

1. Describe how you have worked with others to define practical and needed development opportunities and goals?
2. What approaches have you used to help others develop skills and abilities?
3. Describe a situation in which you assisted a peer who was not performing well. What was your approach, and what specific actions did you take?
4. Describe a situation in which you had to coach an employee through a problem they were having with another coworker.

Personal Preferences and Job Fit

1. Describe times when you found yourself most satisfied and least satisfied in your work situation. What specifically was most satisfying and dissatisfying for you?
2. Tell me about a time when you were visibly accountable for the

completion and success of a major assignment. How satisfied were you with this visibility and level of accountability?

3. Tell me about a time when work would have been more enjoyable if certain aspects were different. What would you have changed?
4. Tell me about one of the most difficult and demanding challenges you had to manage. How satisfied/dissatisfied were you with that, and why?

SUGGESTED READING AND REFERENCE MATERIAL

Appendix D

Good to Great: Why Some Companies Make the Leap…and Others Don't
Collins, Jim
New York, New York: Harper Business
ISBN: 0066620996
Leadership that Gets Results
Harvard Business Review,
Boston March/April 2000

The CEO and the Monk: One Company's Journey to Profit and Purpose
Catell, Robert B. and Moore, Kenny Moore and Rifkin, Glenn
Hoboken, New Jersey: Wiley (January 9, 2004)
ISBN: 0471450111

The Five Dysfunctions of a Team
Lencioni, Patrick
San Francisco: Jossey-Bass, A Wiley Company
ISBN: 0-7879-6075-6

How to Invest in Social Capital
Harvard Business Review
Boston June 2001

The Five Temptations of the CEO
Patrick Lencioni,
San Francisco: Jossey-Bass, A Wiley Company
ISBN: 0-7879-4433-5

Nuts! Southwest Airlines' Crazy Recipe for Business and Personal Success
Kevin and Jackie Freiberg
New York: Broadway Books
IBSN: 0-7679-0184-3

The GE Way Fieldbook, Jack Welch's Battle Plan for Corporate Revolution
Slater, Robert
New York; Mcgraw Hill
ISBN: 0-07-135481-6

How Full Is Your Bucket? Positive Strategies for Work and Life
Rath, Tom and Clifton, Donald O
New York: Gallup Press
ISBN: 1-59562-003-6

For Your Improvement, A Development and Coaching Guide for Learners, Supervisors, Managers, Mentors and Feedback Givers
Lombardo, Michael M. and Eichinger, Robert W.
Minneapolis: Lominger Limited, Inc.
ISBN: 0-9655712-0-3

Successful Managers Handbook, Development Suggestions for Today's Managers
Davis, Brian L. and Skube, Carol J. and Hellervik, Lowell W. and Gebelin, Susan H. and Sheard, James L.
North America: Personnel Decisions International
ISBN: 0-938529-03-X

The Human Capital Edge: 21 People Management Practices Your Company Must Implement (or Avoid) to Maintain Shareholder Value
Bruce N. Pfau and Ira T. Kay,
New York: McGraw Hill
ISBN: 0-07-1337883-9

Execution, The Discipline of Getting Things Done
Larry Bossidy and Ram Charan
New York: Crown Business
ISBN:0-609-61057-0

NOTES

Chapter 1

1. Robert Slater, The GE Way Fieldbook, Jack Welch's Battle Plan for Corporate Revolution. New York; Mcgraw Hill, 2000, pages 152-157
2. Jim Collins, Good to Great: Why Some Companies Make the Leap…and Others Don't. New York: Harper Business, 2001, pages 10-11
3. Ibid. page 13

Chapter 2

1. Samantha Wolman and Darby Miller Steiger (2004, July). All Eyes on Ohio, How workplace engagement affects employees' outlook on life and the economy in this key "battleground" state. Gallup Management Journal. Retrieved from http://gmj.gallup.com/content/default.asp
2. Ibid.
3. Ibid.
4. Bradford D. Smart, PhD., Topgrading; How Leading Companies Win by Hiring, Coaching and Keeping the Best People. Paramus, New Jersey: Prentice Hall Press, 1999, pages 45-55.
5. Bruce N. Pfau and Ira T. Kay, The Human Capital Edge: 21 People Management Practices Your Company Must Implement (or Avoid) to Maintain Shareholder Value. New York: McGraw Hill, 2002, page 5
6. Samantha Wolman and Darby Miller Steiger (2004, July). All Eyes on Ohio, How workplace engagement affects employees' outlook on life and the economy in this key "battleground" state. Gallup Management Journal. Retrieved from http://gmj.gallup.com/content/default.asp
7. Ibid.
8. Tom Rath and Donald O. Clifton, Excerpted from How Full Is Your Bucket? (Gallup Press, 2004). The Power of Praise and Recognition, Research shows they are crucial for increasing em-

ployee productivity and engagement. Gallup Management Journal. Retrieved from http://gmj.gallup.com/content/content.asp

9. Samantha Wolman and Darby Miller Steiger (2004, July). All Eyes on Ohio, How workplace engagement affects employees' outlook on life and the economy in this key "battleground" state. Gallup Management Journal. Retrieved from http://gmj.gallup.com/content/default.asp
10. Ibid.

Chapter 3

1. Daniel Goleman (2000, March), Leadership that Gets Results. Harvard Business Review Article
2. Laurence Prusak (2001 June), How to Invest in Social Capital. Harvard Business Review Article
3. Bruce N. Pfau and Ira T. Kay, The Human Capital Edge: 21 People Management Practices Your Company Must Implement (or Avoid) to Maintain Shareholder Value. New York: McGraw Hill, 2002, pages 164-165

Chapter 4

1. Patrick Lencioni, The Five Dysfunctions of a Team. San Francisco: Jossey-Bass, 2002, pages 188-189

Chapter 5

1. Jim Collins, Good to Great: Why Some Companies Make the Leap...and Others Don't. New York: Harper Business, 2001, pages 52-53
2. Bruce N. Pfau and Ira T. Kay, The Human Capital Edge: 21 People Management Practices Your Company Must Implement (or Avoid) to Maintain Shareholder Value. New York: McGraw Hill, 2002, pages 213-214
3. Jim Collins, Good to Great: Why Some Companies Make the Leap...and Others Don't. New York: Harper Business, 2001, pages 20, 21 and 30
4. Bruce N. Pfau and Ira T. Kay, The Human Capital Edge: 21 People Management Practices Your Company Must Implement (or Avoid) to Maintain Shareholder Value. New York: McGraw Hill, 2002, page 14
5. Ibid. page 65
6. Jim Collins, Good to Great: Why Some Companies Make the

Leap...and Others Don't. New York: Harper Business, 2001, pages 41-42

7. Larry Bossidy and Ram Charin, Execution, The Discipline of Getting Things Done. New York: Crown Business, 2002, page 27
8. Kevin and Jackie Freiberg, Nuts!, Southwest Airlines' Crazy Recipe for Business and Personal Success, pages 106-107
9. Bruce N. Pfau and Ira T. Kay, The Human Capital Edge: 21 People Management Practices Your Company Must Implement (or Avoid) to Maintain Shareholder Value. New York: McGraw Hill, 2002, page 210
10. Ibid. page 242
11. Larry Bossidy and Ram Charin, Execution, The Discipline of Getting Things Done. New York: Crown Business, 2002, page 27
12. Ibid. page 131
13. Ibid. page 146
14. Ibid. page 155
15. Jim Collins, Good to Great: Why Some Companies Make the Leap...and Others Don't. New York: Harper Business, 2001, pages 54-57
16. Bruce N. Pfau and Ira T. Kay, The Human Capital Edge: 21 People Management Practices Your Company Must Implement (or Avoid) to Maintain Shareholder Value. New York: McGraw Hill, 2002, pages 92-93
17. Jim Collins, Good to Great: Why Some Companies Make the Leap...and Others Don't. New York: Harper Business, 2001, pages 49-50

Chapter 8

1. Ken Iverson, Plain Talk. New York: John Wiley & Sons, 1998, pages 54-59
2. Tom Peters, Thriving on Chaos. New York: Knopf, 1987, page 382

Appendix B

1. Michael M. Lombardo and Robert W. Eichinger, For Your Improvement, A Development and Coaching Guide for Learners, Supervisors, Managers, Mentors and Feedback Givers. Minne-

apolis: Lominger Limited, Inc., 1996, pages 1-367 (Note: referenced for selective ideas and concepts, Appendix B does not reflect direct word for word references)

8267791R0

Made in the USA
Lexington, KY
19 January 2011